International Political Economy Series

General Editor: **Timothy M. Shaw**, Professor of Political Science and International Development Studies, Dalhousie University, Halifax, Nova Scotia

Titles include:

Leslie Elliott Armijo (*editor*)
FINANCIAL GLOBALIZATION AND DEMOCRACY IN EMERGING MARKETS

Robert Boardman
THE POLITICAL ECONOMY OF NATURE
Environmental Debates and the Social Sciences

Gordon Crawford
FOREIGN AID AND POLITICAL REFORM
A Comparative Analysis of Democracy Assistance and Political Conditionality

Matt Davies
INTERNATIONAL POLITICAL ECONOMY AND MASS COMMUNICATION
IN CHILE
National Intellectuals and Transnational Hegemony

Martin Doornbos
INSTITUTIONALIZING DEVELOPMENT POLICIES AND RESOURCE
STRATEGIES IN EASTERN AFRICA AND INDIA
Developing Winners and Losers

Fred P. Gale
THE TROPICAL TIMBER TRADE REGIME

Keith M. Henderson and O. P. Dwivedi (*editors*)
BUREAUCRACY AND THE ALTERNATIVES IN WORLD PERSPECTIVES

Angela W. Little
LABOURING TO LEARN
Towards a Political Economy of Plantations, People and Education
in Sri Lanka

John Loxley (*editor*)
INTERDEPENDENCE, DISEQUILIBRIUM AND GROWTH
Reflections on the Political Economy of North–South Relations at the
Turn of the Century

Don D. Marshall
CARIBBEAN POLITICAL ECONOMY AT THE CROSSROADS
NAFTA and Regional Developmentalism

Susan M. Mcmillan
FOREIGN DIRECT INVESTMENT IN THREE REGIONS OF THE SOUTH AT
THE END OF THE TWENTIETH CENTURY

James H. Mittelman and Mustapha Pasha (editors)
OUT FROM UNDERDEVELOPMENT
Prospects for the Third World (Second Edition)

Lars Rudebeck, Olle Törnquist and Virgilio Rojas (editors)
DEMOCRATIZATION IN THE THIRD WORLD
Concrete Cases in Comparative and Theoretical Perspective

Howard Stein (editor)
ASIAN INDUSTRIALIZATION AND AFRICA
Studies in Policy Alternatives to Structural Adjustment

International Political Economy Series
Series Standing Order ISBN 0–333–71708–2
(outside North America only)

You can receive future titles in this series as they are published by placing a standing order.
Please contact your bookseller or, in case of difficulty, write to us at the address below with
your name and address, the title of the series and one of the ISBNs quoted above.

Customer Services Department, Macmillan Distribution Ltd, Houndmills, Basingstoke,
Hampshire RG21 6XS, England

Foreign Aid and Political Reform

A Comparative Analysis of Democracy Assistance and Political Conditionality

Gordon Crawford
Lecturer in Development Studies
University of Leeds

palgrave

First published 2001 by
PALGRAVE
Houndmills, Basingstoke, Hampshire RG21 6XS and
175 Fifth Avenue, New York, N.Y. 10010
Companies and representatives throughout the world

PALGRAVE is the new global academic imprint of
St. Martin's Press LLC Scholarly and Reference Division and
Palgrave Publishers Ltd (formerly Macmillan Press Ltd).

ISBN 0–333–91982–3

This book is printed on paper suitable for recycling and made from fully managed and sustained forest sources.

A catalogue record for this book Is available from the British Library.

Library of Congress Cataloging-in-Publication Data
Crawford, Gordon, 1952–
    Foreign aid and political reform : a comparative analysis of democracy assistance and political conditionality / Gordon Crawford.
        p. cm.
    Includes bibliographical references and index.
    ISBN 0–333–91982–3
    1. Economic assistance—Political aspects—Developing countries. 2. Democracy—Developing countries. 3. Human rights—Developing countries. 4. Developing countries—Politics and government. 5. Conditionality (International relations) I. Title.
    HC60 .C669 2000
    327.1'11—dc21
                                                                                00–055685

10   9   8   7   6   5   4   3   2   1
10   09   08   07   06   05   04   03   02   01

Printed and bound in Great Britain by
Antony Rowe Ltd, Chippenham, Wiltshire

To mum and dad for their love and support at all times

Contents

List of Tables

List of Figures

Acknowledgements

I wish to acknowledge and to extend sincere thanks to all those who have helped with completion of this book. Professors David Beetham and Lionel Cliffe provided intellectual guidance and support, including constructive and detailed commentary on draft chapters. Professor Tim Shaw provided encouragement and most useful suggestions. Gratitude is due to the many government officials and other individuals contacted who generously gave their time and provided assistance in a courteous manner, often when faced with more urgent tasks. Any mistakes, of course, are solely mine.

Very special thanks are due to Dan Farrar for his assistance on computing matters. His contribution was invaluable and without his expertise the database analysis and construction of tables and figures would have floundered. A very deep thank you to Dot Moss for putting up with me and for her own most astute intellectual advice. Apologies to Callum for being an absent dad at times when working overtime to meet deadlines.

I am grateful to Frank Cass (Publishers, London) for permission to reproduce material previously published in an article entitled 'Political Conditionality: Issues of Effectiveness and Consistency' in *Democratization*, Vol. 3, No. 4, 1997. Figure 1.1, 'The democratic pyramid', from D. Beetham and K. Boyle (1995) *Introducing Democracy: 80 Questions and Answers*, is reproduced by kind permission of Blackwell Publishers/Polity Press.

Introduction

A striking departure in the early 1990s in the foreign aid policies of Northern 'donor' governments was the linkage of development assistance to the promotion of human rights, democracy and good governance in Southern 'recipient' countries. Similar policies were declared in rapid succession by almost all major bilateral aid donors from 1990 onwards, with a remarkable consensus in both the ends and means pronounced in the policy statements. The stated aid policy objectives were the promotion of civil and political rights, democratic government and an accountable and efficient public administration. It is asserted here that this amounts to an overall goal of democratisation (see Figure 1.2 on page 29). The policy instruments were two-fold: on the one hand, positive support through aid projects aimed at strengthening respect for human rights and democratic practices; on the other hand, negative action in the form of aid restrictions in situations of perceived violations of human rights or reversals in the democratisation process. The whole policy area is sometimes described as 'political conditionality', though this term more accurately refers to negative measures only. The positive measures are often described as 'democracy assistance', although the term 'political aid' is generally preferred here.

This shift in aid policy was part of the increased rhetorical emphasis on 'democracy promotion' within the foreign policies of Western governments that accompanied the end of the cold war. There are clearly a number of tools by which this foreign policy objective can be pursued, of which development assistance is only one. These include diplomatic channels, dialogue in international fora, trade policy (including embargoes), and even military force (or its threat).[1] Nevertheless, foreign aid has probably been the most significant instrument in the 1990s and is the exclusive focus of this book.

Development aid has always been political, of course, with implicit conditionality. Since the 1960s, economic assistance from industrialised countries has been provided in return for political support and geostrategic advantage. Nonetheless, the policy departure in the 1990s did represent a break with cold war practices when donor governments, West and East, were willing to reward compliant regimes with economic support regardless of their authoritarianism or their treatment of domestic populations, with *realpolitik* the only justification needed. While it is a welcome shift from such practices, the more recent policy agenda remains controversial and problematic, as this book explores.

Reservations were expressed in particular concerning the extent to which high-sounding official rhetoric would be translated into practice. How genuine was the stated intent to promote respect for human rights and democratic principles and how seriously would the new policy agenda be implemented? Past precedents were hardly encouraging. During the cold war years, judgement by Western powers of the human rights performance of other governments was based on selectivity and a lack of objectivity, condemning the poor records of opponents while overlooking those of allies (Beetham and Boyle 1995, p. 93). Further, the ideological use and abuse of 'democracy promotion' is most evident in the case of the US government. Successive US administrations throughout the twentieth century have described America's 'mission' in the world as promoting democracy (Smith 1994), while numerous examples demonstrate their subversion of democracy where left-leaning or nationalist forces emerge, notably in Latin America.[2] Indeed, the record of Western governments' intervention in the political affairs of weaker nations is hardly one characterised by altruism or idealism. Has policy implementation in the 1990s displayed a more serious commitment to human rights and democracy than past examples?

The introduction of explicit political conditions to aid was additional to the prevailing economic conditionality that had dominated aid policy in the 1980s, with multilateral lending and much bilateral aid dependent on the adoption of International Monetary Fund/World Bank-led structural adjustment programmes. All forms of aid conditionality can be resented, suggesting a measure of superiority on the part of the donor, knowing what's best for the recipient, as well as reflecting power inequalities (Nelson and Eglinton 1992, p. 10). Post-cold war, the addition of political conditionality appeared to represent an expression of the triumph of West over East, with moves to liberal democracy becoming a requisite of aid provision. The twin aid policy objectives of economic and political reform characterised the promotion by the major powers of a free market economy and a liberal democratic polity as the sole development model. The shift to promoting democratisation represented an increasingly widespread presumption amongst governments and international organisations of a synergistic relationship between democracy and development. This 'new orthodoxy' (Leftwich 1996, p. 4) was itself a change from previous prevailing views that democracy was the outcome of socio-economic development (Lipset 1959) or that the successful implementation of economic adjustment required the firm hand of authoritarian rule (Bangura and Gibbon 1992, pp. 32–6). Was political conditionality part of a wider package that sought to restrict development options to those sponsored by the rich nations, or, alternatively, was it an attempt to enable local populations to have greater determination in the direction of their national development efforts?

Linking aid to political reforms and to democratisation clearly raised a number of wide-ranging questions, which this book seeks to address. It examines both instrumental and normative questions. To what extent *can* external agencies influence the process of democratisation in aid recipient countries? At the same time, *should* donor governments be engaged in such activities? How legitimate is it to intervene in favour of democracy? Political conditionality and aid to political reform has been widely commented on (see Chapter 1), yet there has been less detailed examination of actual policy implementation, with one exception being the path-breaking work of Thomas Carothers on US democracy assistance. My own research is a systematic and comparative examination of the policies and practices of four selected aid donors, the first of its type, as far as is known. It undertakes an investigation of efforts to promote political reform through aid by the governments of Sweden, the United Kingdom and the United States, and includes an examination of the role of the European Union as a donor in its own right. The structure of the book is outlined below.

Part I commences with a review of the literature in this field, discussing the range of issues raised as well as generating a number of specific research questions (Chapter 1). These are addressed in subsequent chapters through the examination of comparative empirical material. The book then traces the evolution of each donor's policies (Chapter 2), probing the meanings given to the three key concepts of human rights, democracy and good governance, and examining the strategies by which policy is operationalised (Chapter 3). Policy implementation through the two distinct instruments, political aid programmes and aid sanctions, is investigated in Parts II (Chapters 4, 5 and 6) and III (Chapters 7, 8 and 9) respectively. Analysis is comparative throughout, while simultaneously seeking to address wider questions and issues.

Some preliminary points remain before I proceed to the main body of the book: (1) a brief survey of the trend in development policy that occurred in the early 1990s, with a global shift to the promotion of democratisation as a developmentally desirable goal; (2) the rationale for the selection of the particular donor agencies.

Promoting democratisation: a new trend in development policy

The issue of a rapid succession of policy statements making democratic reform both an objective and a condition of development co-operation commenced shortly after the fall of the Berlin Wall. The British and French governments were among the first to declare this linkage. In perhaps the first public statement indicating the policy shift, British Foreign Secretary, Douglas Hurd, spoke in June 1990 of the need for 'good government' and political pluralism, and stated that 'aid must go where it will do good' (IDS Bulletin January 1993, p. 7). (British policy is examined in detail in Chapter 2.) Later that same month, at the biannual La Baule French–African Summit, President Mitterand declared that France 'will link its financial efforts to the efforts made towards liberty' (cited in Uvin 1993 p. 66). The intention was stated to be less generous to those 'regimes which conduct themselves in an authoritarian manner without accepting evolution towards democracy' and, in contrast, to be 'enthusiastic towards those who take the step with courage' (cited in ODI Briefing Paper January 1992). This was an unwelcome surprise to some authoritarian rulers in Francophone African states that, erstwhile, had been able to rely on French government support, including militarily.

Other bilateral donors followed swiftly in the declaration of similar policies. In October 1991, the German government introduced five criteria for the allocation of development aid, three of which were politically orientated: human rights, participatory democracy and the rule of law (Randel and German 1994, p. 69). The so-called Like-Minded Group of bilateral donors (i.e. the Nordic countries, the Netherlands and Canada), with a tradition of more 'progressive' aid policies, including a human rights emphasis and a greater orientation towards poverty alleviation, have all incorporated policy objectives in this field. Dutch policy, for instance, includes 'the suspension of development assistance where human rights are violated, where there is stagnation in the democratisation process or excessive military expenditure' (ibid.,

p. 91). Canadian policy built on its 1980's emphasis on human rights to prioritise the promotion of rights, democratisation and good governance in the 1990s. The Japanese government, now the world's largest bilateral donor in aid volume, proclaimed its ODA (overseas development assistance) Charter in June 1992, involving four general principles of aid, one of which was 'attention to democratisation, market economy and human rights' (ibid., p. 87).

In addition to bilateral donors, a number of international bodies also made policy statements in this area. The Development Assistance Committee of the Organisation for Economic Co-operation and Development (DAC – OECD), which has an aid policy co-ordinating role amongst OECD member states, focused attention on 'participatory development and good governance' as priority issues for the 1990s (OECD 1994, p. 28). Its definition of good governance incorporated issues of democratisation and human rights; a DAC expert group was established, which submitted reports in 1997 (OECD 1997a and 1997b). Regional and international organisations, with representation of Southern governments, also endorsed the pro-democracy re-orientation of the early 1990s, with democratic government becoming a requirement of membership in some instances. Member nations of the Organisation of American States (OAS) agreed a 'Commitment to Democracy and the Renewal of the Inter-American System' at their Santiago meeting in June 1991. This affirmed their 'firm commitment to the promotion and protection of human rights and representative democracy, as indispensable conditions for the stability, peace and development of the region'. Mechanisms included an automatic response to illegal interruptions to the democratic process – invoked in a number of instances – in Haiti (1991), Peru (1992), Guatemala (1993) and Paraguay (1996 and 1999) (Santiso 1999, p. 5). At its Heads of State meeting in July 1990, the Organisation of African Unity (OAU) similarly declared its commitment to democracy, human rights and the rule of law, and the need to promote people's participation in both government and development (cited in *IDS Bulletin* January 1993, p. 7). The Harare Declaration of the Commonwealth Summit in October 1991 defined its principles of membership as including political democracy, human rights, good governance and the rule of law, with Nigeria the first member state to incur suspension of membership. Donor governments have tended to quote such statements as evidence of international support (South as well as North) for the new policy agenda, yet aid conditionality did *not* receive 'unreserved approval' from such bodies (Robinson 1994, p. 49). The OAU meeting also expressed concern at the 'increasing tendency to impose conditionalities of a political nature' on the granting of development assistance (cited in ODI 1992, p. 4), and the governments of India, Malaysia and Zimbabwe expressed similar reservations at the Commonwealth Summit (ibid.).

A related shift in the policy orientation of the multilateral development banks has also been evident, something that has be highlighted by the concept of governance. The World Bank has advocated the concept of 'good governance' since the early 1990s. Restrained by its mandate from advancing an overtly political agenda, the Bank's definition of governance is 'the manner in which power is exercised in the management of a country's economic and social resources for development', with four key dimensions of *good* governance: public sector management, accountability, legal framework for development, and transparency and information (World Bank 1992). In focusing on public sector reform and legal reform as the institutional dimensions of 'sound economic management', the World Bank presents its 'call for good governance and its concerns with accountability, transparency, and the rule of law [as] to do exclusively with the contribution they make to social and economic development' (World Bank 1994a, p. vii). This is discussed further in Chapter 1, section 1.2.3.) The IMF similarly stresses that its 'involvement in good governance should be limited to economic aspects of governance' (IMF 1997, p. 3). Somewhat in contrast, the Inter-American Development Bank (IDB) has felt less constrained in asserting a more political stance with its advocacy of the concept of 'democratic governance'. Indeed, according to Santiso, 'strengthening democracy and good governance in the hemisphere has been an explicit and central objective of the IDB in the last decade', with four main areas of reform identified: the executive branch; the legislative branch and democratic institutions; the justice system; and civil society (Santiso 1999, p. 17, citing IDB 1996 and 1997).

One dissenting voice in the early 1990s was that of UNDP (United Nations Development Programme). While itself at the forefront of promoting democracy and political freedom as an essential element of human development, the UNDP expressed opposition to donor pressure and the conditioning of development aid on democracy and human rights, claiming that 'Democracy is a native plant – it may wilt under foreign pressure' (UNDP 1992, p. 25). Latterly, UNDP appears to have drawn closer to the international consensus and advocates its own broad notion of governance, defined as 'the exercise of political, economic and administrative authority in the management of a country's affairs at all levels', with characteristics of *good* governance including participation, rule of law, transparency, accountability, effectiveness and efficiency, and equity (UNDP 1997, pp. 2–3).

Selection of donors

My selection of the four donors was influenced by a range of factors, including size and importance of aid programme, as well as the inclusion of examplars from different points of the spectrum with regard to aid traditions and practices.

As a UK-based academic, the choice of the British government was made for self-evident reasons. In addition, the UK government was one of the first to signal a policy change, has its own distinct concept of 'good government' and regards itself as influential in international circles in such matters.

The inclusion of the European Union (EU) was of importance for two reasons. First, the European Community's own aid programme is substantial in its own right, the fifth largest donor programme in recent years, amounting to over 5 billion dollars in 1997, over 10 per cent of all development aid distributed by OECD countries (Cox and Koning 1997, p. 1). Second, over the last decade, the promotion of respect for human rights and democratic principles has become an increasingly important part of EU foreign policy rhetoric, included within development co-operation.

The governments of Sweden and the United States were selected due to their contrasting aid traditions, anticipated as likely to provide useful comparative material. US foreign aid, which includes military assistance as well as development assistance, was very much an instrument of cold war objectives. This involved the past prioritisation of assistance to a number of right-wing authoritarian regimes, for example, the government of El Salvador in the 1980s; to developmentally discredited and corrupt rulers, for instance, ex-President Mobutu of (former) Zaïre; as well as support for guerrilla opponents of 'Marxist' regimes, for example, UNITA in Angola. In contrast, Sweden's aid programme, particularly under the succession of Social Democratic governments, has emphasised the aims of equality and of national liberation. In consequence, assistance was provided to socialist-orientated regimes during the 1970s and 1980s, for example, Tanzania and Vietnam, and support given to the 'front-line states' in Southern Africa, including the 'Marxist' governments of Angola and Mozambique.

Caveats

Finally, before proceeding to the main body of this book, at least two *caveats* are appropriate. First, in analysing the role of aid in democratisation, there is considerable reliance on quantitative material, especially in the investigation of political aid programmes. While it is maintained that that this provides valuable indicators of the overall orientation and scope of donor programmes, it is acknowledged that there are limitations to analyses based only on quantitative data, especially given the complexity of objectives and the variety of political scenarios in recipient nations. Ideally, the investigation into the contribution of external agencies would be supplemented by the qualitative analysis that detailed country case-studies can provide. Unfortunately, such case-studies are beyond the restrictions of this single volume. Second, criticisms of political aid programmes are largely based on the analysis of empirical material from 1992–94. Since this is an emerging field, it is acknowledged that the situation will have evolved since then. Concluding policy recommendations are included here as a contribution to the learning that is ongoing in this field, and, indeed, it would be gratifying if some of those suggestions were to be implemented.

Part I
The Emergence of the New Policy Agenda

1
Themes and Issues in the 'New Policy Agenda'

The linkage of development aid to the promotion of human rights, democracy and good governance in recipient countries stimulated a range of responses from numerous analysts and commentators during the first half of the 1990s. Dubbed the 'new policy agenda' (M. Robinson 1994), a variety of issues and questions were raised in the literature. In this chapter, the following themes are identified, with differing perspectives are then explored: the origins of the policy; problems of policy (in)coherence and the lack of conceptual clarity; normative issues concerning policy legitimacy; instrumental questions of policy implementation and likely impact. These are examined, in turn, through a survey of the relevant literature. While there exists a more extensive literature on international aspects of democratisation, this book will confine itself to a review of the narrower set of literature on political conditionality and the promotion of democratisation through development aid.[3] One intention of this chapter is to raise research questions that are addressed in the course of the book. Such questions are outlined at the end of each section.

1.1 Policy Origins

While political conditionality was essentially an initiative of the early 1990s, it was not without precedent. In 1975, the US Congress enacted human rights conditionality into the Foreign Assistance Act, prohibiting all development assistance to 'the government of any country which engages in a consistent pattern of gross violations of internationally recognised human rights'. Human rights in this interpretation was largely limited to civil and political liberties. A detailed exploration of this legislation by Forsythe, led to two main conclusions. First, its implementation by the Carter administration was characterised by inconsistent application, with human rights policy undermined by the predominance of cold war objectives. While foreign assistance was cut to a number of Latin America countries, human rights violations elsewhere attracted no punitive response, for instance, in the Philippines, South Korea, Iran and the former Zaïre. This was explained as due to geo-strategic reasons (Forsythe 1988, pp. 51–60; Nelson and Eglinton 1992, p. 28). Second, the intent of the legislation was subsequently not only ignored but 'violated . . . systematically' by the Reagan administration (Forsythe 1988, p. 51). Other precedents of explicit human rights criteria included policies introduced by the Norwegian and Dutch governments in the mid-1970s. These were distinguished, however, by their greater emphasis on economic and social rights, part of a 'social justice' perspective (Stokke 1995, p. 29; M. Robinson 1993a, pp. 58–9).

Despite such exceptions, the predominant political thrust behind development aid was as an instrument of the cold war, used to bolster allies, whether democratic or not: something particularly true of US foreign assistance as well as that of the UK. While not wishing to denigrate the developmental intent and achievements of much development assistance (see Cassen *et al.* 1994 and Burnell 1997 for reviews), the political usage of aid up to 1989 was distinguished more for its support for authoritarian rulers. Such support rendered oppressive governments less vulnerable to domestic pressures – enabling them to exploit financial aid for purposes of regime survival, for instance, as funds for clientelist practices (i.e. the disbursal of patronage to client social groups in order to retain their political allegiance). If development assistance was previously characterised more as aiding non-democratic rulers, what accounts for the striking change in policy in the early 1990s? Three main factors are put forward, distilled from the analyses of the origins of political conditionality found in a number of accounts.

Clearly, the end of the cold war itself, with the fall of the Berlin Wall and the collapse of communism, is highlighted by many writers as the single most significant factor (Moore 1993a; Burnell 1993; Sorensen 1993b, p. 2; Gibbon 1993; Stokke 1995; Cumming 1996). The end of the cold war meant that there was less justification for Western donors to support right-wing authoritarian regimes and that 'the uses of aid need no longer be shaped by geo-political considerations and compromises' (Moore 1993, p. 1). In addition, with the removal of competition for influence between West and East, 'Western governments felt freer than before to pursue basic political concerns *vis-à-vis* the governments of the South' (Stokke 1995, p. 9). Burnell (1993, p. 6) and Uvin (1993,

p. 63) make similar points, the latter also noting how the increased demand for foreign aid resultant from the collapse of the Soviet bloc has made it easier for donors to impose political conditions on recipients and how the granting of economic assistance to former communist countries in Eastern Europe specifically required commitments to democracy and liberal market reform.[4] This context helps to explain the assertive advocacy of democracy and human rights by Western governments, at least in their policy rhetoric. The triumphalism that accompanied the demise of the Soviet bloc afforded an opportunity to pursue 'predominant Western political norms and interests...and the prevailing Western economic system' (Stokke 1995, p. 9). Such triumphalism rapidly disintegrated in the face of the complex problems faced in the post-cold war world, raising the question of how seriously Western governments would continue to pursue this new policy agenda – and which elements of it would be emphasised – as the going became tougher.

A second factor highlighted the interlinkages between economic and political agendas. In a shift from previous prevailing wisdom – that authoritarian governments were better placed to implement harsh economic adjustment measures – the view of a positive interrelationship between democracy and economic liberalisation became widespread. Essentially, democracy was valued as providing the political context most likely to sustain economic reform efforts. In other words, democratisation was desirable not only as an end in itself but also as a means to the end of economic liberalisation. As Wiseman comments concerning Africa, 'The reasoning behind political conditionality was partly economic in that it was argued that economic failure in Africa was in some measure due to the absence of democracy and political accountability and that without political change the imposition of economic conditionality...would not produce the desired economic results' (1997, pp. 287–8). Other analysts have similarly noted the importance of this factor in accounting for both the emergence and wide acceptance of the new policy agenda, (Lancaster 1993, pp. 9–12; Stokke 1995, p. 9). Such thinking emanated in particular from the World Bank, initially contained in a 1989 report on sub-Saharan Africa. In the context of the poor results of structural adjustment programmes (SAPs), the Bank concluded that the policies were correct but not being implemented properly; it then raised the issue of the competence and quality of government. In this report, the Bank's concerns were stated in fairly overt political terms. On the one hand, attention was drawn to problems of the personalisation of power, widespread corruption, the denial of fundamental human rights, and the prevalence of unelected and unaccountable governments. On the other hand, the benefits of pluralism and multi-partyism were noted. As Hydén (1992, p. 5) comments, 'Implicit, if not explicit, . . . is a call for liberalisation and democratisation. Development will only take place if political leaders abandon their authoritarian practices'. Subsequently, the Bank's interest in this issue of 'good governance' has broadened geographically but narrowed definitionally, drawing back from a pro-democracy perspective to focus on the administrative and economic management aspects of government, in accordance with its non-political Mandate (see section 1.2.3). It is important to note, however, that even in their earlier statements the World Bank valued democracy and pluralism less in their own right and more as a *means* to economic reform and development.

While these first two factors are interlinked, a third factor is more distinct. This pertains to the domestic needs of donor government aid agencies to provide a new justification for foreign aid – important for mobilising support, both within government and amongst the general public – for the protection of aid budgets in the context of public expenditure cuts (Burnell 1993; Lancaster 1993; Uvin 1993; Stokke 1995). Rationales as different as 'anti-communism' (US) and 'third world solidarity' (Sweden) had equally become well-worn with time and the changing international context – accompanied by the notion of 'aid fatigue'. Policies emphasising democracy, human rights and good governance provided a new rationale and a fresh profile for development aid in a number of ways. Firstly, human rights and democracy (or 'good government') provide a new principle, unanimously agreed as desirable, on which to base the provision of assistance, and simultaneously to counter the arguments of opponents that it was used to 'aid dictators'. Secondly, in practice, the new policy agenda provided a basis for the re-orientation of aid to a different set of 'worthy' recipients, including a rationale for cutting aid through the application of political conditionality criteria. Thirdly, prioritising good governance serves to reassure both the public and government colleagues that aid is being well spent and not misused. Fourthly, again in practice, it enables the introduction of tighter controls within the aid programme itself on how money is spent, requiring increased 'accountability' of recipient governments.

In sum, the literature suggests that the policy shift to the explicit promotion of democracy and human rights emerged from a diverse set of circumstances, most notably the sea-change in international relations brought about by the end of the cold war, but also from the changed perception that democratisation enhanced the prospects for economic reform, as well as the domestic needs of donor aid agencies themselves. This discussion of policy origins raises the following questions for further enquiry through the comparative investigation of the four donor cases.

- Do the explanatory factors discussed above provide a successful account of actual policy origins in the four cases examined?
- Are some factors more crucial than others in particular instances?
- To what extent is the policy shift linked to a perceived facilitation of economic reform?
- How significant are domestic imperatives?

Such enquiries are the subject of Chapter 2.

1.2   Policy coherence

The three key concepts within the new policy agenda are human rights, democracy and good governance, terms that are used recurrently within donor policy statements. The meanings of all three terms are both complex and contested, something that has led various commentators to express problems at their inclusion in aid policy. The one theme common to all three concepts in fact seems to be the lack of definitional precision. The issues raised by writers concerning each concept are discussed in three separate sections below, with a summary section (1.2.4) outlining the research questions generated.

1.2.1   Human rights

Human rights is potentially the least disputed, benefiting from the relative clarity bestowed by its incorporation into international law through both UN covenants and regional conventions (Crawford 1995, pp. 51–4; Häusermann 1998; Donnelly 1993; Robertson 1989; Blackburn and Taylor 1991).

Nevertheless, Ostergaard (1993) questions which *type* of human rights are being raised within the new policy agenda, noting the lack of differentiation within donor policies and criticising the selective promotion of civil rights under the rubric of human rights (1993, p. 113, citing Kent 1991, p. 32). This point pertains to old debates concerning the relative importance of different sets of rights, with a perceived prioritisation of civil and political rights by Western states in both foreign and domestic affairs, in contrast to an emphasis on economic and social rights by most developing countries as well as by the former communist states of Eastern Europe. Ostergaard argues for an integrated approach in aid policy in which civil and political rights are 'dovetailed with and indivisible from economic, social and cultural rights' (ibid.), thus conceptualising human rights 'in a way that is acceptable to...most non-Western countries' (ibid., p. 129).

Ostergaard would appear to highlight potentially contradictory trends here. On the one hand, the indivisible, inter-dependent and inter-related nature of *all* human rights has become the agreed international discourse, for example, in the Vienna Declaration at the 1993 UN World Conference on Human Rights. On the other hand, civil and political rights have risen in importance in the 1990s, as reflected in donor policy statements in this area, suggesting a continued focus in practice by Western governments on civil and political rights with relative neglect of economic, social and cultural rights. Nonetheless, if the equal status of all rights is accepted, their distinct nature can also be recognised. Whereas civil and political rights are construed as 'rights from' interference by the state in legitimate activities, with the potentiality of immediate realisation, economic and social rights are 'rights to' economic and social needs being met, requiring positive action by the state, and with 'progressive' realisation over a longer time-frame. The indivisibility of human rights certainly implies that respect for civil and political rights and the realisation of economic and social rights are mutually reinforcing, but perhaps does not preclude different instruments being suitable for the promotion of each set of rights.

Human rights may be definitionally clearer through their incorporation into legal instruments as well as through their universality, something agreed by the 171 states at the Vienna Conference, yet their introduction into development co-operation is not uncontested with the main debate concerning the continuation of selective promotion of civil rights as human rights by Western donors.

1.2.2 Democracy

Almost everyone is in favour of democracy, yet, as Hoffman stated, 'Democracy is without doubt the most contested and controversial concept in political theory' (1988, p. 131). The interpretation of the concept by donors was one key concern of commentators in initial discussions of donors' intent to promote democracy as a goal of development assistance.

Before examining the specific issues raised by such writers, a preliminary discussion explores three general debates around the concept of democracy, with the final one of particular relevance here. First, a past debate occurred between advocates of disparate political systems this century, all attempting to enhance the legitimacy of their particular system by labelling it as 'democratic'. These systems ranged from the 'liberal democracies' of the West, the 'peoples democracies' of the communist regimes of the East, to the 'one-party democracies' of a number of post-colonial states, particularly in Africa. Given that the latter two have been discredited and had largely disappeared by the early 1990s, there would now seem to be few alternatives to liberal democracy as 'actual, existing democracy'.

A second and long-standing debate, largely within the framework of liberal democracy, involves a challenge from participatory democracy to the limitations of a narrow, procedural model of democracy, although with the former not having been realised at the level of the nation-state (Held 1987, Chapter 8; Crawford 1995, p. 55; Potter 1997, pp. 3–6). Following Schumpeter, procedural democracy focuses on representative government, with representatives elected in regular, competitive elections characterised by universal suffrage and individual freedoms, with the resultant government's task being to determine policy and to govern, relatively uninterrupted, on behalf of the entire community. These institutional features are laid out by Dahl (1971) as what he terms 'polyarchy'. In contrast, notions of participatory democracy act as a challenge to extend and deepen democracy. Its proponents (for instance, Pateman 1970) highlight the limited participation by citizens (often restricted to casting their vote periodically) in decisions that affect their lives, and advocate, firstly, the extension of democratic decision-making beyond government to other societal institutions – for example, local community organisations and workplace democracy – and, secondly, the democratisation of the ongoing process of government, between elections, by enhancing mechanisms for both influencing policy-making processes and holding government to account. Frequently, social reform is a third element of a participatory approach, integrating 'progressive' change in the direction of reduced economic and social inequalities and the elimination of social relations of subordination (for instance, gender subordination). In other words, participatory democracy is associated with a more egalitarian society, linked more closely to the realisation of economic and social rights.

Thirdly, a related but distinct argument is that the narrow, procedural model of democracy, based on electoral competition and regular elections, cannot itself be effectively democratic without simultaneous democratisation of political institutions and of society as a whole, in other words without the introduction of at least some elements of a

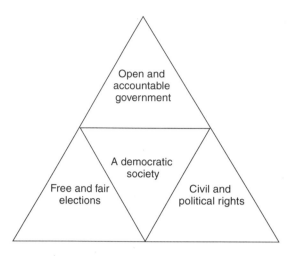

Figure 1.1   The democratic pyramid.
(Reproduced with permission from Beetham and Boyle 1995, p. 31.)

participatory approach. For example, free and fair elections are not possible where the parliamentary opposition has been subject to restrictions
between elections. Such discussions are evident in the work of Beetham
(see Beetham 1993b; Beetham and Boyle 1995; Weir and Beetham, 1999).
He contends that common democratic principles underlie competing
definitions of democracy. In his view there are two key principles of
democracy: *popular control* over collective decision-making, and *political
equality* in the exercise of that control (i.e. equality of rights). Depending
on the extent to which these principles are realised in the decision-
making process of an association of people, it can be called 'democratic',
applicable to all associations in society, though most commonly concerned with control of national and local government. Beetham
expounds three implications that arise from these two key principles.
The first is that democracy is not an all-or-nothing affair; rather, it is a
continuum, and countries can be assessed according to the degree to
which the principles of popular control and political equality are realised
in practice. Second, it is evident that no state realises these principles
fully and popular struggles to consolidate and extend democracy will
take place in all societies, including Western established democracies.
Third, and most importantly for this research, the two principles are
realised through the four essential components of a functioning democracy. These are: free and fair elections; open and accountable government; civil and political liberties; a democratic (or civil) society. Each

component is a necessary but insufficient component of democracy. As each element is essential to the whole, the four components can be represented diagramatically as a 'democratic pyramid' (Figure 1.1).

The argument here is less a debate between different competing conceptions of democracy, narrow and broad, and more that the procedural version is itself unrealisable without the broader components. Interconnections between the four components are evident. Guaranteed respect for civil and political rights is a prerequisite for free and fair elections. It is essential that representative government is open and accountable to its electorate between elections in order to sustain its 'democratic' nature. This also requires an active element *outside* of government – in other words a thriving civil society – both to participate in policy-making procedures and to scrutinise government activities. Further, for politics to be played by democratic rules, with governmental change determined through electoral mechanisms, an acceptance of democratic norms throughout society is required. Coming full circle, civil and political rights are themselves best protected within a democratic society. Thus, it is argued that it is not possible to realise one element of democracy – for example, procedural aspects focusing on competitive elections and representative government – without the other broader elements. Rather, all four components are necessary parts of the whole of a functioning democracy. This work largely accepts this argument and the notion of the 'democratic pyramid' is utilised later in the book as a device to evaluate donor efforts to promote democratisation (Chapter 6).

Returning to the issues raised by commentators on the new policy agenda, a common presumption was of a narrow interpretation of democracy by donors, restricted to the formal, procedural aspects, merely involving multi-partyism and competitive elections (Andreassen and Swinehart 1992, p. viii; Sorensen 1995, pp. 395–401; Stokke 1995, pp. 31–2). The limitations of such a restricted notion are criticised by Sorensen, for example, as a 'quick fix', resulting only in 'a thin layer of democratic coating . . . without changing the basic features of the old structure' (1993b, p. 20). In contrast, democratisation is regarded as 'a long-term process of gradual change' (ibid.), requiring 'long-term commitment' to democratic principles and human rights norms by donors (Andreassen and Swinehart 1992, p. viii). The implication is that this commitment may be both wanting – with donor interests limited to the establishment of formal pluralist politics – and transitory. As an alternative to such a 'quick-fix', critics tend to focus on strengthening the participation of civil society in democratic decision-making (Andreassen and Swinehart 1992, p. xii; Sorensen 1995, pp. 399–400).

Similar presumptions of donors' restricted notion of democracy are also apparent in the work of more Marxist-orientated critics, for instance, Barya (1993) and Gills *et al*. (1993). These authors widen the framework of their analysis, however, to understand such limitations as a broader Western project to maintain their hegemonic domination in the post-cold war world (discussed further in section 1.3.2). Barya hypothesised the donor definition as limited to 'mere political pluralism, namely equating democracy with multi-party politics' and that democracy did 'not really seriously refer to the popular participation of civil society' (1993, p. 17). This limited concept is seen less as a consequence of donor inadequacies and policy incoherence, however, and more as intentional and planned.

In a similar critical vein, Gills *et al.*, the editors of *Low Intensity Democracy*, evoke the US counterinsurgency catchphrase to depict their analysis that a restricted concept of democracy is an integral part of Western capitalist powers' objectives, both to maintain their global dominance and to pre-empt more radical change in developing countries, (Gills *et al*. 1993). Their critique of formal political democracy focuses on its detachment from social reform, rendering the term 'democracy' 'largely devoid of meaningful content' (ibid. p. 5). In their perception, 'low intensity democracy' is largely confined to 'formal electoral participation', providing cosmetic change only, while protecting the *status quo* and obstructing progressive reform (ibid. p. 21). There is further discussion of donor intent in (section 1.3.2).

Barya's alternative to a narrow concept of democracy again focuses on civil society. His challenge is that for donors to be serious about the promotion of democracy, it would require not just a change of personnel in control of the state through multi-party elections, but a strengthening of autonomous organisations of civil society. However, this is 'not seriously envisaged as part of the programme of the new democracies, whether by the donors who are imposing the conditionalities or by most of the new-breed leaders' (1993, p. 21). This particular contention regarding (the lack of) support for civil society, as well as the wider questions relating to the type of democracy promoted by Western governments, are subjects of the empirical investigation of donor political aid programmes in Part II. However, one remaining issue, pertinent to such enquiries, concerns the notion of civil society itself.

Although having a long history in political thought, the concept of civil society has experienced a renaissance in recent years, particularly with the interest in democratisation, with its strengthening posited by a number of commentators as central to a wider and more substantial interpretation of democracy. Yet, the concept in many instances is as inadequately defined and loosely used as donors' references to democracy itself. What is civil society and what is its role in democracy promotion?

Beetham provides some clarity, with the 'democratic society' component of the democratic pyramid referring to the sphere of civil society, although it is less precisely defined than his other three elements. Above all, civil society involves 'a flourishing network of voluntary associations in all areas of social life' (Beetham and Boyle 1995, p. 31). Its contribution to democracy is two-fold. One is to act as some counterweight to state power, performing both a 'watchdog' role, scrutinising government activities and ensuring its accountability, and an 'advocacy' role, channelling interests and demands to government and influencing policy debates. The other, provided that organisations are internally democratic, is that the democratic society constitutes a significant aspect of the practice of democracy in its own right.

In *The Democratic Revolution*, Diamond identifies six ways in which civil society can promote democracy, focusing again on liberal notions of its function as a check on state power, strengthening political participation and resisting authoritarianism (1991, pp. 7–11). Yet the causal links between civil society and democratisation are not necessarily so straightforward, as both Roniger and White indicate (Roniger 1994b; White 1994). In contrast to the commentators above, including those on the political left, Roniger questions the rhetoric of civil society and the claim that it represents 'genuine, popular democracy' (1994b, p. 209, cited in van Rooy and Robinson 1998, p. 44). He argues that 'both in historical and contemporary terms, this identification is more conceptual than factual', citing evidence that civil society may be weak where democracy flourishes (Japan), or strong where democracy is also strong (India) or detrimental to democracy (Russia), (ibid.). He argues that 'the pluralistic character of civil society neither ensures democracy nor implies a strengthening of the open domain of public life' (ibid., p. 210). In more pragmatic manner, White (1994, p. 379) indicates that social forces can obstruct as well as facilitate democratisation. The large majority of civil society associations are non-political, some pro-democracy and some anti-democracy, tolerant or supportive of authoritarian rule (ibid., p. 380). Civil society can include some 'decidedly "uncivil" entities', for instance, the Mafia or religious fundamentalist organisations (ibid., p. 377). One basic two-fold typology distinguishes public benefit organisations and mutual benefit (or membership) organisations (Thomas 1992, p. 123). The former are more likely to engage in both 'watchdog' and 'advocacy' roles, although the latter are not excluded from doing so, with trade unions often seen as playing an important pro-democracy role. The DAC makes a similar two-fold distinction between economic self-interest groups (for example, business associations, farmers' groups, trade unions), and 'civic advocacy' groups that fulfil more altruistic purposes (for example, human rights groups or environmental pressure groups), (OECD 1995, p. 2, cited in M. Robinson 1996, p. 5). Beetham and Boyle also note that interests groups can become undemocratic in circumstances where wealth, organisation or personal connections give them undue influence to modify or frustrate government policy (1995, p. 108).

Civil society organisations are generally conceptualised as being independent and autonomous from the state. The reality can be quite different. Fowler (1997, p. 32) provides an amusing list of acronyms of 'NGO pretenders', including GRINGO, a Government-Run and Initiated NGO, but the more serious point is that non-governmental organisations can often be closely connected to the state. Dicklitch's study of the explosion of NGOs in Uganda indicated that many were involved in service provision and gap-filling activities left by the retreating state (1998, p. 3), as well as 'briefcase NGOs', set up to tap into foreign aid moneys, but with questionable objectives (ibid., p. 8). In this respect, she argues that 'NGOs are not viable vehicles for African democratisation' as currently structured (ibid., p. 3). In a different linkage, state infiltration of NGOs in Nigeria has been claimed – for example, infiltration of women's organisations by the wives of military leaders.

It can be concluded that there is no guarantee that the simple proliferation of voluntary associations in civil society will serve to promote democracy. This will depend on the nature of the organisations and whether they are committed both to democratic rights and principles and to democratic practices in their own internal organisation. In turn, which organisations 'assume a particular significance for the defence and promotion of democracy' will vary in time and place, dependent on a particular country's context (Beetham and Boyle 1995, p. 108). The enquiry into political aid programmes (discussed in Part II) explores the extent to which donor support for civil society incorporates an analysis of the distinctions between civil society groups and their association with democratisation.

1.2.3   Good governance

In contrast to the centuries of debate regarding the nature of democracy, definitional issues concerning 'good governance' stem from the *newness* of the concept. Indeed, it is only in association with the 'new policy agenda' of the 1990s that good governance emerged into common parlance. Two main themes arise in discussions of good governance within the context of political aid. One concerns the nature and alternative definitions of the concept itself while the other explores the origins and impetus behind its rise into wide usage. These themes are examined in turn.

First, the notion of good governance can be interpreted in relatively narrow or broad ways (Nelson and Eglinton 1992, pp. 12–13). A narrow version focuses on public administration management and institutional development, with associated measures to strengthen the capacity and efficiency of executive institutions. A broader interpretation places greater emphasis on the normative dimension of the openness, accountability and transparency of government institutions. Clearly, promoting efficient public administration can be pursued whatever the nature of the political regime, democratic or otherwise, whereas the broader version of good governance is more closely connected to a democratisation agenda. Measures associated with a broader approach involve not only encouraging relevant procedures and attitudes *within* executive institutions, but also strengthening *external* mechanisms of executive accountability, that is, its political accountability to parliament; financial accountability to national audit bodies; and legal accountability to an independent judiciary (Beetham and Boyle 1995, pp. 66–8). Further, the 'watchdog' role of civil society organisations is also pertinent here, notably an independent media and a thriving sector of pressure groups and voluntary associations. One point immediately arises, however. There is clearly a very large overlap between a broad version of good governance and democracy itself, with the two concepts becoming insufficiently distinguishable.[5] A further distinction noted by Nelson and Eglinton is that better governance can be interpreted relatively broadly or narrowly in respect of the *range* of government activities covered. Improved governance can be pursued across the whole of the public sector, or, alternatively, particular areas may be targeted, for example, budgeting and accounting processes (Nelson and Eglinton 1992, pp. 12–13). The inference here is that those parts of government most crucial to economic policy will be emphasised by a narrow approach to improving governance.

Second, where has the more recent interest in good governance sprung from? Concern with the narrow dimensions of governance is not new within development aid. Strengthening public administration has been a feature of both bilateral and multilateral aid programmes, for instance, those of the UK and Sweden and of the World Bank itself. Such capacity building was viewed both as an end in itself and as a means to improving aid effectiveness. Notwithstanding these pre-existing activities, most analysts point to the 1989 World Bank report on sub-Saharan Africa when charting the emergence of the concept of 'good governance' (Lancaster 1993; Nelson and Eglinton 1992; Waller 1992). The importance of this report was noted above (section 1.1) in marking a shift in thinking about the relationship between economic liberalisation and democracy. Significantly, the report stated that, 'What Africa needs is not just less government, but better government' (World Bank 1989, p. 5). As has been said, the context of the report was the disappointing results of structural adjustment programmes in Africa, and by the late 1980s, attention was increasingly focusing on 'weak, self-serving, and often corrupt governments as the most serious obstacles to renewed economic growth' (Nelson and Eglinton 1992, p. 12), with the emerging view that better government involved democratic government and that democratisation was required for successful economic adjustment.

The World Bank itself vigorously pursued this new emphasis on governance. In a 1992 publication, it identified and defined the key elements, giving them global application, not just in sub-Saharan Africa. Three aspects of governance were distinguished: (1) the form of political regime; (2) the processes by which authority is exercised in the management of a country's economic and social resources; and (3) the capacity of governments to design, formulate and implement policy, and to discharge government functions (World Bank 1992, p. 58). The first, as advised by their General Counsel, lies outside the Bank's mandate which is not to interfere in a country's internal political affairs. Thus their focus has been limited to the second and third aspects only, pulling back from the overtly political implications expressed in the 1989 report, as noted above (section 1.1). Four key economic dimensions of governance were identified as of relevance to the Bank's work: public sector management; accountability; legal framework for development; and transparency and information. Improving public sector management pertains to pre-existing activities, for example, civil service reform, public enterprise reform and privatisation, and financial management. It is noted, however, that such activities have grown in volume and altered in type with the changed perceptions of the role of the state, that is, moves towards a smaller state, with a professional bureaucracy, providing an 'enabling environment' for private sector led economic growth (ibid., pp. 12–13). The other three dimensions involve overlaps with elements of democracy, for instance, open and accountable government and the rule of law. However, the Bank states that it restricts itself to consideration of the economic aspects of these concepts. Thus, its concern with the financial accountability of governments entails strengthening accounting and auditing practices as well as improving capacity for economic policy management (ibid., pp. 13–28). Its interest in greater transparency and information provision is stated as three-fold: improving economic efficiency, preventing corruption, and enabling greater dissemination of economic information, for example, by strengthening government statistical offices, itself enhancing the abilities of nongovernmental institutions to contribute to policy discussions (ibid., pp. 40–7). Finally, its concern for the rule of law is limited to establishing a legal framework for economic activity, for example, property rights, laws of contract, and so on (ibid., pp. 28–39). In sum, the World Bank interpretation of good governance can be characterised both as a narrow and as an economic version.[6]

Both the origins and meaning of the governance concept indicate a distinct economic orientation. At least for the World Bank, poor governance is equated with poor economic performance, while good governance is related to the expectation of improved economic performance (Baylies 1995, p. 326). This has led to debates on the implications of the objective of good governance for neo-liberal theorising on the role of the state.

Role of the state and neo-liberalism

The focus on governance reforms indicated a shift away from the state-shrinking agenda associated with the radical neo-liberal project of the 1980s, and towards a greater emphasis on the importance of an *effective* state. In other words, there was renewed attention on the quality of the state and the efficiency with which it performs its functions. This leaves a key question unanswered, however: what *is* the role of the state? Do its functions remain restricted to the minimalist neo-liberal agenda or is there an expanded role? Considerations of whether the good governance agenda constituted a break or continuity with neo-liberalism provoked divergent responses. On the one hand, it involves for Evans a 'recognition of the state's centrality' (1992, p. 141), while Archer states that the good governance approach marks 'an important break with neo-liberalism' and 'rehabilitates the state' (1994, p. 7). Other analysts (Moore 1993; Sandbrook 1990 and 1993; Leftwich 1994) maintain that governance initiatives remain enclosed within a more minimalist concept of the state's role, with implications for the particular type of governance reforms advocated. Such contrasting views are briefly reviewed here.

Evans' belief in the significance of the rethinking involved is indicated by his characterisation of the new agenda as a paradigm shift. He outlines three waves of theorising the role of the state in the development process: first, the state as the key agent of growth and development in the 1950s and 1960s; second, the perceived failure of the statist strategy leading to the new orthodoxy of neo-utilitarian (or neo-liberal) theory and the 'rolling back' of the state in the 1980s; third, a reconceptualisation of the state's role and a reassertion of the state as a crucial actor, (Evans 1992, discussed in Baylies 1995, pp. 324–5). The third wave occurred due to the inherent paradox within the minimalist model, with the state seen as both the problem and solution in relation to structural adjustment programmes:

> orthodox policy prescriptions . . . contained the paradoxical expectation that the state (the root of the problem) would somehow be able to become the agent that initiated and implemented adjustment programmes (become the solution). (Evans 1992, p. 141)

For Archer, similarly, the new policy agenda 'marks the demise of undiluted neo-liberalism', with government no longer 'to be reduced in size and function as a matter of principle' (1994, p. 13). Indeed, 'government again becomes central to economic development as manager, planner and provider of four services . . . public education, public health, economic infrastructure, and the rule of law' (ibid.). This sits uneasily, however, with the continued evidence of declines in health and education provision in many developing countries, due to the constraints on public expenditure imposed by neo-liberal adjustment programmes.[7]

In sharp contrast to notions of a break with neo- liberalism, Leftwich explained the rise of good governance precisely as a result of the influence of neo-liberal political theory. He pointed out that 'neo-liberalism is not only an economic theory but a political one as well', emphasising 'democratic politics and a slim, efficient and accountable public bureaucracy [as] not simply desirable but *necessary* for a thriving free market economy, and vice versa' (1994, pp. 368–9). Thus it is precisely 'resurgent neo-liberal theory . . . [that] spurred western governments and international institutions to go on from promoting economic liberalisation to making good governance (and democracy) a condition of development assistance' (ibid.).

Moore and Sandbrook also perceived a degree of continuity with neo-liberalism. Moore pointed to the ideological nature of 'governance' as a product and an expression of the doctrine of Anglo-American liberalism that dominates World Bank thinking. As a consequence, he believes, the governance experience of East Asian countries with successful economic performance, 'appears to have been largely ignored' (Moore 1993b, p. 41). In conclusion, he asserts that the World Bank is willing 'to keep a close eye on the state...but...unwilling and unable to take state-building seriously' (ibid., p. 49).

Sandbrook (1990 and 1993) responded with similar criticisms to the 1989 World Bank Report on sub-Saharan Africa. The Bank prescribed a minimalist state yet 'experience has shown...that extensive government involvement is essential for achieving rapid economic development' (1990, p. 681). In this view, the emphasis on the importance of governance is right, but the Bank's concept is too narrow. The state's role should be not only to maintain an 'enabling environment' for private sector development but also 'to undertake the directive, co-ordinating role which...rapid capitalist development requires' (ibid., p. 695). The aim of governance reforms should be 'to foster a public sector capable of effectively intervening in economic life' (ibid.). As evidence, Sandbrook also cites the experience of East Asia – 'The "secret" of East Asia's newly industrialising countries...is a strong, interventionist yet market-conforming state' (ibid., p. 682).

Further and distinctive criticisms of the limitations of the governance agenda, particularly as propagated by the World Bank, have been made by Gibbon (1993) and Leftwich (1994). Separately, they criticised the fallacy of a 'technicist' approach to problems of poor governance, arguing it is illusory to conceive a technical solution independent of the form of political representation (Gibbon 1993, p. 54) or of the *type* of state which can sustain and protect good governance (Leftwich 1994, p. 363). Potentially, this critique could be less applicable to bilateral donors if they interpret good governance in a broader sense, linked to demo-cratisation efforts. This remains to be seen, however.

In sum, the rise of the concept of good governance within development discourse in the 1990s has two main thrusts. One is a recognition that the nature of government matters and involves a shift in catch-phrase from 'minimal state' to 'effective state'. In other words, the state should perform its role effectively, however defined, yet with a particular emphasis on economic management functions. The interest is in the state as a developmental instrument and the focus is on strengthening executive capacity rather than on the nature of the political regime. In this sense an effective state could be realised in a non-democratic state, at least in theory. The World Bank, has maintained its renewed emphasis on the importance of an effective state for development, as is apparent from its 1997 report dedicated to this subject. The other propelling factor, especially evident in the broader interpretation, is the push towards effective governance as essentially *democratic* governance, focusing on greater openness and accountability in government, itself a key aspect of democracy. These are quite distinct agendas and, as Schmitz and Gillies (1992, p. 16) put it, will the main policy orientation in promoting good governance be democratising the state or increasing managerial efficiency? The most striking critique from the literature, however, is that the concept of good governance remains both insufficiently well defined and subject to varying interpretations. Nevertheless, it was noted that the World Bank has provided greater clarity to *its* interpretation of good governance, retreating from democratic implications and focusing more narrowly on the economic dimensions.

1.2.4   Human rights, democracy and good governance: one agenda or three?

Two related questions remain. What is the interrelationship between these three concepts and are donors pursuing three distinct policy objectives or just one?

Differentiation can be made between governance efforts and democracy, given that the former can be narrowly orientated towards public administration and economic reform objectives, irrespective of political system. At the same time, it is possible to emphasise the interconnections between democracy and governance. The normative content of good governance, for instance – accountability, transparency, predictability – espouses the same values as democratic government. Indeed, Santiso (1999, p. 12) argues that 'the essence of functioning democracy is good governance'.

The links between human rights and democracy are complex but have been summarised relatively straightforwardly by Beetham (1995b). Human rights can be divided into the two sets of rights that make up the International Bill of Rights, that is, civil and political rights on the one hand, and economic, social and cultural rights on the other.[8] Civil and political rights constitute an intrinsic part of democracy, and without them democracy would be a contradiction in terms, with the guarantee of such basic rights as freedom of speech, of association, of assembly, and so on as a necessary prerequisite for popular control over government and for public participation in political life (ibid., p. 33). Similarly, the rights declared in the anti-discrimination Covenants – for example, those concerning discrimination against women and racial

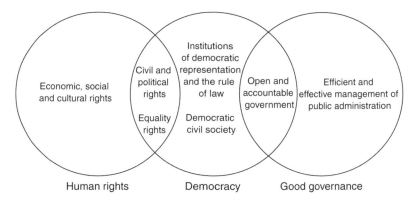

Figure 1.2 Democracy – the central concept.

discrimination – contribute towards the realisation of the principle of political equality, itself underpinning the concept of democracy. The relationship between democracy and economic, social and cultural rights is not so integral, however. It can be argued that they stand in a relationship of mutual dependency (ibid.). On the one hand, democratic rule is claimed to provide a more likely context for the realisation of economic, social and cultural rights, though this is far from guaranteed. On the other hand, the absence of economic, social and cultural rights undermines political equality and the long-term viability of democratic institutions. Nevertheless, economic, social and cultural rights constitute a separate domain from that of democracy, as illustrated in Figure 1.2.

Overall, the malleability of the three terms – in particular those of good governance and democracy – subject to both broad and narrow interpretations, makes definitive statements difficult. Nevertheless, it is proposed here that democracy is the central concept to which the other two are closely interrelated, though less so to each other. This can be illustrated diagrammatically as three intersecting circles, with democracy central, and areas of overlap between democracy and human rights and democracy and good governance respectively. It is asserted here that this amounts to an overall goal of promoting democratisation, with the proviso that there are elements of the governance agenda that are orientated at facilitating economic market reforms and have little to do with democracy.

1.2.5 Summary

A range of analysts have commented that a feature of the main concepts – human rights, democracy and good governance – is their contested nature and that their introduction into development assistance is characterised by a lack of conceptual clarity, with repercussions for policy coherence. The only possible exception is human rights, benefiting from greater definitional specificity through its incorporation into international law. Pertinently, Burnell (1994, p. 488) noted that clarity of aims and objectives is essential for effective policy implementation, with negative implications if concepts are insufficiently well defined.

A number of questions arise concerning the introduction of human rights, democracy and good governance as aid policy objectives. Two general questions are highlighted, followed by questions specific to each concept.

1. What meanings do the donors give to the three main concepts? Have they been clearly defined and what are the differences between their interpretations?
2. What is the relative weight accorded to the three concepts and what are the variations in priorities?
   (a) *In relation to human rights:* do donors restrict their concerns to civil and political rights and is this valid?
   (b) *In relation to democracy:* is democracy promotion restricted to a formal, procedural version, concentrating on multi-party elections? Alternatively, is support extended to all four essential components of a functioning democracy (Beetham's democratic pyramid)? In particular, what emphasis is given to strengthening civil society, how is it defined and what is its perceived role in democratisation?
   (c) *In relation to good governance:* will donors focus on a broad or narrow interpretation? In particular, will the World Bank's interpretation gain increasing influence amongst bilateral donors? Does the governance agenda represent a more extensive role for the state or are its functions still perceived within a neo-liberal framework?

The two general questions are addressed in Chapter 2, while those specific to the three concepts are examined through the investigation of political aid programmes in Part II.

1.3   Policy legitimacy

The linking of development aid to political conditions was clearly controversial and its legitimacy was questioned by commentators in a number of different ways. The normative issues raised can be categorised into three main themes. First, the legitimacy of external intervention; second, the integrity of donor policy; third, the reciprocity of policy application to both recipient and donor governments. These are examined in turn.

1.3.1 External intervention

The legitimacy of donor intervention was scrutinised in several ways. The issue of sovereignty was clearly the most crucial dimension, with a related question concerning claims of donor imposition of a Western political model. These two issues are explored in turn.

Sovereignty

The right to sovereignty and non-interference in internal political affairs is an established principle of international relations, codified in international law. It is included in the *UN Charter* (Article 2.7) and the right of self-determination is the subject of a stand-alone article in both elements of the *International Bill of Rights* (Part I Article 1 in each). Sovereignty has been a particularly valued principle for developing countries in the post-Independence period, given the history of colonialism and issues of neo-colonialism. Political conditionality undoubtedly involves the governments of developed countries in external intervention in the political affairs of developing countries. Does this constitute an infringement of sovereignty?

A number of heads of state of developing countries have certainly argued that this is the case, though the credibility of their claim is undermined at times by their own poor records in treatment of their citizens. Presidents Habré of Chad and Traoré of Mali objected to the introduction of political conditionality by the French government at the La Baule summit in June 1990 as an interference in their domestic affairs (Nwokedi 1993, pp. 172–3). Similarly, President Moi of Kenya unilaterally broke off relations with Norway in 1991, objecting to Norwegian reproaches about alleged human rights violations as interference in internal affairs (Eidmann 1993, pp. 129–30). Discussions of political conditionality also featured prominently at the tenth summit of the Non-Aligned Movement (NAM) in Jakarta in September 1992, with its Final Document declaring:

> However, sovereignty and the principle of non-interference in the internal affairs of other states should not be diluted under any pretext (. . .) No country should use its power to dictate its concept of human

rights or impose conditionalities on others. (Cited in Nherere 1995, p. 291)

On the other hand, legal commentators provide an analysis of the relationship between *human rights* and sovereignty that supports third party intervention under certain conditions as *lawful* interference in the internal affairs of other states, consistent with sovereignty (Nherere 1995, p. 295; Schrijver 1995). This assertion of the primacy of universal human rights over the sovereignty rights of states in international law is broadly supported by most political conditionality analysts (Sorensen 1993b, p. 1; Stokke 1995, p. 35; Eide 1994, p. 170), although Uvin has reservations that it is not yet 'a generally accepted principle' (1993, p. 68). The legal argument focuses, first, on the non-absolute nature and the dynamic nature of sovereignty, with states having progressively agreed to restrictions to their powers through the acceptance of obligations under international treaties, including human rights instruments (Schrijver 1995). Further, it is the essence of human rights that there are limits to what a state can do to its citizens, as defined in international covenants (Nherere 1995, p. 293). As the legitimate concern of international human rights law, what a state does to its citizens 'is no longer within the ambit of its sovereignty' (ibid.). Hence, rather than unlawful interference, Eide contends that third parties are not only entitled but are under obligation to concern themselves with the human rights conditions in other states (cited in ibid.). Such views gain particular force from the fact that the large majority of the world's nations have signed up to both elements of the International Bill of Rights and to regional human rights conventions (see Crawford 1995, pp. 51–4).

Nherere states, however, that such arguments are limited to the justification of *human rights* conditionality, and cannot be extended to the spheres of democracy or good governance, not themselves subject to international agreements. 'There is nothing in human rights law that requires that multi-party elections be held', while 'there is no norm of international law that purports to stipulate or prescribe what constitutes "good governance"' (Nherere 1995, p. 300). While it is formally correct to state that human rights law does not require *multi-party* elections, the right to vote in regular elections is endorsed in Article 25 of the International Covenant on Civil and Political Rights. This states that:

Every citizen shall have the right and the opportunity... to vote and be elected at genuine periodic elections which shall be by universal and equal suffrage and shall be held by secret ballot, guaranteeing the free expression of the will of the electors.

Thus, the right to representative government is established in human rights law, with representatives freely selected through regular elections, even if competition might be limited to individuals as independent candidates and does not necessarily entail multi-party elections.

Overall, the legitimacy of external intervention to promote democracy and good governance is weaker than that for human rights and more susceptible to the allegation of unlawful interference in internal affairs. Two points can be made, however. One is that the 'infringement of sovereignty' argument applies particularly to donor coercion through *negative* measures, that is, to political conditionality as narrowly defined. It is more difficult to apply this argument to positive measures, given that, in principle at least, they are subject to the consent of the recipient state, often through a contractual agreement. Even if conditions are attached to such assistance, it can be argued that the recipient government has consented (ibid., p. 301). To question the legitimacy of donors' actions on sovereignty grounds in such circumstances would be tantamount to querying *all* development aid activities as unwarranted interference in internal affairs.

Second, human rights conditionality, as legitimated by international law, is closely linked to encouraging the emergence of democracy. The overlap between human rights and democracy, with civil and political rights as an essential component of democracy and as a prerequisite for genuine elections, infers that aid made conditional upon respect for civil and political rights serves to promote political liberalisation and to open up political space in which the populace can potentially have a greater influence on national political reforms. Indeed, in recommending that political conditionality be restricted to 'the observance of human rights in general and civil and political rights in particular' and 'to de-emphasize democracy', two specific advantages stated by Moore and Robinson are the increased legitimacy of a human rights approach to conditionality and that 'it does in practice help address many of the concerns of the "democrats"' (1994, pp. 155–6).

The legitimacy (or otherwise) of political conditionality in relation to sovereignty rights has been discussed primarily within an international legal framework, relying substantially on Nherere's analysis. However, there is a more forceful refutation that conditionality constitutes unlawful interference in the affairs of another state. Interestingly, this also comes from Nherere. Having carefully constructed the legal argument to justify human rights conditionality, though not democratisation or good governance conditionality, he then changes tack to say that such arguments are unnecessary in fact and that objections to conditionality as infringing sovereignty are 'both irrelevant and misguided' (1995, p. 301). This is because, 'There is no legal obligation to give aid' and 'there is nothing unlawful' in a donor 'attaching any conditions it likes' or 'choos[ing] to give to such recipients as it selects' (ibid.). This description of the asymmetry of power relations within the aid relationship, at its most flagrant in conditionality, is also explored by other authors, for instance Stokke (1995), though the latter highlights more critically the undesirability of exploiting such power.

In sum, despite the protestations of some rulers, there is a growing consensus in favour of human rights transcending sovereignty rights in international law. This legitimises *human rights* conditionality in principle, if not aid restrictions on democracy or governance grounds. It does not necessarily provide a justification for specific donor practices, however. In an interesting twist, and one which is distinct from the above views of Nherere, Tomasevski criticises aid conditionality for the arbitrary and discretionary way in which human rights are invoked by donors. Conditionality is imposed at the donors' *discretion*, with decisions taken without recourse to the inter-governmental bodies established for that purpose. In this respect, donors are criticised for establishing a ' "parallel track", acting as prosecutor, judge and executor', undermining the existing UN system (Tomasevski 1993, p. 122). In addition, donors' decisions to suspend or restrict aid are *arbitrary* due to the failure to specify the 'criteria for linking human rights violations and donors' responses' (ibid., p. 96). These practices, in Tomasevski's view, 'constitute a breach of the due process of law which undermines the rule of law on which human rights are based' (ibid.). While there appear to be valid aspects of Tomasevski's argument, her emphasis on the UN Commission on Human Rights as the appropriate investigating institution is surprising, given that it is not a Covenant monitoring body and has a reputation as a more 'politicised' body. Her views are echoed by Clayton (1994, p. 3), who criticises human rights conditionality as 'defined by donors, rather than rooted in universal human rights norms'.

The Western model of democracy

A further concern was of donors promoting, if not imposing, a Western model of democracy (M. Robinson 1994, p. 49; Barya 1993, pp. 16–17). Objections can be three-fold.

One is that democracy, however desirable, should not (and cannot) be externally imposed. This was the view of certain African leaders, for example, OAU Secretary General Salim Ahmed Salim and President Museveni of Uganda (cited in Barya 1993, p. 19). Democracy by its very nature must be subject to national level discussion, with local actors determining the form most suitable for local conditions. The extent to which donors actually encourage local participation remains questionable, however. A second and related objection is mistrust and scepticism about donor intentions, with the promotion of multi-party-ism seen as a mechanism through which donor manipulation can be maximised (Barya 1993, pp. 16–17). This argument has particular force when linked to suspicions that 'democracy' is valued more as a means to remove incumbent rulers perceived as obstacles to donor-advocated economic reforms. Third, the appropriateness of a multi-party model for some developing countries is questioned, particularly in the (mainly African) context of ethnically diverse societies. It is claimed that multi-party competition can intensify ethnic divisions, with the emergence of political parties based on ethnic identities. A counter argument, how-ever, is that democracy comprises a *variety* of institutional arrangements and practices. Some, most notably the Westminster model, characterised by majoritarian, winner-takes all politics, may indeed exacerbate con-flict in heterogeneous societies divided along ethnic, religious or cultural lines. In contrast, a consensual model of democracy can moderate such negative aspects of majority rule, providing greater protection to and influence within government to minority social groups.[9]

In sum, clearly any external imposition of democracy is inappropriate and contradicts the very concept itself. It bears repeating that demo-cracy is essentially an internal matter. The objection to the promotion of a Western model, however, does overlook the variety of institutional forms that exist within Western nations themselves. Nevertheless, it remains valid to question the extent to which donors will encourage local participation in determining the most appropriate form.

1.3.2 Donor integrity?

Legitimacy is also questioned through doubts about the integrity of donor policy. Are donors genuinely concerned to promote democratisa-tion in aid recipient countries or is there a hidden agenda? Comment-ators suggest other intentions, some more covert than others. Two in particular are put forward: political reform as a means to economic liberalisation, and political conditionality and democracy promotion as a means of maintaining global dominance and hegemony.

Economic and political liberalisation

First, it is fairly undisputed that the motives behind the introduction of political aid policies were partly economic. There is little attempt to disguise such intentions by donors, given the current orthodoxy in official Western circles of democracy as 'a necessary condition of economic development' (Leftwich 1996, p. 4) and of the mutual compatibility of economic and political liberalisation. Burnell (1993, pp. 11–12) provides examples of such 'current orthodoxy' from UK government ministers, a European Commissioner, and from World Bank officials.[10]

This 'orthodoxy' is not straightforwardly supported by academic research, however. In a fascinating review of 24 cross-national quantitative studies into the relationship between economic development and political regime type, Moore (1995) discovered that nine concluded that democratic governments have a better economic record, whereas the findings of a further nine were that authoritarian governments achieve better economic results; the remaining six could find no definite pattern either way. In other words, the overall findings were inconclusive, a complete stalemate! Turning to the relationship between democracy and economic adjustment, Haggard and Webb do find evidence from an eight-country study that new democracies can successfully implement stabilisation and structural adjustment objectives (1994, pp. 6–8). This is particularly so when economic reforms are introduced shortly after the democratic transition: for instance, in Poland. During this initial period, new democratic governments benefit from a political space ('the honeymoon effect') when the costs of adjustment can be traded against the political gains of democracy. Failure to take swift action, however, meant that success in introducing economic reforms was much less assured: for example, in Argentina, Bolivia and Brazil (ibid.). Somewhat in contrast, Healey and Robinson examined the relationship between economic and political reform through a wide-ranging review of relevant literature and concluded that:

> Third World experience so far does not give any assurance that political liberalisation or more representative government will *per se* result in better economic management or more decisive or effective adjustment policies, faster economic growth or less inequality. (1992, p. 124)

The donors' general assumption that political liberalisation will lead to greater economic reform and development may make most 'sense' in the context of sub-Saharan Africa, given the failure of various forms of non-democratic regimes to deliver economic development, coupled with the belief that incumbent authoritarian rulers and clientelist politics prevail as the main obstacle to economic liberalisation. Nevertheless, this also remains uncorroborated by research. In considering *prospects* in sub-Saharan Africa, Healey and Robinson examine both likely areas of compatibility between political liberalisation and economic reform and potential areas of tension, and conclude that 'there can be no assurance that political liberalisation or multi-party democracy will also ensure better economic management' (ibid., p. 157).

Despite the 'current orthodoxy' in official government circles, a USAID workshop on economic reform in Africa in the era of political liberalisation indicated the lack of consensus amongst academics (USAID 1993). On the one hand, the predominant donor view of overall compatibility was represented, stating that democratic regimes present an improved opportunity for economic reforms, one reason being the increased legitimacy of elected governments to undertake such measures. Baylies makes a comment, pertinent to the issue of donor integrity, that this view suggests 'a more cynical interpretation of donor advocacy of pluralist political systems', with the aim of softening the perception of external imposition of structural adjustment (1995, p. 333). One wonders whether it is not so much democracy that is valued as the change of government that it is surmised will result from democratisation, opening up enhanced prospects for economic reform. Experience indicates, however, that old regimes are often very successful at retaining power in processes of democratic transition.[11] On the other hand, Callaghy offered a dissenting view, questioning that a positive relationship exists between political and economic liberalisation (USAID 1993, pp. 10–11). He argued that the requisites for successful economic reform were more difficult to achieve under democratic conditions, particularly sustained government commitment and technocratic rather than political decision making (ibid.). Common to both predominant and dissenting views, however, was the primary exigency of economic reform, with the contention being whether political liberalisation offered a suitable context for its achievement. Perhaps this emphasis on the primacy of economic reform led Moyo to query whether the donors valued democracy in itself and to question what would happen if an elected government chose to oppose World Bank-type economic reform (ibid., p. 18).

Examining the relationship between the two variables in the opposite direction, that is, the impact of economic reform on democratisation, also highlights some incompatibilities and contradictions between the dual agendas. One claim is that economic liberalisation (in the form of IMF/World Bank structural adjustment programmes) undermines democracy, a point made by Barya and by Oxfam UK. Barya asserts that economic conditionality and political conditionality are 'necessarily contradictory and cannot be successfully be accomplished together', citing the *Codesria Bulletin* that structural adjustment programmes undermine economic sovereignty and strengthen authoritarian regimes who implement inherently anti-democratic socio-economic reforms (Barya 1993, pp. 16–17).[12] Oxfam UK makes a similar point, criticising structural adjustment programmes as responsible for the removal of economic policy choice from national governments to the international financial institutions, supported by Northern governments, and pose the question: 'Is genuine democracy compatible with the *de facto* transfer of economic policy sovereignty to Washington based institutions?' (1993, p. 25). The implementation of structural adjustment programmes since the early 1980s has been characterised by the lack of policy choice, with national governments, in desperate economic circumstances, often having little or no option but to accept the IFIs' packages of economic reforms. Yet the democratic principle of popular control includes *government* control over policy, which the populace in turn influences both through regular, periodic elections and through other mechanisms facilitating ongoing inputs into the policy-making process. Ostensibly, the World Bank seeks to strengthen the latter mechanisms through governance reforms, improving the transparency and increasing the accountability of government. Yet it can be argued that simultaneously they are undermining such processes by the removal of government and local control over economic policy – effectively in their hands and those of the IMF – supported by most donor governments. This raises crucial questions. Governance reforms may bring about improvements in transparency and accountability, but do these measures enhance *popular* control, or rather do they facilitate the better surveillance of a government's economic management and intensify its accountability, not to its own people, but to the IFIs themselves? Are Northern donors, both multilateral and bilateral, now effectively taking over from the state the role of providing strategic direction over the economy, rendering moves to democratic control of national government less than meaningful, as well as raising issues of sovereignty?

At a minimum, these discussions of the interactions between political and economic liberalisation indicate that the relationship remains complex, contested and unresolved, despite the prevailing donor assumption of mutual compatibility. An outstanding question remains, however. If areas of tension and incompatibility do arise, what will take priority in donor programmes: economic or political reform, structural adjustment or democratisation? Clearly, the outcome would depend on donor motivation and whether democracy is valued primarily as an end in itself or as a means to economic reform.

Democracy promotion, global dominance and hegemony

As touched on in discussions of the concept of democracy, a radical left critique views Western democracy promotion as motivated by the aim of defending global power and privilege. The work of key exponents of such views are examined, namely J.-J. Barya, William I. Robinson and B. Gills *et al.*, the editors of *Low Intensity Democracy*; all expound similar arguments at times.

In Barya's (1993, p. 17) view, there is no doubt that the project of the 'new political conditionalities' is nothing but an attempt by the big Western capitalist powers to create a new legitimacy in a new post-cold war world order whereby discredited dictatorial regimes in Africa and elsewhere in the Third World are replaced by new leaders under the ideology of pluralism, democracy and free enterprise, while Western powers maintain hegemony over countries which are economically and politically useful to them.

Similarly, Gills *et al.* interpret the 'current drive towards democracy as an integral aspect of the economic and ideological restructuring accompanying a new stage of globalisation in the capitalist world economy' (Gills *et al.* 1993, p. 4). Their argument focuses overwhelmingly on US foreign policy intervention, past and present, particularly that government's shift in external support away from overt authoritarianism to democracy promotion. In their view, democracy is used as an instrument of intervention, particularly in contexts where authoritarianism is discredited and delegitimised. The intent of 'low intensity democracy' is to provide cosmetic change only, yet sufficient to demobilise popular forces and thus 'pre-empt either progressive reform or revolutionary change' (ibid., p. 8). The attraction of 'low intensity democracy', from the point of view of 'US and conservative domestic elites', is that 'a civilianised, conservative regime can pursue painful and even repressive economic and social policies with more impunity and with less popular resistance than can an openly authoritarian regime' (ibid., pp. 8–9).

A similarly critical perspective is developed extensively by William I. Robinson (1996), seeking to explain the aim of US democracy promotion, described as 'promoting polyarchy', in a wider context.[13] He asserts that the main goal of US foreign policy has remained unchanged since the US emerged as the dominant world power at the end of the second world war. In his view, this goal is to maintain the global disparity of wealth, and the tremendous privilege and power it entails, and which operates essentially in US interests. Various means have been employed to pursue this objective, from coercion through 'straight power' (for example, military intervention), to forms of 'persuasion' (W. I. Robinson 1996, Chapter 1). 'Democracy promotion' is merely the latest instrument used, albeit a 'softer tool' (ibid. p. 5). Echoing Gills *et al.* (1993), W. I. Robinson (1996, p. 6) argues that the intent of democracy promotion is to *co-opt* dissatisfaction and unrest (as expressed through national democratisation movements), to suppress 'mass aspirations' for more thorough-going democratisation, and, thus, 'to secure the underlying objective of maintaining essentially undemocratic societies inserted into an unjust international system'. The theoretical basis of his argument includes Gramsci's concept of hegemony as 'consensual domination' of political and civil society, though extended from national to global levels. In this respect, W. I. Robinson (p. 319) goes further than Barya: for instance, by proposing that the new political intervention will seek not only to develop allies within the formal state apparatus in developing countries, but also 'to advance this agenda... through the organs of civil society in respective countries'. Whereas Barya's proposition was that support for civil society organisations would not be forthcoming from donors, W. I. Robinson postulates their *inclusion* in the hegemonic project, though in a manner which involves their co-option.

In their favour, such radical left critiques do locate policy shifts within the 'big picture' of global changes and do dig deeper to reveal material interests and forces. Nevertheless, they are also subject to challenge. The conspiratorial nature of Barya's propositions may be questioned; one may also query global capital's interest in sub-Saharan Africa, a region which is increasingly economically marginalised in the world economy, and in which the trend is of finance capital's withdrawal (Moore 1993a, p. 3). The emphasis on US élite actors in the works of Gills *et al.* and W. I. Robinson can be criticised on two levels. One, ironically, is its US-centricity and the over-determining influence on global events granted to such actors, with limited emphasis on 'counter-hegemonic' forces, including those within developing countries. Is manipulation so easily achieved? Another criticism concerns the applicability of their arguments to other donor governments whose foreign and aid policies may not complement those of the US government. It is not the intention to outline more detailed criticisms here. Rather, taking W. I. Robinson's

(1996, p. 5) words that 'foreign policy is not to be analyzed on the basis of what policymakers *say* they do, but on what they actually *do*', it is one aim of this research to do just that and simultaneously to assess the accuracy of the propositions put forward by Robinson and other theorists. Are Western governments merely concerned to promote 'polyarchy' and 'low intensity democracy'?

1.3.3   Reciprocity of policy standards?

A third issue of donor legitimacy questions the moral standing of donor policy. At face value, the introduction of human rights and democracy conditionality involves an enhanced ethical dimension to aid policy – in contrast to past policies of aiding authoritarian and repressive regimes. Yet, as Archer (cited in M. Robinson 1995b, p. 373) has argued, this implies that 'Donors should set standards of performance for themselves that are at least as rigorous as those they expect recipient governments to achieve'. Unsurprisingly, a number of writers express scepticism that such reciprocity will occur.

Stokke and Ostergaard both point to Western governments' inconsistent and hypocritical practice in the recent past with regard to human rights and democracy, nothing how both legitimacy and credibility are thus undermined. Stokke cites Southern Africa as one example where 'regimes and terrorist organisations, oppressing fundamental human rights and democracy for years, have been bolstered by today's crusaders of these lofty values' (1995, p. 76). Ostergaard specifically targets the US and French governments, 'both of whom have alarming records of supporting dictatorships', noting how El Salvador was the third largest recipient of US foreign aid in the early 1980s (at the height of state terrorism) and how Mobutu in (the former) Zaïre continued to be propped up by the US as late as 1990/91 (1993, pp. 127–8). While it is clearly relevant to recall such (recent) historical hypocrisy as a pointer to possible unchanged practices, it is also important to acknowledge that government policies can and do change. Ostergaard outlines the implementation standards that are required: 'If democratic principles and human rights are to be a foundation of aid transfers, they have to be applied with consistency, international co-ordination and the necessary dialogue with the country in question' (ibid., p. 128).

The concepts of accountability and transparency recur frequently in donor policy statements. Yet, will such attributes also be applied to donors' own aid programmes? Three aspects are noted. One, will the criteria by which donors assess recipient government performance on human rights and democracy grounds be made clear and explicit? Two, will donor governments improve accountability mechanisms to enable enhanced scrutiny of their own aid programmes, for example, through increased transparency and freedom of information? Three, democratic methods imply a challenge to the practices of donor aid agencies themselves, requiring then to adopt 'more open and more participatory approaches to the planning, design, implementation and evaluation of projects and programs', including greater involvement of intended beneficiaries in decision-making (Sénecal 1993 p. 88).

A tangential view on development aid and human rights is that development policies and projects have themselves been a source of human rights violations within a recipient country, for example, through exploitation of cheap labour, especially of contract and migrant workers, and through forced displacement, especially of indigenous peoples, in large dam projects (Tomasevski 1989; Dias 1994, pp. 53–4). In order to prevent such negative effects, it is argued that all aid projects should themselves be subject to prior assessment according to human rights criteria. Moreover, Tomasevski (1989, Chapter 7) proposes taking this approach a step further by applying human rights criteria in a positive manner to ensure that all aid programmes *promote* human rights, thus guaranteeing the compatibility of aid policies and practices with universal human rights norms and as a corrective against 'maldevelopment'.

Donors are challenged to reform and democratise their own aid programmes. Ul Haq (1993 p. 85), citing UNDP data, points to how many aid programmes are still linked to the cold war past: only 25 per cent of total aid goes to 75 percent of the poorest people; twice as much aid *per capita* goes to high military spenders than to moderate spenders; $370 *per capita* per annum to Egypt compared with $4 to India; in 1992 the US gave as much assistance to E1 Salvador as Bangladesh, despite the latter having 24 times the population and being 5 times poorer. His message to donors: 'You need to reform your own programmes and link them to poverty, link them to human development, link them to restraint on military spending' (ibid.).

Finally, two broader points are made with respect to donor legitimacy, asserting a degree of hypocrisy in political conditionality and challenging the rich governments to change their practices that impair the realisation of human rights in the world. Uvin (1993, p. 7) emphasises the need for donors to 'moralis(e) their own foreign policy', with a starting point being to cut arms exports and military assistance to countries engaged in consistent and gross human rights violations. He notes how such arms from OECD nations often serve to maintain dictators in power

(1993, p. 77). Based on UNDP calculations that development assistance of $54 billion contrasts with a cost of $500 billion from restricted market access in the international economy, Sorensen questions 'whether donor countries practice political conditionality with one hand while upholding an unequal economic system with the other hand, which itself undermines the prospects for sustained progress in human rights' (1993b, p. 5).

1.3.4 Summary

The legitimacy of the new policy agenda has been questioned by commentators in a variety of ways. Of these, the most significant issues are (a) of sovereignty; (b) of the form of democracy that is being promoted; (c) of whether the promotion of democracy conceals hidden agendas; and (d) of whether the same standards and principles are applied reciprocally to donor foreign and aid policies. Some of the questions raised can be answered through empirical research, while others, especially the broader, normative issues, are more matters of judgement which lend themselves less readily to the empirical investigation undertaken here. Questions explored in subsequent chapters through the comparative examination of donor practices include the following:

- Are donor practices sensitive to issues of sovereignty?
- Is the implementation of political conditionality based solely on human rights criteria or extended to grounds of democracy and good governance? Are the mechanisms of the UN human rights system utilised?
- Is a Western model of democracy imposed?
- Is there evidence of hidden agendas operating? In particular, do economic considerations predominate?
- Do donors apply the same standards to their own aid programmes?

Some other issues raised in this section are not included as research questions due to the limited scope of the present study. They may entail distinct questions for empirical investigation that are outside the boundaries of this volume – for example, development assistance and high military spenders. Alternatively, they may encompass themes of such breadth – for example, democracy promotion and the maintenance of global hegemony – that empirical enquiry is less practicable. Nevertheless, from the empirical material gathered, this work does attempt to address the extent to which these latter concerns are justified.

Questions concerning project aid to promote democratisation are examined in Part II, those related to the implementation of aid conditionality are addressed in Part III.

1.4   Policy implementation and impact

Turning to more instrumental issues, a final theme in the literature focused on the implementation of the new policy agenda and its likely effectiveness. Legitimacy aside, would it work in practice?

Policy implementation takes place through two distinct instruments, carrot and stick, described as positive and negative measures. Positive measures (referred to as 'political aid' in this research) entail the provision of development assistance to promote human rights, democracy and good governance, whereas negative measures involve the suspension, wholly or partially, of development aid in situations of abuses of civil and political rights or reversals of the democratisation process. While the objective of both policy tools is to contribute towards democratisation in developing countries, they tend to be utilised in different circumstances. The stick of aid sanctions is mainly applied to help leverage change from an authoritarian to a democratic regime (especially where incumbent rulers are resistant) or to forestall democratic backsliding. In contrast, 'political aid' aims to encourage and assist ongoing political reforms at different stages of the democratisation process from initial liberalisation to democratic transition and subsequent democratic consolidation. There is general consensus amongst commentators that democratisation is fundamentally an internal process and that the role of external agents is to complement internal pressures for reform. However, as regards assessing effectiveness, clearly there are difficulties in separating out the distinct contribution of external actors from the range of other factors. Such factors include not just internal influences, but structural factors (for instance, economic decline) and diffusion effects (for example, regional diffusion). Hence, unsurprisingly, there are different views on the (likely) effectiveness of external agents in democracy promotion activities. Negative and positive measures are examined in turn.

1.4.1   Aid sanctions

With regard to the implementation of punitive measures, two key issues were raised. One pertained to donor consistency in policy application, with a range of commentators all doubting the likelihood of even-handed deployment between countries (Stokke 1995, p. 76; Nelson and Eglinton, 1992 p. 31; Burnell 1993, pp. 28–32; M. Robinson 1993a and b; Uvin 1993; Sorensen 1995; Cumming 1996, pp. 494–5). The other raised the question of the effectiveness of aid sanctions where applied (M. Robinson 1993a and b; Uvin 1993; Stokke 1995).

Regarding the issue of consistency, reference is made to the precedent of selective and uneven application by the Carter administration (1976–79) of human rights conditionality on US foreign assistance (Forsythe 1988, pp. 51–60; Nelson and Eglinton 1992, p. 28, Uvin 1993, p. 65), as discussed above. It is recognised that donor governments pursue a number of competing interests through their foreign policies; this can lead to exampels of double standards, with policy towards China being 'the clearest (but not the only) example' (Sorensen 1995, p. 393). Similarly, M. Robinson notes the lack of systematic application of human rights criteria by donors, especially when in conflict with strategic interests, citing the example of US assistance to El Salvador in the 1980s (1993a, p. 59). The extent to which the end of the cold war will facilitate a more consistent approach is also questioned, with M. Robinson citing early evidence of 'Britain's reluctance to apply strict political conditionality despite evidence of...the suppression of civil and political rights' in Kenya, Malawi and Ghana (1993b, p. 94). For Stokke, however, cases at that point had not provided sufficient evidence to prove or disprove propositions on policy implementation (1995, p. 55). For representatives of recipient nations, concerns are less about the incorporation of the *principles* of human rights and democracy into aid policy, but more about policy *implementation*, again raising the question of consistency (Carl Greenidge, *The Courier*, No. 155, 1996, p. 22).

Although the charge of likely inconsistency by donors in applying political conditionality implies criticisms of hypocrisy and double standards, there is a counter argument, outlined for the sake of balance, by Burnell (1993, pp. 31–2) and by Stokke (1995, p. 76). The claim is that the uneven application of political conditions is defensible in pragmatic terms. An optimum strategy to secure political reform involves applying a combination of measures, both sticks and carrots, in accordance with individual circumstances in particular countries. In contrast to a 'principled' application of threats and sanctions 'across the board', such a strategy implies the application of aid conditionality where it *might work* (for instance, in weak, aid-dependent countries) but not where it is unlikely to succeed (in large, middle-income countries) or the donor costs of applying sanctions are high (where there exist extensive trade relations).

Regarding the likely effectiveness of political conditionality, three writers explicitly addressed this question, Robinson, Uvin and Stokke. Uvin defines effectiveness as 'a recipient country undertak[ing] a policy change it would not have undertaken by itself, that is, without the pressure made to bear upon it by the donor' (1993, p. 72). All three analysts are cautious in their own assessments of likely effectiveness, emphasising limitations and constraints. M. Robinson, however, also surveyed other views on political conditionality's contribution to the political reform process in Africa and found a spectrum of opinions. At the one end, there were those who believed political conditionality had provided the major impetus: 'The principal cause of Africa's wind of change is the World Bank and the donor countries', (*Africa Confidential* 1990, cited in M. Robinson 1993b, p. 92). At the other end, there were those who argued that political conditionality had played a relatively minor role in democratic transition. Robinson's own view is that conditioned aid's contribution to political change in Africa 'probably lies somewhere between these two positions' (M. Robinson 1993b, p. 92). The greatest impact is identified at the early stages of democratisation, 'helping to initiate a process of political liberalisation or to speed up the transition from authoritarian rule if there is resistance from an incumbent regime', and where 'there is an organised internal opposition which favours the imposition of strict aid conditions' (ibid., p. 96). This latter point is reinforced by Uvin (1993, p. 72) and by Nelson and Eglinton (1992, p. 37), who note the potential for 'sham compliance' by recipient governments where internal pressure is weak. The examination of actual cases also leads Robinson to the conclusion that 'political conditionality will only work under certain fairly restrictive conditions', notably donor co-ordination or aid dependency on a single donor (1993a, p. 65).

Uvin examines the constraints that aid conditionality is subject to, both on the donor and recipient sides, and concludes that 'there are many barriers to the exercise of a global and effective policy of political conditionality' (1993, p. 73). These obstacles involve a mixture of both normative and instrumental constraints on effective policy implementation. On the donor side, he identifies problems that will limit effectiveness as: the issue of sovereignty; development assistance as relatively small in volume compared with other sources of income (trade, foreign investment); a hierarchy of conflicting foreign policy objectives; the lack of an operational definition (or minimum threshold conditions) of respect for human rights and democracy; claims that sanctions hurt the poor not the government. On the recipient side, constraints include: élite resistance, particularly if the pressure comes from the former colonial power; government evasion through ability to comply with one hand and undo with the other; access to alternative sources of finance (other donors or capital markets) (ibid., pp. 68–73). To reinforce this view of the probable *ineffectiveness* of political conditionality, Uvin contrasts it with economic conditionality. Expectations of the latter's effectiveness are high, due to the attachment of specific policy conditions which are amenable to definition and measurement. Yet the results have been of low effectiveness, with relatively high levels of 'slippage' regarding actual compliance with economic policy conditionality (see Mosley *et al.* 1991, p. 136 and pp. 300–1; also Chapter 8, section 8.1 of this volume). Given this, Uvin concludes that 'political conditionality risks being extremely ineffective indeed' (1993, p. 73).

Stokke explores the instrumental issue of effectiveness in both theory and practice, by examining actual cases as far as is possible. From a theoretical point of view, he outlines a series of six propositions concerning both, in his words, 'the potentials and limitations' of political conditionality. However, the examples of applied conditionality available (Indonesia, Kenya, the Belgian experience in the former Zaïre, Burundi and Rwanda) did 'not provide sufficient evidence either to prove or disprove the propositions' (1995, p. 55). Two preliminary findings are stated, nevertheless. One is the importance of donor coordination as 'almost an essential, although not sufficient, precondition' of success (ibid.). The other is that small, poor and aid-dependent countries are the exception in being much more vulnerable to donor pressure (ibid.). He concludes that there is 'little likelihood that political conditionality will work except in the limited areas already indicated' (ibid., p. 66). Stokke's work is built on in this research, with his six propositions providing a most useful framework for analysis. Their verification (or not) are considered in Part III from the evidence of a much larger dataset of cases of applied aid conditionality in the first half of the 1990s.

Finally, Sorensen adds another dimension to considerations of political conditionality's effectiveness. He concurs with the cautious approach of the other commentators examined here, stating that political conditionality has a limited role to play. However, he points to how the policy of political conditionality and the mere *threat* of aid restrictions can itself positively assist the democratisation process in two respects: 'first, in dissuading rulers, both non-democratic and newly democratised alike, from human rights abuse against opponents'; second, 'in discouraging backsliding towards authoritarian rule, for example in the case of a military coup or an aborted election' (1993, p. 4). This view is supported by M. Robinson that conditionality could have a role in '*deterring* military intervention' (1993b, p. 97, emphasis added). Thus, this suggests the possibility of political conditionality being more effective than may initially appear, yet difficult to empirically verify.

1.4.2   Political aid

Donor preference for positive measures was noted, something that was reaffirmed by most commentators as preferable to conditionality (Stokke 1995, p. 66; Uvin 1993, p. 77). Nevertheless, both quantitative and qualitative issues were raised, as well as, overall, the question of effectiveness.

The likely quantity of aid dedicated to political objectives was queried in two main respects. One was that rewards of increased aid for progress towards democratisation, as pledged by the British government, for instance, were thought unlikely in the context of aid cuts. Referring specifically to assistance designed to strengthen civil society, M. Robinson describes the volume of aid as 'rather paltry' (1993b, p. 97). The other was that a degree of re-labelling of old activities as support for new democracy and governance objectives was anticipated (Robinson 1993a, p. 61). In line with general expectations of a narrow interpretation of democracy, a qualitative critique foresaw that aid would be concentrated on governmental institutions, particularly the process of democratic transition and support for multi-party elections. In other words, assistance would be predominantly top-down, with a more limited focus on bottom-up measures.

Sorensen distinguished this twofold approach to democracy promotion as support at 'macro' and 'micro' levels. Citing India, he notes how a formally democratic political system at the national level does not mean its introduction at the local level, and personally recommends that donors concentrate on the micro level without disregarding the macro level (1995, pp. 397–9). In expanding this proposal, he advocates support for grassroots development organisations engaged in what is commonly described as 'participatory development', for instance, 'self-help groups involved in housing, health care and education, consumer and producer co-operatives' (ibid., p. 401). While acknowledging that such activities can simultaneously promote both development and democracy, 'empowering participants' through attempts to gain more influence on local decision-making processes, such an apparently radical approach is itself not unproblematic. Potentially, aid to promote *political* objectives could be diluted through its assimilation into participatory development programmes. While there is a clear area of overlap between 'participatory development' and a broad interpretation of democracy, there are also distinct elements, with self-help local development projects often having little or no connection to democratising the state. Highlighting the importance of strengthening groups in civil society as a necessary element of promoting democratisation would appear a most valid point, especially given an anticipation that donor support for such measures would be limited. However, it would seem most pertinent for donors to concentrate on those organisations within the extremely diverse realm of civil society that play a specific and explicit role in the democratisation process.

With regard to the issue of effectiveness, there is a fairly wide expectation that external agencies can play a role in the democratisation process in developing countries, albeit a secondary one. Echenique provides the example that, 'External aid to Chilean NGOs was crucial to the bringing of democracy to Chile', given that these NGOs played such a key role in the pro-democracy movement and the defeat of the dictatorship (1994, p. 111). Yet, simultaneously, most analysts advise caution and that 'too much should not be expected from the new (agenda)' (Stokke 1995, p. 69; also see Carothers 1995, p. 67). In general, however, there has been relatively little commentary on the likely impact of political aid on democratisation processes, probably for two reasons (a significant exception being the writings of Thomas Carothers, providing important analysis of US democracy assistance). One reason is the newness of democracy assistance within overall aid programmes, and the other is that positive measures have aroused less controversy than the imposition of punitive measures. Nevertheless, a number of themes pertinent to the issue of effectiveness can be identified from both academic sources and from initial donor evaluation reports. Five themes are outlined below, providing hypotheses for the examination and evaluation of donors' political aid programmes.

First, the political will of a recipient government is a necessary condition for successful institutional reform (Carothers 1995, p. 67; OECD 1997b, p. 24; USAID 1994; Heinz 1995, p. 41). In other words, donor support for the reform of governmental institutions is unlikely to be effective unless there is political commitment to reforms by the recipient government.

Second, strengthening civil society is a necessary element of external support for democratisation, important not only as an arena of democratic practices itself, but with civil society organisations performing a key role in democratising governmental institutions (Carothers 1995, p. 67; Sorensen 1995, p. 401; M. Robinson 1995a). For Stokke, 'facilitat[ing] the vitality of civil society is the most obvious area where foreign aid can play a role in fostering democracy' (1995, p. 69). It is also acknowledged by the OECD DAC that democratisation involves societal change, and hence that change through state institutions is insufficient – 'Civil society is at the heart of the process' (1997a, p. 4).

Third, the effectiveness of donor assistance increases the more it is directed at supporting endogenous reform processes (Stokke 1995, p. 82; Carothers 1995; Heinz 1995, p. 40, 42; Heinz *et al.* 1995). This stems from the recognition that democratisation cannot be created or imposed from outside and that support for ' "home-grown" initiatives is likely to be more successful than donor-driven reform efforts' (OECD 1997b, p. 24). Greater awareness is needed of how donor democracy promotion activities are perceived within host countries. Donors may feel their efforts are an assertion of democratic principles, whereas recipients may experience them as an assertion of power (Carothers 1996, p. 117).

Fourth, effectiveness is enhanced through long-term donor commitment to support for political reform (OECD 1997a, p. 4; Sorensen 1993b, p. 20). This arises from an understanding that democratisation is a long, slow process, with no 'quick fixes'. Attempts to achieve the latter are liable to failure. This is indicated most clearly in post-conflict societies where often democracy is particularly fragile. Premature withdrawal of support, for instance after transition elections, could lead to renewed conflict and democratic reversal, as occurred in Angola after the elections of 1992, for example.

Finally, effectiveness is increased by avoidance of unintended negative effects (OECD 1997b, p. 27). The positive impact of donor efforts is not assured. Intervention in complex social and political processes can produce outcomes other than those intended. One issue pertinent to democratisation is the potential intensification of ethnic or religious divisions, leading to violent conflict. Another negative outcome, though less dramatic, is the creation of dependency on donor funds amongst civil society organisations.

1.4.3   Summary

In sum, a range of issues concerning the manner of implementation of both negative and positive measures have been examined in the literature, with serious doubts raised concerning the effectiveness of both policy instruments. The most common view is that political conditionality will be effective in restricted circumstances only. There is somewhat less caution about political aid measures, often welcomed as preferable to aid restrictions. Yet the role of external agents in the democratisation process is generally perceived as limited to secondary support for endogenous processes. Questions that focus on the *impact* of external agencies on national democratisation processes clearly require answering through country case-studies, and hence are beyond the scope of this study. Other questions, however, are explored in subsequent chapters through the comparative examination of donor practices, including the following:

- What are the similarities and differences in donors' application of *aid sanctions?*
- Are aid restrictions applied in an even manner or is implementation characterised by inconsistency?
- To what extent are human rights criteria in aid policy subordinated to competing foreign policy demands?
- How effective are sanctions at leveraging political change?
    (a) What accounts for relative (in)effectiveness?
    (b) In what circumstances are sanctions effective?
- What are the similarities and differences in donors' *political aid programmes?*
- Is expressed intent to promote democratisation matched by financial input?
- What are the main focal areas of support?
- Is there concentration of support in particular phases of the democratisation process?
- Is there evidence of long-term support or merely short-term projects?
- Is there evidence of unintended, negative effects?

Again, questions concerning positive measures are examined in Part II, while those related to aid sanctions are addressed in Part III.

1.5 Some concluding (and preceding) remarks

Through an exploration of the wide-ranging literature that the donors' new policy agenda has evoked, this chapter has generated a substantial number of research questions. From the detailed examination of the policies and practices of the selected donors that ensues, the aim is to provide answers to these questions where possible, or, where issues remain complex, at least some clarification and elucidation of the problems involved.

The first two themes contained in the literature are examined in the remaining chapters of Part I, policy origins in Chapter 2 and policy coherence in Chapter 3. The former looks at how policy emerged in each of the four donor cases; the latter examines in detail how the four donors have each defined human rights, democracy and good govern-ance.

Parts II and III examine policy implementation through the two policy instruments, firstly, political aid projects, then, aid sanctions. Questions arising from the literature are explored within each. In Part II, the detailed examination of political aid programmes facilitates extensive discussion of both quantitative and qualitative issues raised in the literature. In Part III, questions concerning the legitimacy and the effectiveness of aid sanctions are examined.

Finally, some of the broader questions raised in the literature, particu-larly by more radical critics, are returned to in the conclusion. Are Western governments merely promoting 'low intensity democracy'? To what extent is democracy promotion linked to neo-liberal economic restructuring and part of a wider Western hegemonic project of global domination? Assessments of the accuracy of such propositions are made as far as possible from the evidence gathered.

2
Policy Evolution

This chapter looks at the emergence of the political aid policies of the four selected donors. Initially, it traces for each donor the evolution of policy and examines their policy statements. From this information, the questions raised above (section 1.1) concerning the explanatory factors that account for the emergence of the new policy agenda are then addressed.

2.1 Donor policy shifts

2.1.1 European Union aid[14]

The EU's own development assistance programme, administered by the European Commission, is both financially significant and institutionally complex. It has been the fifth largest donor programme in recent years, amounting to over 5 billion dollars in 1997, over 10 per cent of all development aid distributed by OECD countries (Cox and Koning 1997, p. 1).[15] Aid is divided into three main 'regional' programmes: the 71 African, Caribbean and Pacific (ACP) countries, signatories of the Lomé Convention; Asian and Latin American (ALA) countries; and the 12 Mediterranean countries of North Africa and the Middle East. Aid and trade co-operation agreements between the EU and third parties constitute contractual arrangements, commonly signed for five-year periods. Additionally, there are sectoral programmes (for example, food aid, emergency relief, NGO fund, etc.) open to all developing countries. Historically, the ACP countries have been the main beneficiaries of EU development aid (Crawford 1996, pp. 514–15), though one notable reorientation has been the strengthening of relations with the Mediterranean countries, with the Barcelona Declaration of November 1995 setting out a new 'Euro-Mediterranean Partnership'.[16] Development assistance to each 'regional' grouping entails distinct legal, financial and administrative frameworks, although policy developments tend to impact on all.

The process of policy formulation is complex, involving a number of distinct but interrelated channels. First, member states can proclaim new agendas through *declarations* at the bi-annual European Council meetings of heads of state and their ministers. Second, the inclusion of policy aims in *treaties* provides a legal basis for activities, though often stated at a level of generality and comprising broad guidelines only. Finally, *resolutions* of the Council of Ministers, in which the Commission plays a key initiation role, tend to entail greater specificity. Policy then has to be legally incorporated into the various development co-operation agreements between the EU and regional groupings, either unilaterally through a new Council Regulation or through a revised agreement with third party states, an example being the Lomé Convention. Such mechanisms are examined below.

Over the last decade, the promotion of democratic principles has become an increasingly important part of EU policy rhetoric, including within development co-operation. This emphasis on democratisation arose itself out of the overall evolution of an essentially economic Community into a body with political objectives, including the advocacy of human rights and democracy (European Commission 1995b, p. 2). Post-1989, this process gained momentum rapidly, initiated largely by the member states, with a series of declarations at European Council summit meetings, notably that of Luxembourg in June 1991 on human rights.[17] The Luxembourg Declaration proclaimed respect for human rights, the rule of law and democratic political institutions as the basis for equitable development, and signalled an intent to include human rights clauses in economic and co-operation agreements with third countries. The consolidation of this shift to explicit political aims is further evident in the Maastricht Treaty on European Union (TEU), signed in February 1992 and entered into force in November 1993, with respect for human rights made a general principle of Community law, hence informing *all* its activities [Article F(2)]. Regarding external relations and the (then) new pillar of Common Foreign And Security Policy (CFSP), one of the principal objectives was stated as the development and consolidation of democracy and the rule of law, and of respect for human rights and fundamental freedoms [Article J.1(2)]. Additionally, for the first time, the TEU provided a legal basis for Community development co-operation by defining its goals and objectives (Title XVII, Articles 130 u-y), and included the general objective of promoting democracy and human rights as a priority aim (Article 130u, paragraph 2).[18]

While the Amsterdam Treaty of October 1997 (amending the TEU and entering into force on 1 May 1999) introduced no innovations concerning the specific promotion of human rights and democracy in external policy, the institutional framework of the CFSP has been strengthened by the new post of High Representative (with Javier Solano, former NATO Secretary-General, as the first appointee) and a CFSP 'troika' consisting of the Council President, the High Representative and the Commissioner for External Relations. Further, the introduction of the possibility of a member state being suspended from the Union for violations of human rights or democratic principles (Article 7), perhaps strengthens the legitimacy of including such conditionality in agreements with non-member nations.

Prior to the Maastricht Treaty, the European Commission had initiated discussions on the promotion of democratisation specifically within development co-operation policy (Communication to the Council and Parliament of March 1991). With further impetus from the Luxembourg European Council Declaration of June 1991, this led to the Resolution of the Council of Ministers (Development) on 'Human Rights, Democracy and Development' of November 1991. The Resolution made promotion of human rights and democracy both an *objective* and a *condition* of development co-operation, not only for the European Community but also for member states. Such policy innovations were supported, and indeed advocated, by the European Parliament.[19]

The Council of Ministers' Resolution of November 1991 was, and remains, the pivotal policy statement. It delineated four political elements as part of a larger set of requirements to achieve sustainable development: human rights, democracy, good governance and decreased military expenditure. This represented a notable broadening of any political dimension within development co-operation, previously limited to human rights only, for instance, Article 5 in the fourth Lomé Convention, signed in late 1989, which stated that development 'entails respect for and promotion of all human rights' and that development co-operation 'is conceived as a contribution to the promotion of these rights' (paragraph 1).[20] The Council of Ministers' Resolution outlined two main policy instruments, a 'carrot' and a 'stick.' 'High priority' was accorded to 'a positive approach that stimulates respect for human rights and encourages democracy' through the provision of financial resources, yet with the warning that negative or punitive measures would be taken 'in the event of grave and persistent human rights violations or the serious interruption of democratic processes', up to and including suspension of co-operation agreements (EU Council of Ministers 1991). The intent was also stated that 'human rights clauses will be inserted in future co-operation agreements' (ibid.). Such a clause spans the division between positive and negative measures. In itself it can act to encourage respect for human rights and democracy, while simultaneously serving as a means to take punitive measures if deemed to be violated.

2.1.2   Swedish aid

Democracy and human rights

Policy-making processes in Sweden are a mixture of parliamentary legislation and government decision-making. Swedish aid is unusual in that 'democratic development' has been implicit as one of its objectives since its development co-operation programme began in 1962.[21] In 1978 the Swedish parliament explicitly laid down four goals of development assistance which included the development of democracy in society.[22] Since 1993, 'respect for human rights' has been added to the democracy goal (Swedish Ministry for Foreign Affairs 1993a, p. 6).

How has the democracy goal been pursued historically? Swedish aid, particularly in the 1970s, gave priority to economic and social equality and not to the nature of political systems. A major review of Swedish aid in 1977 stressed that 'equalisation' and 'economic and social justice must be the principal aim of development co-operation', with assistance being directed not only at the poorest countries, particularly those with egalitarian aims, but at the poorest people in those countries (cited in Ljunggren 1986, p. 77). It was thought that economic and social equality could be achieved in diverse political systems, both single-party and multi-party. The same review devoted only one page in fact to the goal of democratic development, indicating its low priority.[23] It is generally acknowledged that in terms of Swedish aid the meaning of democratic development was never specified and little emphasis was given to this objective for over two decades.[24]

An early sign came in 1988 of the shift in thinking that was to increasingly characterise many governments' aid policies over the next few years. In a Swedish government-sponsored study entitled *Recovery in Africa*, Göran Hydén pointed to the importance, in the context of economic crisis and structural adjustment, of getting 'not only prices but also politics right' (Hydén 1988, p. 145). He saw the poor performance of one-party states and a state-centred approach to development (in many African countries) as due partly to shortcomings in political rights and the system of governance, and asserted that:

The notion of development that is emerging today is highly political. Bringing about an enabling environment is an act of political reform. If donors take this concept seriously they also accept that foreign aid is potentially a means of bringing about political reforms. (ibid., p. 155)

Post-cold war, in September 1990, the Nordic Ministers of Development Co-operation meeting at Molde in Norway, signalled their support for the rapidly evolving policy shift. A substantial part of their Communiqué was devoted to the 'new challenge' of support for democracy and human rights initiatives. They declared that:

The connection between democracy, human rights and sustainable development has become more and more evident. . . . It has now been recognised that open democratic systems and respect for human rights give impetus to efforts to achieve development, economic efficiency and equitable distribution.

They stressed the need for giving 'moral and economic support' to the process of democratisation and for dialogue with partner countries about such matters. However, the Communiqué also warned that lack of progress in democratisation will affect the willingness of donors to provide aid.

Thus, in common with other donor governments in the early 1990s, the Swedish Social Democrat government focused increasingly on issues of democracy and human rights within development co-operation. Its approach was distinct, however, favouring dialogue rather than conditionality. The then Minister for Development Co-operation, Lena Hjelm-Wallén, expressed doubts about 'democratic conditionality' and 'democracy on demand' (Swedish Ministry for Foreign Affairs 1990, p. 373), and stated the appropriateness of promoting democratic development in programme countries 'through dialogue' (ibid., p. 359).

In addition, aspects of the 'good governance' agenda were highlighted at this time by Mrs Hjelm-Wallén. The need for governments to be accountable to their people and for transparency in decision-making was strongly stated, including an implied threat: 'In donor countries it will become increasingly difficult to justify co-operation with countries pursuing wasteful and ineffective policies. As donors we must require accountability of the governments with which we deal' (Swedish Ministry for Foreign Affairs 1990, p. 373). This also indicates the pertinence of the domestic agenda in reassuring Swedish constituencies that aid monies are being efficiently spent, as well as raising the question of whether recipient governments are required to be accountable to their own citizens or to donor governments.

In October 1991, the new Conservative-dominated coalition government (in power until 1994), stated the promotion of democracy and market economies as the guiding principles of development co-operation. The Minister for Development Co-operation, Mr Alf Svensson, affirmed that the Government was putting 'the goal of democracy development at the centre of the process of change underway in Sweden's development assistance programme', valued both as an end in itself and as a means to development more generally. Not only are 'respect for human rights and development of greater democracy of value in their own right', but they provide the best conditions for development. The rule of law, freedom of expression and political pluralism, and multi-party systems were seen as universally valid, 'as relevant in poor nations as in rich' (Swedish Ministry for Foreign Affairs 1993b). In addition, the Minister made clear that respect for human rights must extend to women and children, including such social and economic rights as better education and health care. Additionally, a conditionality approach featured more prominently, targeted particularly at left-orientated single-party states, with the new government duly announcing a reduction in aid to Vietnam and the cessation of aid to Cuba.[25]

Good governance

The concept of good governance also gained greater prominence at this time. Good governance, defined in narrow terms as public administration reform, is regarded as essential for economic and social development, with good governance, democracy and human rights perceived as 'intimately and closely related' (Swedish Ministry for Foreign Affairs 1993c, p. 10). In practice, however, a distinction is drawn between activities in the area of public administration and those concerning democracy and human rights. Public administration development has been a particular concern of SIDA (the Swedish International Development Agency), the government aid agency, for a considerable number of years, initially in its work with government institutions in Southern Africa. Thus, the programme in this field was well established, in contrast with the one promoting democracy and human rights, only instituted in the early 1990s. Although linkages between public administration development and democratisation are recognised, the main concern of the former programme is to increase the effectiveness and efficiency of the state, which may or may not be democratic.

2.1.3 United Kingdom aid

The research outlined in this book covers the period of Conservative governments in power in the UK. Since May 1997, the Labour government has introduced significant changes to the administration of development aid. Prior to 1997, the Overseas Development Administration (ODA) was part of the Foreign and Commonwealth Office (FCO), although comprising a distinct entity. The minister responsible for overseas development, not a Cabinet post, was one of five answering to the Foreign Secretary. The Labour government has upgraded ODA to a separate Ministry, renamed the Department for International Development (DfID), under the Secretary of State for International Development, a Cabinet post. It is also acknowledged that the Labour government has introduced aid policy changes, including in the realm of good governance, but these are outside the timeframe of this study. The departmental title of ODA is used here where the period under examination is that prior to mid-1997.

UK development aid policy is neither laid down in legislation nor contained in a comprehensive policy document.[26] It is proclaimed by governments and found in Ministers' speeches and in annual reports. The promotion of 'good government' as one of the priority objectives of the British aid programme emerged under the Conservative government in the early 1990s, as highlighted in two ministerial speeches.

In June 1990, Foreign Secretary Douglas Hurd, in one of the first indications of the policy shift by Western governments, introduced the concept of good government, its connection to economic development, and the consequences for aid policy.[27] Apparently influenced both by the recent World Bank report on sub-Saharan Africa (World Bank 1989), in which the relevance of governance to prospects for economic reform was first given prominence, and by the 'recent dramatic events in eastern Europe', Hurd spoke of 'the need to move away from the inefficient and authoritarian models of the past' as 'centralised political, economic and social structures have failed to deliver the goods' (Hurd 1990, p. 2). Eschewing the term 'democracy', and with an emphasis on good government as a *means* to economic development, Hurd declared that, 'Economic success depends to a large degree on effective and honest government, political pluralism and observance of the rule of law, as well as freer, more open economies' (ibid.), with Eastern Europe providing 'ample evidence that economic and political liberalisation are inseparable' (ibid., p. 7). Further, a causal relationship is virtually asserted with the statement, 'Political accountability is increasingly seen as a *pre-condition* for economic reform' (emphasis added) (ibid.). The consequence for aid recipients is that political criteria, that is, countries' tendencies towards 'pluralism, public accountability, respect for the rule of law, human rights and market principles' (ibid. p. 2), will influence aid allocation.

A year later, in June 1991, the Minister for Overseas Development, Baroness Chalker, outlined in more detail the three aspects of good government, regarded as universal principles by which all governments should be guided (Chalker 1991, pp. 2–3):

- the promotion of *sound economic and social policies*, including the introduction of market forces and facilitation of private sector activity, economic reform with a human face, and the avoidance of excessive military expenditure;
- the *competence* of governments and other institutions, the need for open and accountable systems, requiring pluralism and democracy;
- *respect for human rights and the rule of law.*

In discussing political systems, Lady Chalker explicitly used the term democracy, stating that 'democratic rights are fundamental human rights' and that 'democratic reforms are necessary in many countries for broad-based sustainable development' (ibid., p. 3). In response to some of the criticisms that Douglas Hurd's speech had met with, she also stated (ibid., p. 1) that good government policy was *not*:

- an attempt to promote Westminster-style democracy;
- an excuse to cut the aid programme;
- neo-colonialist or neo-imperialist – 'we cannot directly impose good government on developing countries: we can only support their own efforts'.

Lady Chalker argued that elements of good government, such as accountability, helped to ensure the effective use of aid. In forthright terms, she stated, 'Some might call this conditionality. I call it common sense' (ibid., p. 4). The Pergau dam affair in early 1994, however, brought the ease of such policy rhetoric into sharp contrast with the realities of the uses and abuses of development aid for commercial purposes by donor governments.[28]

In implementing good government policy, an emphasis on positive measures was stressed, aiming to help governments improve their performance. Nevertheless, where good government criteria were not adhered to, the intention to take negative measures by reducing or suspending aid was clearly stated, as had already occurred with Sudan and Burma.[29] It was noted that improvements in good government can also be achieved through instruments other than aid, through, for example, dialogue, diplomacy and démarches. In concluding, Lady Chalker summarised the aims of the new policies as 'to ensure respect for fundamental human rights while increasing aid effectiveness and enhancing development', re-stating the claim that 'the link between good government and development is firmly established' (ibid., p. 8).

2.1.4 United States aid

US policy is again a mixture of Congressional legislative mandate and government initiative. In March 1990, the US Secretary of State, James Baker, stated the post-cold war mission of the US government to be 'the promotion and consolidation of democracy' (cited in Gills *et al.* 1993, p. 11). Subsequently, in December 1990, the US Agency for International Development (USAID), the principal US government agency administering bilateral development assistance, created its 'Democracy Initiative'. This was one of four policy initiatives announced by USAID at this time following its new Mission statement of September 1990, which included 'support for democracy'.[30] Both the Mission statement and the policy initiatives indicated a re-focusing by USAID on its activities.

The legislative mandate for support for democratic development had existed since the enactment of Title IV of the Foreign Assistance Act of 1961, which, as amended, remains the current legislation. It was acknowledged, however, that prior to the new Mission statement, 'support for democracy was not a principal focus for A.I.D.' (USAID 1990, p. 3). In fact, US development assistance activities were subordinated to strategic and military considerations during the cold war years, with US support for 'a number of regimes that were clearly undemocratic in the name of anti-communism' (Morfit 1993, p. 18). Nevertheless, there were antecedents for the policies declared in 1990, two of which deserve brief mention.

Aid and human rights

One antecedent of change was the linkage in the mid-1970s of foreign assistance to human rights. In 1975, the US Congress passed an amendment, section 116, to the Foreign Assistance Act, known as the Harkin amendment after its sponsor. This prohibited development assistance to the government of any country which engages 'in a consistent pattern of gross violations of internationally recognised human rights...' (s. 116a). An exception is that assistance can be provided where it 'will directly benefit the needy people in such a country', something that is expected to be channelled mainly through non-governmental agencies. Further sections mandate that USAID take certain human rights considerations into account in setting development assistance levels (s. 116c), and authorise funds for the promotion of civil and political rights through project support, as long as they do not influence an election or support a political party (s. 116e). Some degree of implementation of this legislation was undertaken by the Carter administration (1975–79), albeit in an inconsistent manner, but abandoned by President Reagan (Forsythe 1988; Nelson and Eglinton 1992, p. 28).

Reagan and 'Project Democracy'

The second was the Reagan administration's request for a global democratic assistance programme, entitled 'Project Democracy', presented to Congress in 1983. Although interpreted as a propaganda exercise on the evils of communism and the virtues of US democracy and rejected by Congress (Carothers 1991, p. 203), two linked outcomes were significant. One was the creation by Congress of the National Endowment for Democracy (NED) in 1983, formally independent of government but wholly dependent on US government funding, as an alternative that attracted bipartisan support. The NED has subsequently engaged in democracy promotion activities globally through an annual grant from Congress, working primarily with political parties, labour and business through its core constituents, and described by W. I. Robinson as operating 'as a specialized branch of the US government' (1996, p. 93).[31] Criticisms have included the ideological orientation of its support (Forsythe 1988, p. 19) and its partisan approach to work with political parties, especially that of the International Republican Institute, one of the core grantees, which overtly seeks to assist 'like-minded' parties in their attempts to gain power (Carothers 1991, p. 229; W. I. Robinson 1996, pp. 93–9; Council on Hemispheric Affairs 1990). The other outcome was the commencement of a democracy assistance programme by USAID's Latin American and Caribbean Bureau (Carothers 1991, pp. 205–26). Projects focused initially on electoral assistance during the redemocratisation process in the 1980s, but with the largest element becoming legal system assistance, entitled 'administration of justice' programmes. In many respects, this relatively small programme was a forerunner of the much larger democracy building programmes of the 1990s.

The 'Democracy Initiative'

USAID's 'Democracy Initiative' of 1990, nonetheless, represented a more significant policy departure, reflecting the perceived triumph of 'market democracies' accompanying the end of the cold war. It saw democracy as complementary to the transition to market-orientated economies and supportive of sustained economic development, though without citing evidence in support.

Discussions within USAID led to the publication, in November 1991, of the 'Democracy and Governance' policy paper. The objective of the Democracy Initiative is stated to be support for democratic political development, both as a fundamental value in itself and as a means to broad-based economic growth. The primary areas of focus were defined (USAID 1991, p. 1) as:

- strengthening democratic representation;
- supporting respect for human rights;
- promoting lawful governance;
- encouraging democratic values.

The Clinton administration and aid

The change of Presidency and Administration in January 1993 resulted in a number of policy developments. The promotion of democracy and human rights was accorded a higher profile under President Clinton, stated to be one of the three pillars of US foreign policy. (The other two were 'economic competitiveness' and 'national security'.) In addition, Clinton affirmed foreign assistance as a central component of effective foreign policy.

USAID redefined its strategy and reorganised its programme, with the overall goal of 'Sustainable Development' incorporating four fundamental objectives:

- broad-based economic growth;
- protecting the environment;
- stabilising world population growth and protecting human health;
- building democracy.

In what could be regarded as a cost-cutting exercise, 21 country offices were closed, with assistance concentrated on fewer 'sustainable development' countries, stated to be those offering the best prospects for attaining objectives, including building democracy.[32]

2.2   Explaining donor policy trends

Questions for further enquiry were raised in the discussion of policy origins (Chapter 1). What answers can now be drawn from the analysis of how policy evolved in the four cases examined? There is confirmation of the significance of the three explanatory factors, influential in some if not all cases.

First, the change in global circumstances that accompanied the end of the cold war is the most crucial factor in accounting for the *initial* policy shift in the cases of the US, UK and the EU, though less so for Sweden. Having witnessed the defeat of communism, US Secretary of State Baker was proclaiming the promotion of democracy as the US post-cold war mission in the world within weeks of the fall of the Berlin Wall. Similarly influenced by events in Eastern Europe, British Foreign Secretary Hurd was extolling the attributes of Western pluralist political systems as representing 'good government' by mid-1990, and stating that such criteria would affect aid allocation. Declarations at both European Council summit meetings in 1990 highlighted the promotion of democracy and human rights in external relations. Somewhat in contrast, the initial shift in Swedish policy can be traced less to the collapse of communism and more to the emerging new orthodoxy of a positive correlation between democratisation and prospects for economic and social development.

This leads directly to the second factor, the perception of democracy as a means to economic liberalisation and the match between market economies and liberal democracies. Economic overtones were most evident in the policy statements of UK government ministers, with political liberalisation perceived as a 'pre-condition' for economic reform and with the first element in the definition of good government as 'sound economic policies', itself a euphemism for market-orientated policies. In US policy, the integral link between the economic and political dimensions is summed up by their intent to promote 'market democracies'. In Swedish policy shifts, the economic agenda is also very visible, though in distinctive ways associated with changes in government. Initially, under the Social Democrats, democratisation was seen as offering improved economic prospects, especially in sub-Saharan Africa where Swedish assistance is concentrated, while the Coalition government in Sweden adopted the new orthodoxy in a more assertive manner. In power again from 1994, the Social Democrats have placed more emphasis on the importance of democracy as an end in itself, linked to issues of international security and conflict prevention. The EU is a possible exception, placing greater emphasis on democracy and human rights as valuable in their own right and seeking a more moderate correlation with economic development.

Finally, the relevance of domestic imperatives is evident as an influential, if secondary, factor for the bilateral donors. In the programmes of all three bilaterals, there are indications that the new emphasis on democracy and good government addressed aid agency needs to defend their budgets by seeking to persuade domestic constituencies of the more effective use of aid through its re-orientation to democratic governments and of its more legitimate use to promote objectives regarded as universally desirable. How can anyone take exception to the British ODA's promotion of *good* government, for example? For USAID, threatened with ever greater budget cuts by a sceptical Republican-controlled Congress, the prominence given to bipartisan democracy building could only be beneficial. In Sweden, however, the domestic imperative was more clearly party political. In highlighting democracy and human rights within development co-operation, and consequent cuts in aid to Cuba and Vietnam, the Conservative-dominated coalition government was motivated to demarcate their policies from their Social Democrat predecessors (something that is discussed further below).

The three explanatory factors are all very distinct: events in the real world, shifts in prevailing ideas, practical domestic needs. While all have been shown to be influential, perhaps their relative importance has varied as the policy agenda has evolved. Initial policy shifts were largely due to the momentous events in Central and Eastern Europe in the late 1980s, with consequences for North–South relations, as well as East–West. The change in the conventional wisdom concerning the relationship between democracy and development has served to reinforce and maintain the objective of political reform as a policy priority, but with negative implications when further shifts in prevailing ideas occur. Finally, budgetary cuts, such as those that occurred in the first half of the 1990s, provide a strong motivation for aid agencies not only to change policies, but also to improve their public presentation. The extent to which practices change is a matter for investigation later in this volume.

3
Policy Operationalisation

The linking of aid to political reform in the 1990s introduced not only a new and very broad agenda, but also a problematic one. It is recalled that commentators in this field drew attention both to the contested nature of the main concepts and to how they are subject to varying interpretations. In three main sections, this chapter addresses the questions raised in those discussions of definitional clarity and conceptual coherence. First, donor definitions of the key concepts of human rights, democracy and good governance are explored and compared. Second, the question of strategy is examined, examining the means by which policy is translated into practice.

3.1 Defining concepts

The definitions of human rights, democracy and good governance provided by the four donors are presented in Table 3.1. The degree of conceptual clarity and of agreement between donors is greatest for human rights, decreases regarding democracy, with most divergence concerning the notion of good governance. A lack of distinctiveness between the three concepts is also evident, with elements of overlap between the three terms.

3.1.1 Human rights

There is a reasonable degree of consensus amongst the four donors regarding their definition of human rights, reflecting the relative clarity and agreement achieved through the incorporation of human rights into international law. All four donors define human rights in this context as *civil and political liberties*. Sweden is the most specific, defining such rights as those in the International Covenant on Civil and Political

Table 3.1 Donor definitions of human rights, democracy and good governance

European Union aid	Swedish aid	United Kingdom aid	United States aid
1. Human rights Human rights in this context defined as civil and political liberties, to be promoted 'in parallel with economic and social rights', presumably seen as supported through the overall development co-operation programme. (EU Council of Ministers 1991)	**1. Human rights** • Civil and political rights, as defined in the ICCPR • Economic and social rights seen as supported by Sweden's development assistance programme generally (SIDA 1993a)	**1. Human rights** • protection of civil and political rights, including freedom of expression and association • promotion of institutional pluralism, i.e. economic and social interest groups in civil society, particularly those representing disadvantaged groups Rule of law: • framework of known and fair law • impartial legal processes • independent judiciary • legal information and representation • arti-discrimination legislation • minority rights protected (ODA 1993)	**1. Human rights** Reference made to the Universal Declaration of Human Rights, and a distinction made between three categories of rights: • integrity of the person, i.e. freedom from torture, arbitrary arrest or imprisonment etc. • civil and political rights • social and economic rights Not clarified which human rights are the focus of AID's programme, although those which protect the 'integrity of the person' are given prominence. (USAID 1991)

Table 3.1 Continued

European Union aid	Swedish aid	United Kingdom aid	United States aid

2. Democracy
No definition of the main components of democracy, although attention is drawn to the following:
• elections
• establishment of new democratic institutions
• the rule of law
• strengthening the judiciary and the administration of justice
• NGOs, necessary for a pluralist society
• equal opportunities for all
(EU Council of Ministers 1991)
	2. Democracy
	Defined as:
	• a political system in which decision makers selected in regular, free and fair elections, with universal franchise
	
	Free elections imply a number of civil and political rights, e.g.:
	• freedom of speech and association, of religion etc.
	• political opposition as legitimate
	• an effective legal system to protect rights
	(SIDA 1993a)
		2. Democracy
		Covered by the terms 'legitimacy' and 'accountability'
		
		Legitimacy criteria:
		• multi-party democracy
		• or other means of consultation and responsiveness to popular needs and aspirations, where multi-party system 'impractical or unsustainable'
		• Other requisites:
		  • healthy civil society
		  • basic education and literacy
		
		Accountability:
		• of executive to legislature
		• of government officials to politicians
			2. Democracy
			Characterised by:
			• Political participation and peaceful competition, involving:
			  • free and fair elections
			  • freedom of expression and association
			  • free flow of information
			  • healthy civil society
			
			Strong democratic values, notably:
			• tolerance and political compromise
			• majority rule and minority rights
			• civil authority over the military
			• peaceful resolution of differences
			(USAID 1991)

- between government institutions, e.g. of parastatals to central ministries
- of government institutions to external audit institutions
- of government institutions to society

Accountability criteria:

- definition of expected performance standards
- transparency of decision-making
- availability of information, including free press
- mechanisms to hold responsible individuals to account

(ODA 1993)

Table 3.1 Continued

European Union aid	Swedish aid	United Kingdom aid	United States aid
3. Governance[34] Uses the term 'good governance' very broadly as an umbrella covering all major policy elements: • sensible economic and social policies • democratic decision-making • governmental transparency and financial accountability • a market-friendly environment • measures to combat corruption • respect for human rights and the rule of law (EU Council of Ministers 1991)	**3. Governance** Narrow concept of governance covering public administration and management. Support for 'capacity building' of public sector institutions preceded democracy and human rights concerns. Scope of pre-existing policies included: • improving efficiency and effectiveness of public administration • strengthening policy-making capacity • re-building government legitimacy, through increasing citizens' participation and by protecting the most needy • making more effective use of local initiative and resources (SIDA 1991, pp. 43–4)	**3. Governance** Covered by the term 'competence' Defined as government 'capacity' or 'capability' to plan and manage services, (not service provision), including: • formulating policies • taking decisions, both long- and short-term • managing service delivery Competence criteria generally not concerned with policy content, although 'command economic model' not appropriate, and other exceptions are excessive military expenditure and excess luxury consumption by elite, where government competence would be questioned (ODA 1993)	**3. Governance** Uses the term 'lawful governance' Its key characteristics are: • a just and responsive judicial process to which all state officials (including military and police) are subject • a system of laws impartially enforced by an independent judiciary • accountability of the executive through transparency of its actions and established procedures for public scrutiny (USAID 1991)

Later definition of 'good governance' as:

- increasing the efficiency of the state apparatus
- increasing its responsibility and accessibility to citizens
- promoting public contrcl over state operations
- increasing service-orientation and democratic work methods

(SIDA 1993b, p. 3)

Rights (ICCPR). The US is the least clear and most removed from the consensual view, both with its three-fold category of human rights and its apparent emphasis on rights involving 'integrity of the person', essentially a sub-division of civil and political rights.

Where do economic and social rights fit in? Three of the donors, Sweden, the EU and the UK, claim that the realisation of economic and social rights are advanced through the aid programme as a whole. Britain specifically states that economic and social rights are the subject of *other* aid policy objectives, thus justifying the emphasis on civil and political rights within the 'good government' programme.[33] Therefore, it is asserted that both main sets of rights are promoted, but through different policy instruments in the aid programme.

3.1.2   Democracy

Table 3.1, above, reveals considerable variation and some confusion amongst donor agencies with regard to the concept of democracy. Some clarification is attempted through use of Beetham's democratic pyramid (Figure 1.1, above) as an analytical device.

As part of their definitions, all donors include two of the four components, free and fair elections and civil and political liberties, though with the latter under the separate heading of human rights. There is almost unanimity on free and fair elections within a multi-party system as a minimal, necessary condition of democracy, although with the UK adding a qualification, indicating a preparedness to legitimise other means of consulting the population where multipartyism is 'impractical or unsustainable' (ODA 1993, para. 2.5).

The degree to which the other two components, 'open and accountable government' and a 'democratic society', are included in donors' definitions, varies from sketchy inclusion to omission, revealing substantial differences. USAID provides the broadest definition of democracy, if short on detail, of the four donors examined here. Their definition is based around the principles of political participation and peaceful competition, the defining characteristics of which include the free flow of information (essential to open and accountable government) and a healthy civil society, as well as free and fair elections and civil and political liberties. In addition, a democratic society requires the fostering of certain values, such as tolerance and compromise, majority rule and minority rights. In this respect, the US is the only donor to highlight the importance of a democratic culture. In contrast, Sweden restricts itself to a minimal definition of democracy, confined to free and fair elections and civil and political liberties, plus a legal system necessary to protect such rights. The European Union does not attempt a definition of democracy, but instead mentions various elements of democracy in what can be thought of as a rather *ad hoc* and incoherent way, with little attention to detail.

3.1.3 Good governance

To what extent have the four donor agencies defined 'good governance' and how broad or narrow are their interpretations? What is most evident from Table 3.1 is the lack of agreement over the broad parameters of what constitutes the area of governance, far less a common definition. The only clarity is provided by SIDA's pre-existing work in the sphere of public administration which 'sets out a strategy for the development of what is known as good governance' (SIDA 1993b p. 3), while the UK's terms of 'competence' and 'accountability' cover similar terrain. In contrast, the European Union uses the term governance very loosely, without definition. Although USAID changed their policy title from 'Democracy Initiative' to 'Democracy and Governance', its definition of 'lawful governance' is quite distinct from that of the other donors, being more concerned with the dimensions of democracy described here as legal and political accountability, and more commonly discussed by the other aid agencies under the heading of democracy.

This lack of an agreed definition is perhaps not surprising given that it is not a term with a legal definition (as human rights), or with centuries of literature behind it (as democracy), but rather that its very origins are recent, interrelated with the new policy agenda itself. Yet, it also indicates the same danger as that observed by van Rooy and Robinson regarding the concept of civil society, that is, 'a rush to vocabulary rather than a rush to comprehension' (1998, p. 54). What is particularly ambiguous about the use of good governance is the extent to which it constitutes a separate sphere of activity or whether it merely duplicates much of what is already encompassed by the term democracy. This confusion is evident in the comparison between the four donors. The broad usage by the US is insufficiently distinguishable from democracy, whereas the narrow interpretation of Sweden, and to some extent the UK, at least has the advantage of entailing a discrete set of activities.

3.1.4 Findings

Recalling questions posed in Chapter 1 (section 1.2.4) concerning donor definitions and prioritisation, what answers can be provided from the examination of the four donor cases?

First, have the three concepts been clearly defined and what are the differences in interpretations between donors? A reasonable degree of clarity and consensus has been achieved with regard only to human rights. There is agreement amongst donors that, in the context of political aid, human rights refers to civil and political liberties. These are largely defined as those in the ICCPR, though all donors do also stress the rights of women, children and minority groups. Such definitional clarity is clearly facilitated by the incorporation of human rights into international law. In contrast, no adequate conceptualisation has been attained regarding democracy or good governance. Definitions of democracy tend to consist of *ad hoc* lists of various elements of democratic political systems, differing between donors in comprehensiveness and in overall coherence. One exception was the UK's definition of accountable government, clearly outlining the different aspects of *political* accountability, despite eschewing the term 'democracy'. Inconsistency in donor interpretation was at its worst with regard to good governance, attributed with widely different meanings and at times used loosely and in an undefined manner. An exception was SIDA, applying a narrow interpretation of good governance to its established and clearly defined activities in the area of public administration. The UK's concept of 'competence' has a similar orientation, integrated as one of the four components of 'good government'. The EU fails to define good governance, using the term in a broad and vague manner, with little practical meaning or application. Somewhat confusedly, the US term 'lawful governance' combines the rule of law with the accountability of the executive.

Second, what are the differences in prioritisation accorded to the three concepts? The differential emphasis and comprehensiveness accorded to each in the strategy documents largely confirms the initial indications from the titles of programmes in this field, (see Table 3.1). The EU concentrates on promoting human rights and democracy, with little or no focus on governance aspects. The US prioritises democracy, with a broader range of proposed measures in this area, in contrast with the relative lack of clarity concerning its focus on human rights and governance. A Swedish prioritisation of human rights is strongly suggested by the extensive range of activities outlined, distinguishing those appropriate for different contexts, in contrast with a less coherent list of measures to support democracy. In addition, good governance, as narrowly defined, is clearly a well-established priority within Swedish development co-operation. The UK outlines fairly comprehensive sets of measures by which to promote the four dimensions of good government, with no clear focus or priority. Nevertheless, a concentration on strengthening *governmental* institutions seems certain and avoidance of the term 'democracy' could be significant for its practice.

3.2 Developing strategies

Following the establishment of the objectives of the new policy agenda in the early 1990s, subsequent developments concentrated initially on elaborating a strategy by which to operationalise policy, which task fell to the government aid agencies. SIDA and ODA both produced a 'strategy document' in June 1993 and October 1993 respectively. USAID produced its more detailed 'Democracy and Governance' policy paper in November 1991, and a Strategy Paper in March 1994. The original resolution of the EU's Council of Ministers in November 1991 doubled as a policy statement and a strategy document, and further developments in EU strategy can be gleaned from the first two annual 'implementation reports', dated October 1992 and February 1994.

Carothers (1997, pp. 112–17; 1999, pp. 86–90) has identified the 'core strategy' applied in US democracy assistance, with three key parts. First, the model of democracy, which he terms the 'democracy template', consists of a set list of institutions and processes, primarily institutions, with the three main categories of elections, state institutions and civil society, based on what are perceived as the essential components of established Western democracies. Second, a 'natural sequence' model of democratisation follows the relatively set path of political liberalisation leading to transition elections followed by democratic consolidation. Third, the concept of 'institutional modelling' by which democracy assistance programmes aim to reduce the deficit of institutions from ideal Western forms. From the documents examined, it appears that a similar core strategy has been adopted in common by donor agencies, with evidence of the first and third elements in particular. Policy operationalisation has entailed the identification by each donor of a range of pertinent sectors, both state and non-state, to which assistance programmes could be directed. If the strategy was a common one, however, Table 3.2 indicates both similarities and differences in the content of the 'check-lists', as well as raising further issues of policy implementation.

3.2.1 Human rights

Similarity between donors is most evident here, though with distinct emphases and attention to detail. There are also important differences.

Table 3.2 Donor strategies – checklists of measures

European Union aid	Swedish aid	UK aid	United States aid

1. Human rights
Support to local human rights organisations
 	
Educational schemes (human rights information or awareness-raising)
 	
Support for vulnerable groups, i.e. victims of discriminatory and violent practices (minorities, political prisoners, children, torture victims). In particular:
• Legal and other material support to target groups through:
  • local NGOs
  • public-sector establishments (e.g. universities, human rights ombudsmen)
 	
Support for conflict prevention or resolution, including:
• support to victims of conflict
 	
Cross-cutting focus on the rights of women, children and indigenous communities.
 	
(European Commission 1994a)
	1. Human rights
	In countries where the government is involved in human rights violations, support to:
	• organisations, national and international, which document violations of human rights
	• activities, national and international, which create public opinion against the type of government
	• victims and their families
	• conflict solving and national reconciliation measures, in civil war situations
	
	In countries where governments aspire to respect human rights, measures to strengthen the rule of law could include the following:
	• legislative capacity and law-making
	• police training re. human rights
	• prosecution authorities, courts and prisons
	• state organisations for enforcement of court decisions
		1. Human rights
		Measures to promote human rights and the rule of law
		• drafting of laws
		• strengthening civil society, through support for organisations representing the following:
		  • the disadvantaged, including women, the poor, minorities
		  • business associations and unions
		  • professional associations
		  • community groups
		  • the media
		  • community-level conflict resolution
		• The courts including:
		  • the judiciary
		  • prosecution and defence services
		  • courts administration
		• legal advice, assistance and representation
		• the police
			1. Human rights
			Promoting respect for human rights by supporting:
			• the establishment of a framework of law and legal procedures
			• human rights education
			• the rights of women, children, cultural and religious minorities
			• institutions that monitor and advocate respect for human rights
			
			(USAID 1991)
			
			The latter institutions can be local, national, regional or international
			
			(USAID 1994)

- legal advice and assistance,
- legal aid
- ombudsman institutions
- anti-corruption measures and institutional arrangements
- training of lawyers

Other measures, as follows:

- information programmes to increase citizens' awareness of legal rights and responsibilities, including through the media
- to create public opinion in favour of ratification of international human rights conventions
- to strengthen the situation and rights of women
- to strengthen the situation and rights of the child, particularly 'street/working children', in war situations, handicapped children
- to strengthen the situation and rights of ethnic minorities
- to strengthen the situation and rights of disabled people and other vulnerable groups

(SIDA 1993a)

- initiatives addressing inequalities, e.g. gender, race
- limiting arbitrary power by officials through Ombudsman or community organisations
- initiatives to strengthen community level conflict resolution
- school education for a democratic society

(ODA 1993)

Table 3.2 Continued

European Union aid	Swedish aid	UK aid	United States aid

2. Democracy
 	
Activities to support democratic transition:
 	
• pre-election measures
• elections
 	
Activities to strengthen the rule of law, including support for:
 	
• newly-founded parliaments
• independent judiciary
• draft constitutions and electoral codes
• regional decentralisation and participatory local government
 	
Activities to strengthen civil society:
 	
• Support to local NGOs, including:
  • local associations that promote democracy
  • grass-roots development organisations
• Literacy campaigns
• Support to independent media
 	
Particular attention given to rights and position of women as cross-cutting issue.
 	
(European Commission 1992a)
	2. Democracy
	
	Also see measures to strengthen respect for human rights, above, regarded as simultaneous support for democracy.
	
	Measures specific to promoting democracy include support for:
	
	• freedom of speech, including the media and culture
	• constitutions and other statutory instruments on forms of government
	• elections, including pre-electoral support and election supervision
	• parliament
	• local government
	• popular participation in political life, e.g. voter registration campaigns
	• transfer of knowledge of democratic network and procedures to local community organisations
	• citizen's awareness of how their country is governed, e.g. through the media or the education system
		2. Democracy
		
		Measures to promote legitimacy include:
		
		• electoral activities, including pre-elections
		• institution building for legislatures, including both national and local institutions, e.g. training for legislators, parliamentary clerks
		• assisting the transition from military to civilian rule, e.g. demobilisation
		• encouraging participation in government, both local and national
		• curriculum development for civics teaching in schools
		
		Measures to enhance political accountability include:
		
		• restructuring of government, e.g. decentralisation
		• strengthening information systems within government, particularly for disadvantaged people, e.g. the illiterate
		• development of the media
		
		(ODA 1993)
			2. Democracy
			
			Strengthening democratic representation through:
			
			• Elections, including activities to:
			
			  • strengthen electoral systems and institutions
			  • observe and monitor elections
			  • educate and register voters
			  • improve professionalism of political parties
			
			• Representative political institutions, including activities to:
			
			  • enhance professionalism of legislators
			  • strengthen legislative research and drafting capabilities
			  • strengthen accountability of local government
			
			• Civil society, including activities to:
			
			  • support professional associations, civic groups, labour organisations, business groups, advocacy groups

Activities to support democratic consolidation stated as future priority.

(European Commission 1994a)

- greater transparency of public administration systems, to allow public control

(SIDA 1993a)

- Free flow of information, including activities to:
  - support independent policy research institutions
  - support independent mass media
  - reduce censorship
  - support transparency of government decision-making
- Encouraging democratic values through:
  - civic education
  - leadership training

(USAID 1991)

Democracy Building – the later strategy document includes the following additional areas:

- constitution drafting
- political parties and other national political organisations, (though subject to statutory prohibitions against influencing election outcomes)
- improved civil-military relations, including civilian control of military

(USAID 1994)

Table 3.2 Continued

European Union aid	Swedish aid	UK aid	United States aid
3. Governance Activities to promote good governance do not appear to have received much detailed attention. In the Commission's 1992 Report, 'Good Governance' is included as part of activities to strengthen the rule of law, but only one measure listed, 'greater openness in the management of public finances', corresponds to the concept of governance, as narrowly defined. Along with the rule of law, good governance is stated as a second priority area, but then discussion moves on to how structural adjustment support programmes are contributing to good governance. (European Commission 1992a) The 1993 Report, in the conclusions, lists good governance as a future priority. Governance is now more narrowly defined as open and transparent public administration, and examples given on governance reforms are:	**3. Governance** Earlier support focused on government agencies that perform 'core functions', i.e. Ministries of Finance, Planning, Public Administration, etc. Within such 'systems development', the following specific areas are prioritised: • financial policy-making and management, e.g. budgeting, accounting, taxation, central banking • services to assist government planning, e.g. national statistical services • administrative development and reform, (i.e. organisation and reform of human resources), e.g. personnel administration, management training • decentralisation and support for local government • promotion of women in the public sector • public administration co-operation at regional level (SIDA 1991, pp. 21–32)	**3. Governance** Measures to promote public accountability include: • clarification of definitions or responsibilities and standards • strengthening systems of financial planning, accounting and audit • anti-corruption measures • reform of systems of procurement and tendering • encouraging institutions to be outward looking and more responsive to their clients (ODA 1993) Measures to increase competence include: • policy making skills, particularly macro-economic planning • improving the management of government itself, e.g. the Cabinet Office, civil service reform • strengthening budget/resource allocation systems	**3. Governance** • Promoting lawful governance by support for the following: Legal and judicial systems, including: • legal education • judicial reforms • independent judiciary • legal advice and assistance services • Accountability of the executive, including: • formal constraints on all state officials • establishing ombudsmen • procedures for financial accountability • anti-corruption measures • monitoring of military budgets by civil authorities (USAID 1991) The later strategy document also highlights support for institutions that increase government accountability at state (regional) and local levels, as well as national. (USAID 1994)

- decentralisation
- effective supervisory bodies
- tax reform

It is also noted that good governance is a priority area in the Commission proposals for the Lomé IV mid-term review.

(European Commission 1994a)

The context of economic and political reform has led to the development of new areas of support, including outside the public sector.

- Support for the development of a market economy:
  - establishment of a legal framework to regulate private business, plus state instruments to monitor and supervise the private sector
  - development of policy analysis capacity, e.g. support to research institutions
  - support of educational efforts in strategic sectors, e.g. training of bankers, managers

- Strengthening of important institutions outside the public sector, i.e. the development of competence in strategic civic organisations, e.g. bar associations, institutes of chartered accountants, in order to facilitate an equal interplay between the public sector and civil society

- a range of institution building activities to enhance effectiveness
- developing the capacity to review and redefine the role of government, e.g. substituting private sector activity for government intervention

(ODA 1993)

Table 3.2 Continued

European Union aid	Swedish aid	UK aid	United States aid
	• Support for the development of the legal system (however, no distinction is made between activities in this area relevant to good governance and those promoting democracy and human rights) • Higher education, particularly support to relevant university departments, e.g. law, economics, politics, business and administration (SIDA 1993b, pp. 5–6)		

The US has dealt most cursorily with measures to promote and strengthen civil and political rights. In contrast, Sweden has drawn up the clearest framework for its support, being the only donor to differentiate distinct sets of measures in different contexts, namely in countries where the government is involved in human rights violations and in countries where governments aspire to respect human rights. Identifying activities in the former context is particularly important if the commitment to re-channel aid to non-governmental organisations, in the event of government-to-government aid being suspended, is not to remain merely rhetorical.

3.2.2 Democracy

The lists of measures put forward by the aid agencies to support democracy (see Table 3.2) generally reflect and underline the tendencies of emphasis and omission identified in the definitions. Support for electoral activities is widespread, including pre-election activities. In contrast, support for some of the less tangible aspects of democratic consolidation is not so apparent.

'Accountability' and 'transparency' are terms which feature strongly in donor policy statements, particularly in the speeches of British government ministers. Yet, both concepts appear to receive less attention in strategy documents, as well as variable interpretations. The espousal of open and transparent government by Northern governments to their Southern counterparts is a sensitive issue, raising questions of paternalism. To do so with justicity, and without hypocrisy and double standards, depends on their own practice and on their willingness to be judged by the same standards, as with human rights. In this respect perhaps Sweden has the greatest legitimacy with its open government tradition of almost all documents being on the public record. The US has its Freedom of Information Act, but with an Executive Presidency accused of conducting actions unbeknown to Congress far less the US public, especially in foreign affairs (for example, the Iran-Contra Affair). The UK could be said to have a particularly poor record with its culture and tradition of government secrecy (under the Official Secrets Act), and lack of access to information (as yet, no freedom of information legislation). If Northern governments do not 'practice what they preach', this not only undermines policy legitimacy, but suggests less likelihood of policy rhetoric being translated into a concrete programme of activities.

As regards accountable government, activities to enhance political accountability include the strengthening of national legislatures and decentralisation to local government. This latter measure entails controversial aspects, with two related issues. First, decentralisation in itself is not sufficient to ensure accountability, and could lead to the concentration of power in the hands of local élites (Edwards 1994, p. 69). Thus, attention must also be paid to the *democratic* character of local government. Second, although decentralisation of power is often perceived as beneficial in development terms (for example, in 'basic needs' literature), promoting the restructuring of government raises the issue of the sovereignty of the recipient country to determine the nature of its political system. A shift in the respective roles and responsibilities of central and local government is particularly contentious in the context of the state-shrinking reform agenda advocated by the IFIs and many Northern governments.[35] Perhaps a more legitimate activity for donors is to strengthen *democratic* local government and its capacity to carry out ascribed functions, as determined by the recipient nation.

Donors all explicitly emphasised the strengthening of civil society, yet with limited attempts at defining what this entails, with the US as the single exception. In the initial strategy documents, there was little attempt to differentiate pro-democracy elements from others within civil society. For example, the UK and US merely list a diverse range of civic organisations from business associations to local community groups that are deemed eligible for support. Sweden alone highlights the encouragement of local organisations to be internally democratic. In a later study for USAID, Fox (1995, pp. 10–12, cited in M. Robinson 1996, p. 5) provides a typology of civil society organisations. He offers a three-fold distinction between primary level associations, multi-purpose civic organisations, and specialised civic organisations. Primary level associations (for example, local community organisations, credit unions), are membership organisations that have grassroots development as their primary function. Multi-purpose civic organisations combine civic or political functions in addition to developmental activities, for example, federations of primary level associations at the regional or national level, religious bodies, or development NGOs providing support to community based organisations. Specialised civic organisations serve the public interest and undertake specialised tasks to assist democracy building, for example, media organisations, human rights organisations, civic education groups, policy centres and research institutes. Such clarification led to greater emphasis on what USAID termed 'civic advocacy organisations', those public benefit groups within civil society that concentrate on seeking to influence government policy.[36]

Support for 'civil society' remains a relatively new area for donor agencies. However, unless the concept is adequately defined and the relation to democracy of its components addressed, there are negative implications for both the focus of implementation strategies and for the effectiveness of programmes. The enquiry into the proportion of resources channelled to civil society and to what types of organisations is undertaken in Part II.

3.2.3   Good governance

The degree of diversity in interpretations of good governance in the four donors is such that meaningful comparison is only feasible between the Sweden and the UK, between whom there is a relatively high degree of congruence in the policy measures outlined. Yet, there are also some differences in emphasis, traced back to somewhat differing conceptions of the role of the state. The UK's ODA appears to have few positive words to say about the state's role, with the exception of its 'enabling role' for private sector development. In contrast, SIDA's starting point in its 1991 document on Africa is a more favourable perception of the state as the most important actor in dealing with crises of development with their declared objective as supporting and strengthening the state. Its later strategy document (1993b) reflects more the pro-market climate and includes a new area of support as the development of a market economy. Yet even here measures involve, firstly, *support for the state* to stimulate private institutions, and, secondly, the need for *regulations* to enable the state to monitor and supervise the private sector. The question of the role of the state in development underpins the issue of governance. Will the promotion of good governance involve a state-building exercise, or, alternatively, remain within a neo-liberal agenda, aiming at creating an effective state but one whose activities are kept strictly in check? Again, the empirical investigation into policy implementation in Part II addresses such questions.

Part II
Political Aid

A comparative investigation of the implementation of the new policy agenda by the four selected donors is undertaken in Parts II and III, examining the two main policy instruments respectively. Part II investigates the implementation of positive measures through project aid to support democratisation; Part III explores the application of aid sanctions on human rights and democracy grounds as an attempt to leverage political reform.

In linking development assistance to political reform, all four donors examined stressed the priority given to positive measures to promote greater respect for human rights, democracy and good governance. Part II investigates the implementation of such measures in three chapters. Chapter 4 examines the introduction of political aid programmes and overall patterns of expenditure. Chapter 5 conducts a detailed comparative analysis of policy implementation based on a census of all projects over a two year period. Finally, Chapter 6 carries out an evaluation of donors' programmes.

4
Implementing Political Aid Programmes

This chapter is structured in two main parts. First, background information on the introduction of political aid programmes into development co-operation is provided through an examination of the relevant financial instruments and institutional structures of each donor agency. Second, patterns of total expenditure are explored and compared.

4.1 Financial instruments and institutional structures

For most donors, political aid was a new departure requiring the establishment of new financial instruments and institutional structures. More detailed coverage is required of the EU and the US due to the greater number of financial instruments involved and the complexity of institutional arrangements.

4.1.1 European Union

Financial instruments

Financial resources for positive measures in support of democratisation are available from two main sources: dedicated budget lines and mainstream regional development co-operation funds. Although the November 1991 Council Resolution created a budget line to support 'human rights and democracy in developing countries' (see B7-7020 below), its clear message was to encourage the use of funds from mainstream regional budgets. The budget lines are intended to have an 'innovative' or 'catalyst' effect, providing initial support for short-term, pilot projects, potentially leading to mainstream funding. Nevertheless, the main emphasis in the 1990s has been on budget line funding and the plethora of these are outlined below, although this research focuses only on those to developing countries.

At the instigation of the European Parliament, budget lines specific to the promotion of human rights and democracy were grouped together in 1994 as Chapter B7-70, the 'European Initiative for Democracy and Human Rights', covering a number of themes and geographical areas. At the time of going to press, Chapter B7-70 includes the following nine budget lines:[37]

- B7-7000 *Support for democracy in the countries of Central and Eastern Europe, including Republics formerly part of Yugoslavia* (including the PHARE Democracy Programme). Established in 1992 with a budget of EUR 15 million in 1999.
- B7-7010 *Support for democracy in the New Independent States* (of the former Soviet Union) *and Mongolia* (the TACIS Democracy Programme). Established in 1993 with a budget of EUR 10 million in 1999.
- B7-7020 (formerly B7-5220) *Human rights and democratisation in developing countries, especially ACP countries.* Created as a direct result of the November 1991 Council Resolution, initially as a resource for all developing countries *except* Latin America. It has subsequently become more orientated to ACP countries with the later establishment of budget headings for the Mediterranean region and for Asian countries. It had a budget of EUR 17 million in 1999.
- B7-7030 (formerly B7-5230) *Democratisation process in Latin America.* The first regional budget line, created in 1990 at the initiative of the European Parliament. Its original aims were to support the democratisation process in Chile and the peace process in Central America, but was extended from 1991 to cover all of Latin America.
- B7-7040 (formerly B7-5240) *Grants to certain activities of human rights organisations.* Established in 1979 with a global remit, including member states, this was the original human rights budget line with a focus on torture. By 1999, thematic coverage had expanded considerably, including women's human rights, minority groups, human rights education and training, abolition of the death penalty, although 40 per cent remained allocated to support for torture victims. It had a budget of EUR 15 million in 1999.
- B7-7050 *MEDA* [Mediterranean] *Programme for Democracy and Human Rights.* Established in 1996 at the initiative of Parliament, with a budget of EUR 9 million.
- B7-7060 *Support for the activities of International Criminal Tribunals and to the setting up of a permanent International Criminal Court*, with a budget of EUR 3.3 million in 1999.

- B7-7070 *Human rights in Asian countries.* Established in 1998 with a budget of EUR 5 million in 1999. Current focus on China.
- B7-7090 *Support for, and supervision of, electoral process.* Established in 1997, with a budget of EUR 2 million in 1999. Emphasis on funding of international electoral observation in countries where electoral assistance is *not* available from other instruments.

Budget lines have been created in the 1990s in a largely piece-meal and haphazard manner, differentiated by regional and thematic foci.

Institutional structures

The management of both dedicated budget lines and the mainstream regional development co-operation programmes reflects the institutional fragmentation of the European Commission in this field. For the period of this research and until September 1999, when a new and re-organised Commission was confirmed by the European Parliament, there were five Directorates involved in the management of development co-operation, each headed by a different Commissioner, as follows:[38]

- DG VIII (Development) – ACP states, plus some budgetary lines benefiting all developing countries, for example, non-emergency food aid and NGO co-financing;
- DG IA (External Relations) – Central and Eastern Europe, former Soviet Union, Mongolia, Turkey and other European countries outside the EU;
- DG IB (External Relations) – Southern Mediterranean, Middle East, Latin America and most Asian developing countries;
- DG I (External Relations) – China, Korea, Macao and Taiwan;
- ECHO (European Community Humanitarian Office) – all humanitarian aid.

Responsibility for the implementation of human rights and democracy measures is split between the 'Human Rights and Democratisation Unit' located in DGIA, with overall responsibility for all aspects of human rights policy, and separate units for each geographical region.

4.1.2 Sweden

Financial instruments

There are two main sources of political aid funds. A Democracy and Human Rights Fund was established in 1992/93, administered by SIDA, and open to all developing countries. This was not all new money however. It incorporated what had previously been called 'humanitarian assistance', involving substantial and somewhat concealed support for liberation movements in Southern Africa and for opponents of military dictatorships in Latin America. The South African ANC and Chilean exiled groups were the main beneficiaries historically. This accounted for approximately 40 per cent of the Democracy and Human Rights Fund until the mid-90s, disbursed almost exclusively to the ANC.[39]

Assistance to what became known as 'good governance' had been a part of Swedish development co-operation since 1983/84, when the Public Administration Section was established. Support for public administration began initially with government partners in Southern Africa, then expanded to other regions and continents, though limited to Sweden's 'programme countries'. Projects in this field are funded out of the overall country budget, with projects decided jointly with recipient governments.

Institutional structures

A section was created within SIDA, the Democracy and Human Rights Unit, to administer the new fund, while the Division for Public Administration and Management continued to deal with good governance projects. In 1997, the two sections were merged into a single division responsible for democracy, human rights and public administration.

4.1.3   United Kingdom

The promotion of 'good government' became one of the priority objectives of the British aid programme in 1991.

Financial instruments

No new budget line was created for the specific purposes of promoting good government. Rather its establishment as a key objective signalled its general incorporation into country programmes. As encouragement, Lady Chalker set a target in June 1991 of £50 million in new project commitments in this area within the following year.

Institutional structures

Responsibility for policy implementation lies with the 'Government and Institutions Department' within ODA. Rather than administering a budget, their role has been to disseminate information and assistance on policy implementation to country and regional desk officers and to in-country aid 'missions', offering both general guidance and country-specific advice as appropriate, including project design. The Human Rights Unit within the Foreign Office has responsibility for policy matters, but with no direct involvement in aid project design.

4.1.4 United States

Financial instruments

No specific budget line has been created nor a budgetary earmark established by Congress. USAID's political development programmes can be traced back to relatively small-scale assistance to elections and judicial reform in Latin America from the early 1980s (Carothers 1991, Chapter 6). Subsequently, in the 1990s, democracy promotion has increasingly become an integral part of country and regional programmes. Since 1991 there has been a steady incorporation of multi-year democracy and governance (D/G) projects in most of the 50 'sustainable development' countries, deemed to offer the best prospects for development. Expenditure in this field has been institutionalised since FY 1995 by the inclusion for most countries of a 'Building Democracy' component in USAID's annual funding request to Congress.

Only programmes administered by USAID are included in this analysis of US democracy assistance. USAID D/G projects comprise the largest element of US government activities in this field by far, but there are a number of other financial sources, mainly from other US government agencies (US Department of State 1995a). The Department of State, in conjunction with US Embassies, administer a 'Democracy and Human Rights Fund' (Section 116[e] Fund). This was established in 1979 to provide small grants to local NGOs working to promote civil and political rights in Africa, as required by the same section of the Foreign Assistance Act, with available funds rising from $500,000 in FY 1989 to $3 million in FY 1993 and 1994, (ibid., p. 4). The United States Information Agency (USIA) provides a range of programmes which proclaim to advocate democratic values, focusing on education and technical assistance, for example, exchange visits and scholarships (ibid., p. 7). Additionally, the Departments of Justice and Defence have some programmes that purport to promote human rights and democracy, for example, military training in respect for human rights and the apolitical role of the military in a democracy (ibid., p. 8). These smaller and separate sources of democracy assistance from US government agencies are not included in the data analysed here.

Institutional structures

USAID describes itself as a decentralised organisation in which the regional bureaux for Africa, Asia and the Near East, and Latin America and the Caribbean have relative autonomy, including responsibility for implementation of democracy promotion activities. Each regional bureau has a democracy and governance section to develop its activities in this field. In addition, a Center for Democracy was established in 1994 within the Bureau for Global Programs with the stated intention of providing technical and intellectual leadership in the democracy and governance area. The concept of human rights is less spoken of within USAID than those of democracy and governance. Within the State Department, however, human rights are accorded a more explicit profile, particularly through the Bureau for Democracy, Human Rights and Labor, whose tasks include the production of the respected 'Annual Country Reports on Human Rights Practices'.

4.2   Total expenditure

The promotion of normative political goals through development aid was introduced with considerable fanfare in the early 1990s, yet one expectation was that policy rhetoric would not be matched by a comparable input of resources. This section examines the proportion of overall aid budgets allocated to the promotion of human rights, democracy and good governance.

Taking aid agency expenditure figures on political aid as a primary objective, Table 4.1 demonstrates the relatively small proportion of total aid budgets that have been channelled to promote political objectives.[40] Despite this sector constituting one of a small number of priority objectives for all donors here, only Sweden had achieved an expenditure level of over 5 per cent of the total aid budget. UK government expenditure is the lowest, failing to devote even 2 per cent of its aid programme to promoting 'good government' as a principle objective, despite its status as one of seven priority objectives. While there was sizeable growth in EU resource provision, it remained at only 2.6 per cent of total aid in 1994, despite being a key element of development policy outlined in the Maastricht Treaty. The US pledged less than 5 per cent of its funds in 1994 on one of its four fundamental objectives, with the increased proportion due more to a decline in overall foreign aid than to an increase in resources committed to democracy promotion. Sweden was the only donor examined to allocate a more respectable proportion of its

Table 4.1　Total expenditure on political aid – a comparison (currency units x 1 million)

Donor	Year	Total bilateral aid	Total political aid (domestic currency)	Total political aid (US $)[41]	Political aid as a percentage of total aid
EU[42]	1993	ECU 3164	ECU 39.2	$45.9	1.24
	1994	ECU 3639	ECU 95.3	$113.4	2.62
Sweden[43]	1992/93	SKr 10037	SKr 773.0	$99.3	7.70
	1993/94	SKr 10327	SKr 955.7	$123.9	9.25
UK[44]	1992/93	£1127	£18.6	$27.9	1.65
	1993/94	£1156	£22.4	$34.3	1.94
US	FY 1993	$7167	$225.0	$225.0	3.14
	FY 1994	$5917	$284.2	$284.2	4.80

Sources: EU: European Commission 1994c, p. 5 and p. 7; European Commission 1995c, p. 7 and p. 11; Sweden: SIDA 1994b, Tables 1 and 6; SIDA 1995, Tables 1 and 6; UK: ODA 1994, Table 1; ODA 1995, p. 84; US: USAID 1994a, Table 1.

NB: All figures are 'current' (i.e. not adjusted for inflation). See note 41 for exchange rates.

overall expenditure to this field, almost 10 per cent in 1994. It is notable that a relatively small country like Sweden (population 8.7 million) is devoting over $100 million annually on promoting democratisation internationally, whilst the UK (population 54.9 million) could muster less than one-third of that amount.

Two questions arise from this analysis. First, although it is acknowledged that political aid programmes often consume relatively small amounts of finance (elections are one exception), nonetheless it remains pertinent to ask whether less than 10 per cent and in most cases less than 5 per cent, of expenditure is appropriate for one of the priority objectives of all donors? The answer would appear to be self-evident. Second, *why* is there such a disjuncture between the reality of expenditure and the emphasis placed on this area in policy rhetoric? One explanation pertains to donors' own domestic needs to generate a new rationale for aid, highlighted in the analysis of policy origins, with policies emphasising democracy and human rights providing a more favourable profile for development aid. This domestic agenda perhaps requires aid agencies to *say* that they are promoting human rights and democracy more than to demonstrate that they are actually *doing* it, and could explain why political aid policies are high in public salience yet low on real expenditure.

5
Political Aid: a Comparative Analysis

This chapter contains a comparative analysis of the implementation of political aid by the four selected donors. It is based on a census of *all* projects supported within this field over a two-year period, not a sample. Therefore the analyses conducted are representative of *actual* policy implementation, providing information on the distribution of political aid across broad sectors, across countries and regions, by implementers and by beneficiaries. Interesting and significant variations are revealed, as well as some common features. The chapter is in five main parts. First, the methodology is outlined, including the series of hypotheses that are used to structure the analysis that ensues. This is followed by analysis of expenditure by the four categories of: purpose (or objective); region and country; implementing agency; and beneficiary.

5.1 Methodology

5.1.1 Project database
The comparative analysis is based mainly on quantitative data of donor assistance in this field. Information on political aid projects was obtained from each donor for a two-year period between 1992 and 1994, depending on differences in financial years.[45] Only projects in developing countries were examined, with those in Central and Eastern Europe excluded. A total of 1573 projects were categorised in this way. Well over 50 per cent were Swedish (900 projects), compared with 338 EU projects, 174 UK projects and 161 US projects. However, this considerable variation in numbers of projects reflects bureaucratic differences in project classification, more than differences in expenditure commitments. In fact, examination of overall expenditure (above) showed that the US had the greatest expenditure in this field, followed

by Sweden. USAID supported a small number of large projects, within which there are various components, while Sweden funded a large number of small projects.

Information from donor project data was entered onto a database, comprising the project title, recipient country and region, and expenditure per financial year. This was supplemented by 'interpretative' categories. Given that donor categorisation of their projects varied, a common categorisation was required in order to conduct a comparative analysis. Thus, each project was categorised by the author according to:

- its purpose;
- the type of implementing agency;
- the beneficiary by sector.

Purpose

The overall purpose (or objective) of political aid is divided into six categories. First, a three-fold distinction is made between projects which promote human rights (i.e. delimited to civil and political rights in this context), democracy and good governance (i.e. the open and accountable nature of public administration). Second, each main category then is sub-divided into measures which strengthen state institutions and those which strengthen non-government bodies and societal organisations. Two supplementary categories were needed: 'miscategorised' and 'unknown', the former for projects which appeared to promote objectives *other than* human rights, democracy or good governance, and the latter for a minority of projects which were unclassifiable due to insufficient information in the data provided.[46]

Implementer

The implementing agents are those to whom funds are disbursed by donor agencies and who are responsible for project implementation. Three main types of implementing agency were identified, recipient government institutions, non-governmental organisations and multilateral organisations, with various sub-divisions. (See Appendix.)[47]

Beneficiary

The beneficiary was categorised as the *sector* in the host country to which the assistance was targeted.[48] A basic distinction was made between state and non-state beneficiaries.[49] State beneficiaries were sub-divided into central and local government, with the former separated into the main branches of the constitution, electoral system, legislature, executive and legal system. Non-state beneficiaries were sub-divided into human rights groups, pro-democracy groups and interest/pressure groups. This division is based somewhat on the DAC's distinction within civil society between advocacy groups, pursuing more altruistic purposes, and economic self-interest groups (OECD 1995, p. 2) with human rights and pro-democracy groups in the first category and interest groups in the latter. In total, over 100 beneficiary sectors were identified, with the full list provided in Appendix 1.

In general, the categorisation of each project involved a mixture of factual and interpretative categories, with 'beneficiary' as the main interpretative one. To facilitate analysis, each category was given a numerical code (see Appendix 1).[50]

Hypotheses

The following hypotheses were stated concerning possible directions of political aid implementation in relation to the different areas explored. These are generated from the literature on the 'new policy agenda' explored in Chapter 1. They are not intended to be a coherent and consistent package; rather they are utilised separately as tools for examining and analysing the various dimensions of policy implementation.

Purpose

1. Of the three linked objectives, the promotion of democracy, human rights and good governance, the greatest focus will be on promoting democracy.

This proposition arises from the analysis of the origins of the new policy agenda. A key factor was the end of the cold war and associated Western triumphalism concerning a liberal democratic polity and a market economy as the sole development model. This is likely to lead most immediately to the promotion of formal democratic institutions, rather than a revived espousal of civil and political liberties, given that the latter have changed little since their incorporation in UN declarations half a century ago. Initially, less focus is anticipated on good governance, as the least well defined concept. Additionally, democracy was regarded as the central and overriding concept (see Figure 1.1, above) in the overall agenda of promoting democratisation.

Geographical distribution

By region

2. Of the three main developing areas, political aid will concentrate on Africa, with lesser expenditure to Latin America and Asia.

Two factors account for the anticipated concentration on Africa. First, a focus on democracy promotion, [as outlined in hypothesis (1)], is likely to entail a prioritisation of support to sub-Saharan Africa, given the period of democratisation in that region from early to middle 1990s. Second, another key factor in the emergence of the notion of 'good governance' was the World Bank's shift to perceive democratic government as positively correlated with 'good' economic management and the implementation of structural adjustment programmes. As noted, such discussions occurred initially in the context of adjustment in Africa and have continued, to a large extent, to focus on this region. It is anticipated that Latin America and Asia will receive less funding relative to Africa, though with Latin America featuring more prominently in EU and US assistance, given the EU dedicated budget line and the priority accorded to hemispheric programmes within US foreign assistance.

By country

Two contrasting hypotheses are outlined here, with the intent to investigate which has most explanatory value.

3a. Assistance is concentrated on countries undergoing political reform in the direction of democratisation, along with NGO support in countries where non-democratic governments are responsible for abuses of civil and political rights.

3b. Countries are selected where donors seek to influence the nature of government in their own economic and political interests.

Hypothesis (3a) is based on an expectation that donors will seriously pursue their stated aims of political reform, focusing on those countries where potential impact and effectiveness is greatest. In contrast, the questioning of donor integrity in Chapter 1 gives rise to hypothesis (3b). The possibility of hidden agendas evokes the potential for donor manipulation of political aid as a means to ends of economic or political self-interest.

Implementers

4a. Political aid will be disbursed predominately to recipient governments to implement, with a much smaller proportion to NGOs.

4b. Of the proportion to NGOs, the larger part will be channelled to Northern NGOs, with limited aid disbursed direct to Southern NGOs.

The core proposition (4a), that a large majority of funds will be channelled to recipient governments, anticipates that donors will limit their support to a narrow and formal notion of democracy, focusing on elections and the trio of state political institutions, the executive and the legislature and judiciary. In contrast, endorsement of the view that democratisation requires simultaneous progress not only at the level of political institutions but also throughout society as a whole, as conceptualised in Beetham's democratic pyramid, would require inclusion of democratic elements of civil society on a proportionate basis. Additionally, assuming a level of support for civil society, it is anticipated that donors will feel more comfortable channelling resources through Northern NGOs, more familiar to them and perhaps perceived as more accountable. Finally, expectations are that bilateral links will be emphasised, with donors reluctant to transfer resources, with some loss of control, to multilateral implementers.

Beneficiaries

Hypotheses here concern the support offered to the range of sectors, both governmental and societal. The anticipated proportions of support to different types of beneficiary is again based on the premise, outlined above, of donor focus on a narrow, formal model of democracy, with an emphasis on democratic transition and support for newly established legislatures. In addition, it is felt that the traditional donor–recipient links between *central* government agencies will remain predominant.

5a. Donors will concentrate on strengthening public authorities, with limited support for civil society.

5b. Despite policy statements stressing 'decentralisation', central government will receive by far the largest share of assistance, with very limited support to local government.

5c. Assistance will concentrate on the electoral system and new legislatures, with less support to the executive and judicial branches.

The nature of civil society support has remained largely undefined by donors, despite civil society itself being composed of many disparate and heterogeneous elements. A pro-democracy agenda would require donor practice to concentrate on those elements that carry out democratic functions (i.e. the DAC's 'civic advocacy groups' (see section 1.2.2) or Fox's 'specialised civic organisations' (see section 3.2.2)). The hypothesis below is proposed as a means of examining the extent to which donors have directed their assistance to such organisations, or, alternatively, disbursed support to civil society in a more haphazard and unfocused manner.

> 5d. With regard to civil society support, donor assistance will focus on those public benefit organisations that specifically promote democratisation.

5.2 Purpose of political aid

Given that different donors categorised the overall objective or purpose of their projects in different ways, all projects were classified by the author according to the common categorisation outlined above. One problem encountered was the classification of many USAID projects with a single purpose category, given their large and multisectoral nature. Fortunately, USAID (1994a, Table IV) provided supplementary information for 1994 democracy projects, categorised by 11 *activity* codes. This was converted into the six purpose categories used here for comparative purposes.[51]

The results of the purpose categorisation are given below. Firstly, expenditure by each donor by the initial three-fold categorisation is presented in Figure 5.1, excluding the 'miscategorised' and 'unknown' projects. Expenditure for both years is combined for all donors except the US (1994 only). Secondly, the more detailed analysis by the six-fold categorisation, plus 'miscategorised' and 'unknown' projects, is presented in Table 5.1.

5.2.1 Expenditure by purpose

Different priorities are noted between donors. The EU and the US both prioritise democracy assistance (59.8 per cent and 55.8 per cent of expenditure respectively), while the UK emphasises the promotion of good governance (46.4 per cent). In contrast, the EU pays scant attention to public administration issues with only 2.6 per cent of expenditure, whilst democracy assistance is accorded the smallest proportion of UK funds (22.0 per cent). Swedish expenditure is divided more equally

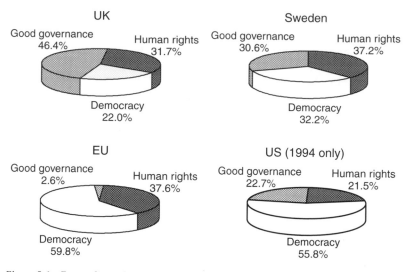

Figure 5.1   Expenditure by purpose: human rights, democracy and good governance (1992/93–1993/94 combined).[52]
Sources: Project database (EU, Sweden and UK) and USAID 1994a, Table IV (US only).

between the three main purpose categories, though ranked in the order
of, first, human rights, second, democracy and, third, good governance.[53] Such differences tend to reflect the different political cultures
of each donor country, with the US as self-appointed 'beacon of democracy' in the world, despite its own contradictory practices, the Swedish
government's record of support for victims of human rights abuses, and
the UK's traditional emphasis on an efficient civil service.

Six-fold classification

The lack of distinction between state and non-state activities limits this
analysis, however, and a fuller picture is provided by the six-fold categorisation presented in Table 5.1, again both years combined, except for
the US.

The benefits of the six-fold analysis are demonstrated by the example
of human rights. From the initial three-fold analysis, one element of
apparent consistency is that each donor allocates approximately one-
third of its expenditure to the human rights sector. Dividing this
into state (1.1) and non-state sectors (1.2) reveals very significant differences, especially when presented as a percentage of human rights expenditure only (see Table 5.2). Less than 1 per cent of UK human rights

Table 5.1 Distribution of political aid by purpose (percentages)

Purpose	EU	SWEDEN	UK	US[54]
1.1 Legal/judicial institutions	5.1	2.6	22.2	16.4
1.2 Human rights NGOs	23.7	25.6	0.1	5.1
2.1 State political institutions	34.9	3.9	12.6	16.6
2.2 Civil society	11.0	20.5	2.8	39.1
3.1 Public administration	2.0	22.0	32.5	22.7
3.2 Private sector/professional bodies	0.0	1.2	0.1	0.0
Miscategorised by donor	6.5	11.2	25.9	N/A
Unknown	16.7	12.9	3.8	N/A

Sources: Project database (EU, Sweden and UK) and USAID 1994a, Table IV (US only).

Table 5.2 Proportions of human rights expenditure to state and non-state institutions (percentages)

Support for human rights	EU	SWEDEN	UK	US
1.1 Legal/judical institutions	17.8	9.4	99.6	76.4
1.2 Human rights NGOs/legal professions	82.2	90.6	0.4	23.6

Sources: Project database (EU, Sweden and UK) and USAID 1994a, Table IV (US only).

expenditure goes to human rights NGOs, whereas the large majority of Swedish and EU assistance is channelled to this sector, 90.6 per cent and 82.2 per cent respectively. Thus, there is evidence of a division amongst donors in the manner of promoting human rights. On the one hand, the UK and the US prioritise assistance to state judicial institutions and administration of justice. On the other hand, Sweden and the EU concentrate on supporting non-government bodies which protect and promote respect for civil and political rights.

Similarly, the analysis of expenditure by the other purpose categories indicates considerable differences in the priorities and foci of donors, not only in human rights support. (See Table 5.1, above). The prioritisation of EU expenditure is on state democratic institutions (34.9 per cent) and on human rights NGOs (23.7 per cent), with less than 10 per cent expenditure on each of the four other categories.[55] Swedish priorities are human rights NGOs (25.6 per cent) and public administration (22.0 per cent). UK expenditure is concentrated on the three elements of the state sector, public administration (32.5 per cent), judicial institutions (22.2 per cent) and democratic political institutions (12.6 per cent). Non-state categories account for a total of 3 per cent only. What stands out from the analysis of US government assistance is its relatively high level support to civil society, accounting for over one-third of total expenditure.[56] State institutions are also targeted by the US, notably the legal system and public administration.

5.2.2 Miscategorised projects

The proportion of 'miscategorised' projects is a finding of particular note and concern (see Table 5.1). Motivated presumably by the wish to augment total expenditure on a relatively new area of support, donor agencies have tended to 're-label' existing activities. It is contended here that this has resulted in the wrongful inclusion by donors of projects which do not, in fact, promote the stated political objectives. These amount to a considerable proportion of total expenditure. The UK and Sweden were the worst offenders, with 25.9 per cent and 11.2 per cent respectively of total expenditure miscategorised, while the EU had a lower proportion of 6.5 per cent. The US D/G programmes also contain a number of anomalies, although their multisectoral nature means that it is not possible to quantify the exact percentage of miscategorised expenditure.[57]

Summary of findings

Hypothesis (1) suggested that:

> Of the three linked objectives, the promotion of democracy, human rights and good governance, the greatest focus will be on promoting democracy.

The findings are of a mixed profile of donor support for these three objectives, and, hence, do not confirm this hypothesis unequivocally. While the EU and the US prioritise the promotion of democracy, the UK focuses on good governance and Sweden on human rights, though the latter less emphatically. Rather than the donors sharing a common focus, the varying priorities of the three bilateral donors tend to reflect their differing political cultures.

5.3 Geographical distribution

This section analyses the geographical distribution of political aid, first by region and then by country.

5.3.1 Regional distribution

The regional breakdown of total expenditure by *all* donors combined is displayed in Figure 5.2, with that of each *individual* donor shown in Table 5.3.[58] Commentary addresses the question of why political aid has been concentrated in some regions and not others.

Two related points emerge from the regional distribution of political aid. The first is the concentration of assistance to Africa and Latin America. Combining these two regions, they account for 83.4 per cent of political aid from the four donors, and at least three quarters of total assistance provided by each one, (see Figure 5.2 and Table 5.3, below). The other point, conversely, is the relative neglect of support to Asia, accounting for only 9.2 per cent of donors' combined aid, with only the UK providing a significant slice (24.7 per cent) of their total good government support to Asia. The receipt of such a small proportion of overall political aid is especially remarkable given Asia's size, accounting for the majority of the world's population.

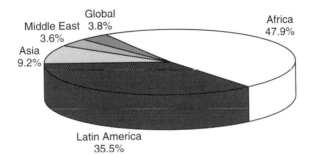

Figure 5.2 Regional distribution of political aid (all donors, 1992/93–1993/94 expenditure combined, US$m).
Source: Project database.

Table 5.3 Regional distribution of political aid (by individual donor, 1992/93–1993/94 expenditure combined) (percentages)

Continent	EU	SWEDEN	UK	US
Africa	34.8	58.4	61.2	44.9
Latin America	58.4	22.9	12.8	36.9
Asia	1.8	6.4	24.7	11.8
Middle East	2.8	5.3	0.0	3.4
Global	2.1	6.9	1.3	3.0

Source: Project database.

What accounts for both this concentration of assistance to Africa and Latin America and the low level of support to Asia? Two factors are suggested to account for the regional prioritisation, followed by three propositions to explain the relative neglect of Asia.

Why has there been such prioritisation of support to Latin America and Africa? The primary explanation concerns political events in the actual world, to which donors have responded. In the 1980s, Latin America experienced a widespread resurgence of democracy, notably the replacement of military dictatorships by elected, civilian governments in South America. Few formally non-democratic governments remained in Latin America by the end of the decade, yet democracy was far from fully achieved. In virtually all countries democracy remained fragile and in need of consolidation, with military élites often retaining 'reserved' power and authority. In the early 1990s, the wave of democratisation in Africa left few countries untouched, with moves to multi-partyism and transitional elections in many countries. However, similar to Latin America, the establishment of limited democracies in some countries left considerable uncertainty regarding their prospects for consolidation. In addition, the pressure for democratisation was unsuccessful in other African countries, stalled or reversed by existing authoritarian regimes (Luckham 1995). Hence, in both Latin America and sub-Saharan Africa, there was a clear role for external support of the democratisation process. Indeed, in Latin America, US and EU involvement was evident prior to the much-heralded shift in donor policies in the early 1990s. As discussed previously, USAID's democracy assistance programmes were initiated in Latin America in the early 1980s, and the EU's first democratisation budget line, specific to Latin America, was established in 1990. Regarding sub-Saharan Africa, the new policy declarations by donors in the early 1990s coincided with the democratisation phase that was commencing then, making it an obvious target and priority for donor support.

A secondary explanation for the concentration of donor assistance in Africa and Latin America pertains to the regional priorities of the overall aid programmes of the donors examined, combined with their general political orientation. For different reasons, Africa is a priority region for both Swedish and European Commission development aid. Africa has long been the biggest recipient of Swedish development assistance, the location of the large majority of 'programme countries'.[59] The Lomé Convention between the EU and ACP states (the large majority of whom are in Africa), accounts for the largest single portion of EU aid (Crawford 1996, p. 518).[60] Yet, Latin America also emerges as a priority region for the disbursement of *political* aid by Sweden and the EU. This is particularly due to Sweden and the EU's frequently voiced concerns for the victims of human rights violations, particularly in Central America. In the EU context, such concerns have been expressed in particular by the European Parliament, initiators of the Latin America democratisation budget line. For the US government, Latin America has always been a main focus of its foreign assistance, traceable back to the Monroe Doctrine of 1823 aimed at 'keeping extrahemispheric powers out of Latin America' (Carothers 1991, p. 1). In addition, the promotion of democracy in Latin America has been a recurrent, stated theme of US governments, though often disguising anti-Communist and pro-US business policies, for instance, during the Reagan and Bush presidencies. Ironically, the US government has often provided support to the same right-wing, military-dominated governments in Central America criticised by Sweden and the European Parliament for their human rights abuses.[61] US development assistance to Africa, under threat with the decline of regional strategic interests, has been safeguarded by Congress through the creation of the 'Africa Development Fund', and the US focus on democracy promotion within Africa in the 1990s was unsurprising given the prevailing orthodoxy emanating from Washington that simultaneous economic and political liberalisation lay at the heart of African recovery (USAID 1993). Britain's general aid programme remains highly focused on its ex-colonies in Africa, Asia and the Caribbean, something that is similarly reflected in its good government programme.

In contrast, why has Asia received such a low proportion of overall political aid? Three explanations are offered. First, Asia has not experienced the same clear process of democratisation, influenced by a regional 'demonstration' effect, as was evident in Latin America in the 1980s, in Central and Eastern Europe in 1989, and in sub-Saharan Africa in the early 1990s. Nevertheless, (re-)democratisation did take place in a number of countries in the 1980s, for example, in Pakistan, Bangladesh, Mongolia, South Korea, Taiwan and the Philippines, though additional democratic transitions in the 1990s have been limited to Nepal and the UN-supervised elections in Cambodia (Potter 1997, pp. 1–40). It appears, however, that the lack of a clear regional process of democratisation has meant less attention to Asia, at least by the donors studied. This is particularly unfortunate given the fragile and parlous state of democracy in many countries in the region. The strengthening of democratic elements both within and without government would seem highly appropriate, both in the unstable democracies, for example, Pakistan and Bangladesh, and where representative political institutions are becoming more established, in the Philippines, for instance.

Second, the lack of political aid directed at the longer established parliamentary democracies of India and Sri Lanka suggests an underlying assumption in operation that such assistance is not required where electoral democracy exists. Yet, India's status as the world's largest democracy surely requires support for processes of democratic deepening, as well as combating instances of alleged human rights abuses by both military and police.[62] Furthermore, the situation of civil war in Sri Lanka would appear to make it an appropriate target for donor support for conflict resolution and mediation between governments and guerrillas, highlighted as a priority area by the EU.

Third, a further proposition applies particularly to East and Southeast Asia, providing a persuasive explanation as to why this region has not been targeted with political aid. The economic growth and developmental success that has occurred in this region contrasts with the negative growth and de-development experienced in much of Africa and Latin America, especially in the 'lost decade' of the 1980s. It would appear that the promotion of democracy and human rights is less of a priority for donors in conditions of developmental success. This raises the question of donor motivation. Is democratic government seen as an end in itself, or, alternatively, is it valued primarily as offering the best prospects for economic development in areas of low growth? Certainly, issues of good governance are strongly linked to those of economic management, and have been raised most prominently in relation to problems of weak authoritarian government in sub-Saharan Africa. Improved governance through democratic, accountable rule is seen as essential for economic reform and renewal in Africa and, to a lesser extent, in Latin America. In contrast, in much of East Asia, although a transition to democratic rule may be viewed as desirable in the longer-term, the authoritarian state has been a *developmental* state and hence subject to less external pressure to politically reform. Economic success and much less aid dependence in East Asian countries also implies a lack of donor leverage to achieve political reform, even *if* donors were so motivated.

The UK is the only donor of those examined to provide a significant proportion of its overall political aid to Asia, almost 25 per cent. Yet, a country breakdown reveals Indonesia, China and Pakistan to be the main recipients, none noted for their progress in democratisation in the period examined (see Table 5.3, above). This suggests that the aim of pursuing Britain's economic interests in these countries was as crucial a factor as promoting democracy.

Summary of findings

Hypothesis (2) stated that: Of the three main developing areas, political aid will concentrate on Africa, with lesser expenditure to Latin America and Asia.

This has been confirmed quite emphatically, with expenditure in fact in inverse proportion to population. Expenditure figures confirm not only the anticipated focus on Africa, they also highlight the remarkable neglect of political reform in Asia.

5.3.2 Country expenditure

The major country recipients of each donor's political aid programme are examined here. Table 5.4 presents the top ten recipients for each donor, analysing each year's expenditure separately, while Figure 5.3 identifies the top twenty recipient countries for all donors combined, aggregating both years' expenditure[63]

Table 5.4 indicates that the priority recipients of political aid vary considerably between donors, as well as showing a small number of commonly supported countries. The commentary that follows focuses on each donor separately, examining the main recipient countries and addressing why they have been targeted for political aid.

Table 5.4 Top ten recipient countries of political aid (by individual donor) Year 1 (1992/93)

EU		SWEDEN		UK		US	
Recipient	*(%)*	*Recipient*	*(%)*	*Recipient*	*(%)*	*Recipient*	*(%)*
Ecuador	9.3	South Africa	26.6	Zambia	17.3	South Africa	13.4
El Salvador	7.0	Zimbabwe	4.3	Indonesia	9.9	Colombia	8.6
Chile	6.6	Tanzania	4.2	Uganda	9.8	Mozambique	7.4
Uganda	6.5	Mozambique	4.2	Kenya	8.3	El Salvador	5.1
Burundi	5.5	Namibia	3.8	Pakistan	6.8	Guatemala	4.6
Malawi	4.7	West Bank & Gaza	3.7	Ghana	5.7	Nicaragua	4.3
Colombia	4.4	Botswana	3.6	China	5.4	Haiti	4.1
Ethiopia	3.7	Vietnam	3.4	Nigeria	3.7	Cambodia	3.2
Guinea	3.4	El Salvador	2.1	Zimbabwe	3.5	Panama	2.6
Brazil	3.4	Lesotho	1.5	Swaziland	3.2	Bolivia	2.3
TOTAL	54.5		57.4		73.6		55.6

Year 2 (1993/94)

EU Recipient	(%)	SWEDEN Recipient	(%)	UK Recipient	(%)	US Recipient	(%)
Mozambique	27.0	South Africa	33.9	Uganda	22.3	South Africa	20.4
Nicaragua	17.3	Mozambique	6.7	South Africa	9.6	Rwanda	8.3
Brazil	9.0	El Salvador	5.9	China	7.1	Nicaragua	6.8
Colombia	7.3	West Bank and Gaza	4.7	Zambia	6.6	El Salvador	5.5
Peru	6.5	Zimbabwe	3.2	Pakistan	4.9	Egypt	4.4
Guatemala	5.0	Vietnam	3.1	Cambodia	4.2	Somalia	3.8
El Salvador	1.9	Namibia	2.6	Botswana	3.3	Mozambique	3.0
Tanzania	1.8	Botswana	2.4	Montserrat	3.3	Haiti	3.0
Palestine	1.6	Tanzania	2.2	Malawi	3.1	Cambodia	2.6
Chile	1.6	Nicaragua	1.9	Mozambique	2.9	Panama	2.6
TOTAL	79.0		66.6		67.3		60.4

Source: Project database.

European Union

Expenditure is disbursed to 66 countries, as well as to regional programmes, the largest number amongst the donors examined. Such a wide dispersal of limited resources perhaps reflects the application-driven nature of budget line funds, with fewer links to overall development cooperation programmes. All main recipient countries are in Latin America and sub-Saharan Africa, with the exception of Palestine, (i.e. the West Bank and Gaza). The favourable representation of Latin America countries in the top ten, especially in 1994, reflects the budget dedicated to that region. The prioritisation of peace processes in Central America is reflected in the prominence of El Salvador and Guatemala as major recipients.

There is some lack of continuity over the two years. In fact, only three countries feature in both years, El Salvador, Colombia and Chile, perhaps reflecting more use of multiannual programmes of assistance within the Latin American budget line (B7-7030). Discontinuity is mainly due to the presence of short-term projects typical of budget line funding – especially the general democracy and human rights fund (B7-7020) – responding to situations (and applications) as they arise. Most frequently, such contingency situations are elections, accounting for a number of African countries featuring as major recipients in 1993.

The position of Ecuador as the largest recipient in 1993 is somewhat surprising given its relatively small size, non-turbulent political situation and the lack of elections in that year. Investigation, however, reveals that this top position is due solely to one large grant of Ecu 3.57m. to the Ecuadorian government from the mainstream Financial and Technical Co-operation budget line (B7-3010) for a project entitled 'Women's Development in the Rural Areas'. Two observations are pertinent. First, while recognising the developmental relevance of such a project, it does not clearly have democracy and human rights promotion as its primary purpose, although increasing women's political participation could be one of its elements. For this reason, this project was classified as miscategorised under the 'purpose' classification, and thus Ecuador only features at all in this analysis due to taking donor data sets as given. Second, it is indicative of how thinly resources have been spread amongst a large number of countries when Ecuador can acquire the status of top recipient in this manner. Similarly, Ethiopia appears in the top ten in 1993 on the basis of one project only, promoting press freedom.

In 1994, Mozambique is the largest recipient by far, accounting for over one-quarter of all funds, due entirely to the massive financing of the multi-party elections held that year. Nicaragua also received extensive funds, including a more varied range of political aid projects. The bulk of monies disbursed to Nicaragua, however, was for one project entitled 'Consolidation of the rule of law and fostering economic growth in rural areas', with expenditure of over Ecu 14 m. from the mainstream budget for Asia and Latin America (B7–3010), 85.9 per cent of all assistance to Nicaragua that year. There appears to be two quite separate sectoral objectives within this one project, only one of which is relevant to political aid, yet with no financial breakdown of the different elements. Similar to the Ecuadorian example, funding of the rural development component is considered to be miscategorised. The inclusion of such a substantial grant, however, makes a significant difference both to Nicaragua's position as second highest recipient and to the grand total of EU political aid. Interestingly, the error comes from the same source in both cases, serving to increase the total finance allocated to democracy and human rights from the mainstream Latin American budget (B7-3010).[64] The focus on electoral processes remains in 1994, with Tanzania and Palestine as major recipients due to funding of electoral activities.

Colombia is a major recipient in both years, but with assistance channelled overwhelmingly to human rights NGOs, especially victim support and human rights education. In two instances only were funds disbursed to public authorities, one for the establishment of a human rights ombudsman and the other for a community development project, listed under good governance. The much larger proportion of overall assistance distributed to the top ten recipient countries, almost four- fifths in 1994, is again largely accounted for by the above two huge projects to Mozambique and Nicaragua.

Sweden

A total of 54 countries benefited from Swedish political aid. Significant proportions of assistance are also channelled into regional programmes in Central and South America where Swedish aid has much less of a presence in individual countries.

The single, outstanding characteristic of Swedish political aid during this period was the very large proportion disbursed to South African organisations, accounting for 26.6 per cent in 1992/93 and 33.9 per cent in 1993/94. This overwhelmingly took the form of support for the ANC. No other individual country receives more than 5 per cent of total aid, with the exceptions in 1993/94 of Mozambique (6.7 per cent) and El Salvador (5.9 per cent). As discussed earlier, the focus on South Africa, or more accurately on the ANC, was not new, a continuation of the assistance provided by the Swedish government for many years. It was also terminated post-democratic elections in 1994, with funds transferred to a country budget for general developmental use by the new South African government, and hence no longer representative of current practice.

What factors have influenced the selection of the main recipients of Swedish political aid? Two are suggested. First, many of the top recipients are the 'programme countries' to whom the bulk of Swedish development assistance is channelled, for example, Tanzania, Zimbabwe, Botswana, Mozambique, Vietnam. The bulk of assistance to these countries is public administration support (good governance), which is disbursed almost exclusively to programme countries. Second, there is an emphasis on conflict resolution and the achievement of sustainable peace and democracy, as indicated by the fact that most top recipients have emerged out of conflict situations. In some respects, this would appear to be a contemporary expression of the Swedish support, evident from the 1960s onwards, for anti-colonial and anti-imperialist movements. Hence, support is now provided towards: black majority rule in South Africa; the implementation of the Peace Accord in El Salvador (signed in January 1992), along with the establishment of more meaningful democratic institutions; the resolution of the civil war and the transition to democracy in Mozambique; and attempts to bring peace and autonomy to the Israeli-occupied territories of the West Bank and Gaza.

Of those examined, Sweden is the sole donor to make an explicit distinction between 'measures in countries where Governments aspire to achieve respect for human rights' and those in countries where 'violations of human rights are due to actions of Governments', with support to governments being restricted to the former. This policy would appear to have been upheld, with no evidence of political aid disbursed to public authorities where governments are implicated in civil and political rights abuses. For example, in El Salvador, out of 31 projects, those few related to government activities involved the channelling of assistance through UN and other international bodies, notably UNDP, including electoral support and police training. In addition, large-scale assistance was provided to the 'Truth Commission', government-related, but with the mandate to investigate past human rights abuses and to promote reconciliation. From a liberal democratic viewpoint, one inconsistency in policy implementation could be the provision of public administration support to the communist government of Vietnam, where civil and political liberties are indeed restricted. It is perhaps worth recalling, however, that the long-term Swedish support to Vietnam arose from its opposition to US involvement in the Vietnam War and the subsequent isolation imposed by most Western governments after US defeat in 1975.

United Kingdom

Good government assistance is disbursed to 49 developing countries, plus two regional programmes, with a relatively high concentration of aid amongst the top ten recipients, accounting for 73.6 per cent and 67.3 per cent in each year. Uganda (22.3 per cent in 1993/94) and Zambia (17.3 per cent in 1992/93) stand out as the major recipients of UK good government assistance.[65] No other country received more than 10 per cent in either year.

What accounts for the prioritisation of Zambia and Uganda? As ex-British colonies and amongst the world's poorest countries, both are priority recipients of the UK's development aid programme.[66] Yet, it is recent political developments that account for the high levels of good government assistance to these countries. Zambia led the way in Anglophone Africa not only as the first to return to multi-party politics, but also to elect a change of government, with the success of Frederick Chiluba and the Movement for Multi-party Democracy in the elections of December 1991. One consequence of Zambia's early democratic transition was the reward of substantial 'good government' aid from the UK for purposes of civil service reform and financial management, as well as assistance from other donors.

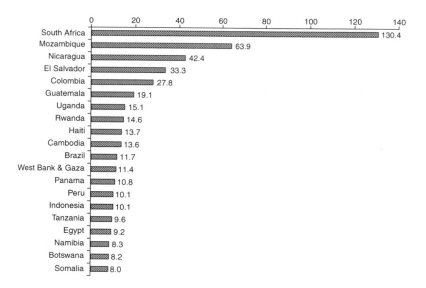

Figure 5.3 Top twenty recipient countries of political aid (all donors, 1992/93–1993/94 expenditure combined, US$m).
Source: Project database.

It is the focus on Uganda that is of particular interest, however. It is not only the major recipient of the UK's good government programme, but also the seventh highest recipient of the four donors' combined political aid (see Figure 5.3). Under President Museveni's National Resistance Movement, Uganda bucked the trend towards multi-partyism in sub-Saharan Africa in the early 1990s, preferring a non-party 'movement' system of representative government. Local representation is provided through a system of Local Councils, claimed to augment local powers and to be a more participatory form of democracy. At the grassroots level, members of the village Local Council (LCI) are elected by universal franchise, but thereafter the representatives to the Councils of successively larger geographical areas, from parish to district levels (LCII–V), are selected by the bodies immediately below. The legislative body is the National Constituent Assembly, formerly the National Resistance Council, the majority of whose members are directly elected by universal franchise, but as individual candidates not political party representatives, with a minority of reserved seats for representatives of different social groups (for example, women, trade unions) as well as the army. Presidential and parliamentary elections were held in May and June 1996, respectively. Political parties are not illegal as such, but under the Constitution of 1995 they cannot be electorally active, and are thus limited in their actions. A referendum is planned for 2000 when the population is expected to choose between a multi-party or 'movement' system, but with Museveni already on record as opposed to multi-party politics (*The Courier* No. 170 1998). Donor emphasis on multi-partyism could have led, if not to aid sanctions, then at least to a lack of support for the 'movement' model. Yet, on the contrary, Uganda's distinct form of political development has generally been given enthusiastic support by the donor governments.[67] What accounts for this? Three possible reasons are put forward. First, donors are intent not to impose a Western model of democracy on recipient governments and welcome the development of an alternative form of democratic representation. However, it is also possible that donors interpreted the 'movement' system of representation as a transitional phase before multi-partyism, making long-term support more uncertain. Second, Museveni has brought political stability and economic growth to Uganda since coming to power in 1986, after the decades of political chaos, human rights abuses and economic decline under Amin (1971–79) and Obote (1965–71 and 1980–86), with Museveni himself hailed as the prime example of a 'new breed' of African leaders, whom Northern donors are more concerned to support than to chastise. Third, Museveni has implemented structural adjustment programmes in line with World Bank and IMF models, including drastic cuts in the number of public employees and a privatisation programme, and has been faithful to the demands of Uganda's international creditors for debt repayments. It is suggested that the latter two reasons have most explanatory weight, especially in accounting for UK support to Uganda. The UK's promotion of 'good government' is often more closely linked to reforms in the public sector and in economic management, than to more explicit *political* reforms. This is reflected in the nature of projects to Uganda, all to public authorities, primarily civil service reform and the police. Thus, it is advanced that the example of Uganda indicates how donors in general, and the UK government in particular, are more prepared to tolerate a different approach to democracy on condition that World Bank/IMF monitored economic reform programmes are maintained and political stability prevails.

What other factors underlie the selection of the major recipients of good government aid? A country's status as a primary recipient of the British bilateral aid programme is clearly significant, with the large majority of the main recipients for 'good government' assistance simultaneously featuring amongst the top twenty bilateral recipients.[68] The country priorities of the overall bilateral programme reflect both ex-colonial interests and newer commercial interests, particularly in East and South East Asia. One apparent outcome is that the major benefici-aries of good government assistance make up a curious collection of countries, with selection at times appearing to be influenced more by *non*-political factors than by the aim of promoting democratic govern-ment. Indeed some of the major recipients are characterised not only by the *lack* of democratic rule, but also by the absence of any real intention on the part of their governments to move towards democratisation, notably the case in Indonesia and China, but also in Pakistan, steeped in political corruption with little evidence of democratic progress, and Swaziland, characterised by monarchical control of the country's pol-itical institutions. This point is especially pertinent given that 90 per cent of UK political aid is channelled to governments and not NGOs.

Indonesia and China, as two of the highest ranking recipients of UK political aid, arouse the greatest incredulity, given the records of both governments as violators of civil and political rights and given that the assistance benefited these governments themselves, not oppositional NGOs. The failure to apply aid sanctions to Indonesia and China will be discussed in Part III. How can the selection of such regimes for positive assistance be accounted for? It would seem that British eco-nomic self-interests are the primary motivation, not political objectives. In the case of Indonesia, the inclusion of police aid turns democracy and human rights objectives on their head, strengthening the very forces responsible for many human rights abuses (something that is discussed further in section 5.5). Closer examination of the projects supported reveals that in both China and Indonesia not only was a large propor-tion of overall good government aid expended on one project only, but also the connection of that project with the promotion of democracy and human rights is, at best, tenuous. In China, by far the largest of good government projects is the aforementioned 'Shanghai Environ-mental Project', with disbursements of $1.42 m and $2.21 m in 1992/93 and 1993/94 respectively, accounting for 99 per cent of all expend-iture. Similarly, in Indonesia, a large proportion of funds is provided to an energy project, developing natural gas resources, with disbursements of $2.05 m and $0.66 m in 1992/93 and 1993/94 respectively, 77.8 per cent of all 'good government' expenditure. This would seem to be an economic development project. In both instances, the good govern-ment link is tenuous, and for the purposes of this research they are regarded as 'miscategorised'. British economic interests would appear to be served, however, directly and indirectly.

Nigeria also features as a major recipient prior to the annulment of the presidential elections of June 1993, with aid focused on civil service reform, but also including expenditure of over $1 m on police training. Other main recipients of British good government aid are accounted for by the occurrence of transitional elections at this time, particularly in sub-Saharan Africa.

Also noteworthy is the appearance of the island of Montserrat, before the volcanic eruptions of July 1995, as the eighth largest recipient in 1993/94, with over 3 per cent of total expenditure, despite a mere 11 000 inhabitants.[69] That such a tiny country can feature as a major recipient highlights the small volume, in overall expenditure, of the UK's good government programme.

United States

As with Swedish assistance, South Africa was the largest recipient of US political aid at this time, with 13.4 per cent of USAID's democracy assistance in 1993 and 20.4 per cent in 1994. No other country received above 10 per cent during this period, although a small number did receive more than 5 per cent of total assistance. As a superpower and large aid donor, the US maintains foreign aid programmes in many countries throughout the developing world, more so than Sweden or the UK, for example. Yet, in contrast, USAID's 'democracy and govern-ance' programmes are concentrated in a smaller number of countries, 45 in the period examined, considerably less than for Sweden or the EU. This concentration is primarily due to USAID having integrated D/G assistance into its mainstream programmes, rather than disbursing funds to small projects in a wider range of countries.

In many instances, the selection of the main recipients of democracy assistance appears to reflect the major geo-political interests of the US government, rather than specific pro-democracy concerns. First, there was a prioritisation of countries in Latin America, seven out of the top ten recipients in 1993, where US economic and political interests are most significant given continental proximity and an assumed 'sphere of influence'. It is notable that El Salvador and Guatemala, whose repress-ive governments received extensive US military support in the 1980s for counterinsurgency activities against left-wing forces, both feature now as major recipients of democracy assistance.[70] Also of note is that post-Sandinista Nicaragua became a major target for 'democracy assistance', something that is especially striking given how earlier the US gov-ernment provided covert support to the anti-democratic 'Contras' in their war against the leftist Sandinista government, destabilising the country and ultimately undermining the Sandinista's electability.[71] US interests predominate in the other priority Central American recipient, Panama, small in size but with the strategically important canal. Given the history of US military intervention in Panama to protect its economic and strategic interests in the Canal Zone, including the much criticised invasion of December 1989, political aid to Panama is probably more accurately perceived as another means to maintain US political influence, rather than the more neutral promotion of democratic institutions. Second, it is interesting that Egypt has a sizeable 'democracy and governance' project in 1994, despite little evidence of democratic progress, and where the extensive US foreign aid programme, second only to that of Israel, is clearly motivated by security and geopolitical interests. Further, it is significant that Somalia and Haiti appear amongst the main recipients, both locations of US intervention in the 1990s.

Colombia, the second largest recipient in 1993, deserves particular attention. The large bulk of US democracy assistance is an extensive six-year 'administration of justice' project. This can be criticised on two counts. First, the lack of commitment of the Colombian government to judicial reform undermines its effectiveness. This is a prime example of Carothers' criticism of the neglect of power relations in democracy assistance. Questions of whose interests the current judicial system serves and whose interests would be threatened by reform are not asked (Carothers 1997, pp. 122–3). Second, the commitment of the US government itself to serious judicial reform in Colombia is doubted by criticisms of the specific content of the project. Human Rights Watch has drawn attention to the project's support for the controversial Public Order courts, criticised for violation of due process norms and their misuse against legal political actors, for instance, striking workers or other demonstrators (Human Rights Watch 1992, pp. 92–3).

It is somewhat surprising that Rwanda is the second largest recipient of USAID's democracy assistance in FY 1994, given both the country's small size and the lack of historical links.[72] This was one of the earliest of USAID's 'Building Democracy' programmes, commencing in October 1993 shortly after the signing of the ill-fated Arusha peace accord in August 1993 and prior to the genocide of April 1994 onwards. It arose out of general donor pressure from the early 1990s, including that from the French, on the Rwandan government to move towards democratisation (Klinghoffer 1998, p. 19). The extent of US support can perhaps be explained as part of wider attempts to gain influence in the Great Lakes region, in competition with the French, with favourable outcomes likely to accompany regime change. Yet, whether such ulterior motivation was present or not, the case of Rwanda, and similarly Burundi, dramatically and tragically indicates the dilemma of external intervention in complex internal political processes, with dangers of unintended consequences. Such dangers are multiplied where knowledge of local conditions and circumstances are limited, as would seem to be the case with US involvement in Rwanda. Indeed, President Habyarimana is described as a 'reluctant partner' in the move towards democratisation being pushed upon him, and that he simultaneously operated on a 'second track' with strong ethnic and militarist overtones, leading to the establishment of the extremist Hutu militias (ibid., p. 20). In particular, it has been argued more generally that the promotion of multi-partyism *per se* can be inappropriate in situations of ethnic divisions or other social cleavages, with the emergence of ethnically identified political parties, for example, likely to intensify existing social divisons and even fuel armed conflict. While the causes of the Rwandan genocide are clearly more complex than a simple attribution to multi-partyism, it can be claimed with some substantiation that the resistance to external pressure to democratise led to a parallel government-backed build-up of armed militias. This has led to the concept of 'Do No Harm', requiring Northern donor governments to scrutinise their political aid programmes to identify any such unintended but harmful effects, particularly an aggravation of human rights violations. It is perhaps noteworthy that the militia killings and human rights abuses, pre-genocide, did not instigate donor action or any aid restrictions, despite international investigations critical of the Rwandan government at that time (ibid., pp. 22–3).[73]

All donors

Combining all donor expenditure gives the 'top twenty' of recipient nations for the years examined. Clearly, countries supported by the US, and to a lesser extent by Sweden, will tend to feature most prominently, given that their expenditure is greatest. Figure 5.3, above, shows South Africa in number one position, in receipt of over twice as much assistance as second-placed Mozambique, with donor funds directed particularly at the transition to democratic rule in both countries at that time. Also of interest is that three Central American states, Nicaragua, El Salvador and Guatemala, feature in the top six, despite their relatively small size. In El Salvador and Guatemala, support is driven by the implementation of peace processes. The high position of Colombia is initially surprising, given the degree of human rights violations perpetrated by the military and the lack of commitment of the Colombian government to democratic reforms (see Part III, section 9.3). Assistance is a mixture of valid EU support to the NGO sector, including the local branch of the International Commission of Jurists, author of much of the documentation placing responsibility for human rights abuses, and a questionable US 'administration of justice' project, itself subject to criticism (see above and section 9.3). Rwanda appears almost solely due to the extensive US 'democracy building' programme initiated prior to the genocide in 1994. Similarly, Haiti's high position is due mainly to the substantial and continued US involvement in the country after the restoration of President Aristide in September 1993. Support for Cambodia and for the West Bank and Gaza is accounted for by multi-donor assistance to the UN-supervised Cambodian elections in May 1993 and by the implementation of the 1993 Israeli–Palestinian peace accord, culminating in the transfer to Palestinian self-rule. Finally, the surprising inclusion of Indonesia is due mainly to UK assistance, though perceived as having little to do with promoting democratisation.

Summary of findings

It is recalled that two contrasting hypotheses were constructed in order to facilitate an analysis of why certain countries are selected as major recipients, as follows:

3a. Assistance is concentrated on countries undergoing political reform in the direction of democratisation, along with support for NGOs in countries with non-democratic governments responsible for abuses of civil and political rights.

3b. Countries are selected where donors seek to influence the nature of government in their own economic and political interests.

To what extent are either of these two hypotheses confirmed or refuted by the practices of the respective donors?

In the case of the EU, there is little evidence to suggest donor manipulation of political aid for ends other than the promotion of a democratic polity, and, hence, hypothesis (3a) would appear to be most appropriate. The selection of countries appears to be determined primarily by the aim of strengthening peace building and democratic reform. This is reflected particularly by support for peace processes in Central American and in the Occupied Territories and for elections in sub-Saharan Africa. In countries where governments have a poor human rights record, for example, Colombia, assistance is channelled to the non-governmental sector. The analysis of the main recipient countries does focus attention on three other issues, however. First, the lack of continuity in country support over the two years suggests a selection process which is application-driven and short-term in outlook.[74] Second, the short-term nature of support is emphasised most clearly by one-off grants for electoral assistance. The development of a longer-term strategy is necessary if democratic elections are to be the foundation of a continuing process of democratisation, rather than a facade behind which power structures show minimal change. Third, longer-term promotion of democracy and human rights by the EU is more achievable if integrated into mainstream development co-operation programmes, with more substantial funding available, and moves in this direction are encouraging. It must be noted, however, that such moves also involve the inaccurate labelling of activities in other spheres as political aid, as the examples of Paraguay and Nicaragua demonstrated.

Regarding Swedish assistance, hypothesis (3a) is again generally confirmed, with little evidence to suggest hidden agendas influencing the allocation of its political aid. It is true that one aim of good governance assistance is to improve the efficient and effective use of Swedish development aid. This is quite legitimate, however, and there is little to suggest that Swedish economic interests are being pursued through the selection of political aid recipients. What is more evident from the country selection is the continued influence of the Swedish 'tradition' of support for national liberation and leftist movements.

When examining the major recipients of British good government aid, it is very difficult to explain their selection solely on grounds of democracy promotion. On the contrary, hypothesis (3b) has greater credibility in accounting for why a number of authoritarian governments feature amongst the major beneficiaries. The prioritising of assistance to the governments of Indonesia, China, Pakistan and Nigeria, none of whom show commitment to democratisation, can be explained more convincingly by the use of political aid to maintain British influence and economic interests in the two former colonies and to promote business opportunities in the large and expanding economies in East Asia. In these instances, the promotion of democratic government is a facade behind which more base motivations predominate, with the strengthening of authoritarian regimes a consequence. On a less critical note, the emphasis on support to the Ugandan government indicates flexibility in policy implementation, consistent with the stated intention of not imposing a Westminster model (Chalker 1991).

Positively, the US has contributed substantial financial assistance to the democratic transition in South Africa, upholding hypothesis (3a). Nonetheless, there are also a number of examples that confirm the pertinence of hypothesis (3b), with many major recipients of US democracy assistance corresponding with countries where the US has pursued long-standing economic and strategic interests, often with little concern for matters of democracy.

This finding is perhaps unsurprising given the ambiguity surrounding the US and democracy throughout the post-1945 period. For half a century the US government has presented itself as the standard bearer of democracy in the world. Whether this image was purposeful facade or self-deception, the reality has been quite different. In attempting to extend its hegemonic influence world-wide, the US government has readily jettisoned proclaimed democratic principles in active support of right-wing forces, frequently anti-democratic, either in the perceived 'struggle against communism' and/or when US business interests were threatened. Examples abound from the 1950s onwards, for instance, the overthrow of President Arbenz in Guatemala in 1954, democratically elected by the Guatemalan people but unacceptably reformist to the US government, ushering in decades of US-supported, repressive military rule.

Have US claims to promote democracy changed in the 1990s? The concentration of assistance to Central American countries indicates an ongoing intent to sustain US influence in this proximate region. Is the intention of such influence now to promote democratic government or to maintain hegemony, as charged by W. I. Robinson (1996)? It is acknowledged that US policy in El Salvador and Guatemala has shifted, especially after the defeat of successive Republican administrations (1980–92), and with the signing of Peace Accords to end the long-running civil conflicts in each country (Barry 1992, part 8; Murray with Barry 1995, part 8). Yet, it is unlikely that US political aid to either country is solely altruistic assistance for democratic institutions, given the massive support to military governments and to counterinsurgency activities in preceding decades. Democracy assistance can be interpreted more credibly as part of ongoing regional efforts to ensure that governments and their policies remain favourably disposed to US government influence and to US commercial interests and other activities, for example, drug control efforts. Similarly, US 'democracy building' in Nicaragaue cannot be regarded with other than a jaundiced eye, given their role in undermining the Sandinista government, itself responsible for introducing a democratic constitution, but 'unacceptable' to the US government for its leftist policies. In the cases of these three Central American countries, suffice it to say that the 'jury remains out' on whether there are genuine attempts by the US government to assist the process of democratisation, immaterial of who is in power, or whether the primary motivation is securing governments that act in accord with US political and economic interests.

The status of Colombia and Egypt as major recipients of US democracy assistance is of particular curiosity. Both are highlighted in Part III as examples of the non-application of aid sanctions, despite evidence of gross and persistent abuses of human rights by their governments. In both cases the US is the principle donor. It would appear that the intent of the US government is to maintain large-scale development co-operation programmes with both governments, motivated by other dominant foreign policy concerns, as outlined in Chapter 9. In the current policy climate, there is doubtless some pressure to include a 'democracy and governance' component. Two points are pertinent, however. One is that the D/G element can act as 'window-dressing', serving to partly conceal and partly legitimate the substantial economic and military support provided by the US to governments with little or no democratic credibility. The other is that any 'democracy assistance' to governments with so little commitment to improve their human rights and democracy performance will be compromised from the outset.

It was suggested that the extent of US assistance to democratic transition in Rwanda, pre-genocide, was motivated by the wish to gain greater influence in a region dominated internationally by the French. One question posed in Chapter 1 concerned evidence of unintended negative effects. While this is most suitably answered by country case-studies, the Rwandan example, whatever the intent of US and other donor involvement, does demonstrate the potential gravity of negative outcomes from external intervention where motives are mixed and where external efforts are not based on broad knowledge of the local political context. The danger was also highlighted of ignoring the warning signs of human rights abuses by government.

In sum, in accounting for why certain countries have been selected as major recipients of political aid, there are a number of instances, particularly with UK and US assistance, where hypothesis (3b) offers a more convincing explanation. Conclusions are two-fold. First, donor motivation can be complex and multiple, including pursuit of self interests. Second, where such ambiguity exists, at best the stated goals of promoting international standards of civil and political rights and democratic governance are compromised and, hence, less likely to be achieved. At worst, the potential for negative and unintended consequences, that is, for doing harm, are increased.

5.4   Implementers

This section examines the range of organisations to whom political aid has been disbursed, here described as implementers, and discusses the implications for the nature of donor political aid programmes, especially the types of activities that are included and excluded through

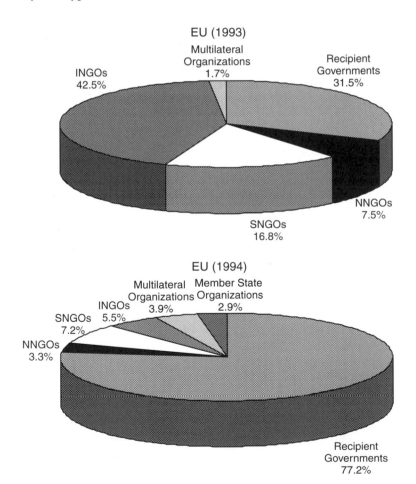

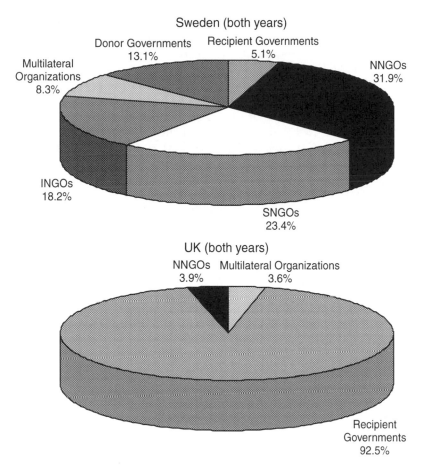

Figure 5.4 Political aid expenditure by implementer (by individual donor).
Source: project database.

channelling support to particular kinds of organisations. In some cases, implementing agencies are also the aid recipients, for example, developing country governments or southern non-governmental organisations (SNGOs), and thus simultaneously the beneficiaries. In other instances, implementers act as intermediary organisations who themselves distribute funds to selected projects, for example, multilateral organisations or some northern non-governmental organisations (NNGOs). Implementers are distinguished from beneficiaries in that the former are *agencies* and the latter are the *sectors* of government and society supported by the aid received, for example, the legal system, women's participation in politics, an independent media, and so on. Beneficiary sectors are examined in the next section (5.5).

The comparative analysis of donor practice in their disbursal of funds to implementing agents again reveals significant and interesting variations. Figure 5.4 presents graphically the differing proportions of expenditure by implementer for three of the donors. The percentages for Sweden and the UK are aggregates for the two-years period, whereas separate pie-charts are required for EU assistance to show the apparent substantial changes in implementing agencies between years. Precise quantification of US expenditure by implementer is not possible due to USAID's large projects commonly having multiple implementers, with the breakdown of funds to each agency generally unspecified. A more general discussion of US implementers remains possible, however.

Commentary on the findings focuses initially on the ratio of funds disbursed to government and to non-government implementing agencies, and then on the proportions channelled to different types of NGO implementers. Brief analysis and commentary is also provided on the use of multilateral organisations and of donor government organisations as implementing agencies.

5.4.1 Government: NGO implementers

A significant distinction between donors is the proportion of assistance distributed to governments or to NGOs. The sharpest contrast is between the UK and Sweden. Whereas the UK distributes over 90 per cent of its assistance to governments and less than 4 per cent to NGOs, Sweden disburses almost three-quarters of its political aid through NGOs and only 5 per cent direct to recipient government implementers.[75] Regarding EU assistance, a remarkable change would appear to be the shift from NGOs to governments as the main implementing agent over the two year period (see Figure 5.4). This change is due mainly to increased funding of political aid projects from mainstream development co-operation budgets, generally used to finance recipient *government* activities. As such, it could be interpreted as a longer-term trend, a consequence of policy decisions to gradually incorporate political aid projects into mainstream development co-operation programmes. The European Commission comments favourably on this trend as 'a step in the right direction', illustrating the success of the 'incentive' role of the budget lines (European Commission 1996, p. 12). It is said to indicate how 'these issues [democracy and human rights] are being taken into account' within mainstream programme implementation, and, given that the use of these resources generally requires the approval of the recipient governments, how such 'considerations are being taken on board by the developing countries' (ibid.). Such claims are cast in a different perspective, however, by the fact that these figures are heavily skewed by two huge projects in Mozambique (Ecu 22 m) and Nicaragua (Ecu 14 m). These two alone account for 51.5 per cent of all funds to governments in 1994, out of a total of 70 projects. In fact, removal of these two projects would leave 1994 figures not too dissimilar from those of 1993.

The Swedish focus on disbursement of political aid through NGOs, particularly funds from the Democracy and Human Rights fund, stems from two factors. First, where the governments are responsible for human rights abuses, support is exclusively to NGOs. Nevertheless, it is also stated that where a government aims to respect human rights, it is 'the natural partner' (SIDA 1993a, p. 22). This strategy has clearly not been fully implemented, with abundant evidence of working with NGOs in the latter context. Second, over many years, Sweden has allocated a significant proportion of its overall development assistance to selected Swedish NGOs, amounting to 13.6 per cent of total aid disbursed through SIDA in 1994/95 (SIDA 1996, p. 19).[76] This 'tradition' has continued with the distribution of democracy and human rights funds. Examples of organisations that receive substantial funding from this latter budget are:

- DIAKONIA (Free Church Council of Sweden for International Assistance), with a justice, peace and equality perspective;
- LO/TCO (Council of International Trade Union Co-operation), supporting trade union education in developing countries;
- Rädda Barnen (Swedish Save the Children).

It is somewhat understandable that the UK's unique policy title of 'promoting good government' leads to the provision of assistance overwhelmingly to government agencies. However, the exceedingly small proportion of funds disbursed to non-state implementers indicates that the important role of NGOs in improving the quality of government, for example, in holding governments to account, is largely ignored.

Although the exact percentages of US funds distributed to government and non-government implementers cannot be specified, it can be reliably stated that a significant proportion is disbursed to NGOs. Where host countries are targeted with a large D/G project, usually this includes both governmental and non-governmental components.

Two examples demonstrate this. In Mongolia, the democracy project involves support to three areas: 'the parliament, the press and local NGOs' (USAID Democracy Projects Inventory). In Guatemala, the 'strengthening democratic institutions' project has four targeted areas: the National Congress; the Office of the Human Rights Ombudsman; the Supreme Electoral Tribunal; and 'private sector groups dedicated to democratic government, human rights and civic education' (ibid.). Government-related projects may commonly receive the lion's share of D/G funds in any single country programme, but NGOs are also routinely included.

5.4.2   Types of NGO implementers

There are also differences in the *type* of NGOs to whom donors distribute funds. Each donor is examined in turn.

Sweden disburses large proportions of its total funds to all three main kinds of NGO, Northern (31.9 per cent), Southern (23.4 per cent) and International (18.2 per cent). Swedish (i.e. Northern) NGOs act as implementers in 193 projects (out of 900), with expenditure of $64.2m. In addition to the above examples, other Swedish non-governmental implementers included the following:

- research institutes (for example, the Olof Palme International Centre, Dag Hammerskold Centre);
- solidarity groups (such as, the Swedish Committee for Kurdish Human Rights, Africa Groups in Sweden);
- Swedish civil society associations, particularly church and trade union related (for example, Swedish Ecumenical Centre, Metal Workers Union).

Democracy and human rights funds are disbursed directly to SNGOs in 194 projects, one more than to NNGOs, but with less overall expenditure of $47.1m. Almost half of such projects are in South Africa, however, with assistance here amounting to $32.2m, over two thirds of SNGO expenditure. Elsewhere, examples of a diverse range of implementers included:

- Free Legal Assistance Group in the Philippines, providing legal aid and human rights education;
- Zambian Youth Council, for a conference on democracy;
- a co-operative of journalists, Mozambique;
- Women's Legal Aid and Consultation Centre in the West Bank and Gaza;

- CIPAF (Centre for Feminist Action) in the Dominican Republic;
- organisations challenging child prostitution and sex tourism in Thailand.

In South Africa, in addition to the large sums disbursed directly to various sections of the ANC, a range of other organisations are also supported, including:

- political organisations, such as COSATU Peace Monitoring Project;
- educational institutions, for example, University of the Western Cape's gender project;
- local civic groups, such as Soweto and Alexandra Civic Associations.

International NGOs also feature strongly, involved in 118 projects, with expenditure of $36.5 m. The most common implementers included:

- large, humanitarian organisations (for example, International Committee of the Red Cross);
- campaigning and advocacy bodies (such as, Penal Reform International, Anti Slavery International);
- international human rights groups (for example, Minority Rights Group, Index on Censorship, InterRights);
- religious-based bodies (for example, World Council of Churches, YWCA/YMCA);
- educational trusts, such as the World University Service.

Along with Sweden, the EU is the only other donor to disburse significant assistance to International and Southern NGOs. It channels relatively little assistance, however, to NGOs based in specific member states, (i.e. NNGOs). INGO implementers included:

- International Commission of Jurists, for electoral activities in Madagascar, Guinea and Malawi;
- HURIDOCS, for an international workshop on human rights documentation;
- Anti-Slavery International, for their work with groups in various countries;
- Penal Reform International, for work in Caribbean islands and in Zimbabwe;
- World Council of Indigenous Peoples, for a seminar in Central America;
- International Alert, for various training programmes in conflict prevention and for specific work in Sudan;

- Reporters sans Frontières, for a study of the independent press and training needs in North Africa, and for the establishment of a rapid response network to attacks on press freedom;
- Defence for Children International, to conduct legal training in the West Bank and Gaza.

SNGOs included:

- Andean Commission of Jurists – Colombian section (CAJSC);
- Human Rights Office of the Archbishopric, Guatemala, for an analysis of political violence;
- 'Sólo para mujeres', for a project on street girls' rights in Guatemala;
- National Indian Council, Venezuela, for a workshop on human rights;
- 'Fundacion Argentina de Medicina Social', providing psychological assistance to torture victims;
- Task Force Detainees, the Philippines, providing legal aid to political prisoners;
- Joint Council of Churches, Uganda, for civic education;
- Palestinian Independent Commission for Citizens' Rights.

These examples give rise to two comments. First, the EU focus on *human rights* NGOs is evident, yet one which includes the protection of social groups vulnerable to abuse, notably the rights of children and minorities. Support for media organisations is also notable. Second, it is apparent from the geographical locations of selected SNGOs that the budget line for *Latin America* (B7-7030) places a particular emphasis on channelling support to human rights organisations.

Much greater support to INGOs and to SNGOs is shown by the EU and Sweden, compared with the US and, in particular, the UK. A number of the same INGOs feature as implementers of both EU and Swedish assistance, yet some difference is perceived in the sort of SNGOs supported. Swedish assistance to SNGOs tends to focus on legal aid projects and on women's projects. An impression, however, is that the European Commission appears more willing to disburse funds to more radical groups, engaged in more challenging stances with their governments. Examples from the above projects include: the Andean Commission of Jurists – Colombian section (CAJSC), known for its annual analysis of political murders in Colombia, with regular findings that government forces are responsible for the majority of human rights violations (see Chapter 9 below); the Human Rights Office of the Archbishopric, Guatemala, one of whose number, Bishop Gerardi, was brutally murdered in April 1998, immediately after publication of his report which placed responsibility on the armed forces for 80 per cent of human rights crimes committed in the previous decade; and Task Force Detainees of the Philippines, overtly supporting political prisoners detained by a formally democratic government. It could be, however, that more radical activities are supported through Swedish NGOs and hence less evident. One such example is DIAKONIA, a non-conformist free church organisation. It operates globally, providing financial assistance to local NGOs working in the field of human rights and democracy. They have a history of involvement with human rights organisations in Latin America from the time of the military dictatorships in the 1960s. One organisation funded is 'Forensic Anthropologists and Archaeologists', an Argentinean group working with relatives of the 'disappeared' in the identification of bodies, and whose expertise was required in El Salvador and in Bosnia in the mid-1990s. DIAKONIA's activities in Asia includes support for human rights organisations in Burma.[77]

Of the minimal amount of UK assistance implemented by NGOs at this time, all was disbursed to British NGOs, totalling 13 projects only. No funds were distributed to INGOs or SNGOs. Moreover, when projects are examined more closely, it becomes clear that the UK assistance to NGO activities contrasts sharply with that provided by the Swedish government and the European Commission. With the exception of three trade union education projects implemented by the UK Trade Union Congress, NGO projects within the good government programme almost all concern rural development and community development, often with a tenuous link to democracy and human rights. Project descriptions include:

- 'Rural development' in Angola;
- 'Agricultural and Women Support' in Benin;
- 'Community Irrigation' in Peru;
- 'Crime Prevention and Rehabilitation' in Swaziland;
- 'Livestock Sector Review' in Paraguay.

It is recalled that, quite extraordinarily, these are all projects where 'good government' is the principal objective. A generous explanation could suggest that they have a local, participatory element, yet, even this is hard to sustain from some project titles.

With regard to US democracy assistance, it is clear from the project information that implementers commonly include both US PVOs (private voluntary organisations) and SNGOs, though with the former accounting for much larger financial sums. Almost no assistance is disbursed through INGOs. The role of US PVOs is distinct in that they play a significant role as project implementers where both government institutions and non-governmental sectors are beneficiaries. The example of Malawi demonstrates this dual role. The Malawian democracy project, pre-1994 elections, had three main components. First, assistance to the new electoral commission, implemented through the US-based International Foundation for Electoral Systems (see below), and to the six political parties, implemented by the National Democratic Institute (NDI). Second, support for related legal and constitutional reforms involved assistance to the (Malawian) National Consultative Council and judiciary, but implemented by a US university (Howard University, Washington DC) and a private consultant (Checchi and Company Consultancy). Third, support to local NGOs 'committed to democracy' included a direct grant to the Christian Council of Malawi for human rights activities, autonomous from US organisations.

The widespread use of US PVO implementers is in accord with the USAID's 'New Partnership Initiative' of contracting out the implementation of development projects to the voluntary and private sectors.[78] Large-scale providers of democracy assistance include:

- the Africa–America Institute (AAI), a key organisation in the disbursal of the Africa Region Electoral Assistance Fund (AREAF);
- the International Foundation for Electoral Systems (IFES), a provider of technical electoral assistance to a number of governments, especially in Africa, funded from the Africa Democracy and Human Rights Fund;
- The Asia Foundation (TAF), an active participant in virtually all the countries of USAID's Asia Democracy Program;[79]
- the Asia-America Free Labor Institute (AAFLI), again heavily involved in the Asia Democracy Program, including a block grant to strengthen 'free and democratic trade unions' in the countries of the region;[80]
- the American Institute for Free Labor Development (AIFLD), similarly the recipient of a block grant 'to promote democratic trade unions in Latin America and the Caribbean', as well as the implementer of specific trade union support projects, for example, in El Salvador;
- the National Democratic Institute (NDI) and the International Republican Institute (IRI), two of the four components of the National Endowment for Democracy, are very significant 'PVO' implementers.[81] Both NDI and IRI contract to provide elements of USAID's D/G programmes, separate from and additional to the block grants received from the US government;

- US universities, for example, Florida International University (Center for Democracy) and the State University of New York, joint deliverers of a project to promote the development of legislatures in selected Latin American and Caribbean countries.

Additionally, US implementers are not restricted to the non-profit sector, with private consultancy firms also heavily involved in the delivery of democracy and governance programmes, for example, 'Associates in Rural Development', 'Checchi and Company Consultancy' and 'Management Systems International'.

A much smaller proportion of funds are disbursed direct to SNGOs. For example, as part of substantial support leading up to the South African elections in 1994, grants were channelled to South African NGOs for voter education activities.[82] However, the $32,000 provided to the Independent Forum for Electoral Education, for example, contrasted starkly with the $1,700,000 granted to NDI, also for voter education, and the $1,907,000 provided to a consortium of NDI, IRI and the Joint Center for Political and Economic Studies (a US organisation) to help South African political organisations prepare for the elections. Questions of 'cost effectiveness' are clearly raised by such figures. In El Salvador, 'strengthening democratic and electoral processes' includes support to Salvadorian NGOs to promote citizen participation, as one of four activities. In Haiti, one of five institutional groups included in the 'democratic enhancement' project is the 'independent sector', particularly trade unions, the media, and women's organisations (ibid.). Other examples of SNGO support include:

- 'indigenous NGO strengthening' in Benin;
- 'institutional strengthening of civic participation' in Bangladesh;
- participation of NGOs in democratic development and grassroots economic development in Indonesia;
- local NGOs and a higher education institution in Nepal;
- the Arias Foundation for projects related to women's rights and conflict resolution in Costa Rica.

The sums involved are of a minor order, however, in comparison with those disbursed to US PVO implementers and to recipient governments.

5.4.3 Multilateral implementers

All donors disburse a small proportion of funds through multilateral organisations. Sweden channels most assistance multilaterally (8.3 per cent), with smaller amounts by the EU (3 per cent) and the UK (3.6 per cent). It is in terms of *number of projects*, however, that Swedish support for multilateral organisations stands out. Out of a total of 70 projects with multilateral implementers, 55 are Swedish financed, nine by the EU, three by the UK and three by the US.

British support was exclusively to UN-related bodies: UNDP's electoral assistance in Mozambique; a UN Trust Fund for the peace process in Mozambique; and UN efforts in Cambodia. US support was to both UN and regional organisations: the UN-sponsored ECOWAS 'peace-keeping' force in West Africa, engaged notably in Liberia; an OAS project in Nicaragua entitled 'human rights strengthening'; and to OAU peace-keeping operations in Rwanda (1994). EU assistance was somewhat more extensive and channelled through a wider range of multilateral organisations. These included: UN bodies involved in electoral activities in Malawi and Mozambique; ONUSAL's wider involvement in the peace process in El Salvador;[83] the OAS's electoral role in Paraguay; and to the Inter-American Court of Human Rights. Notwithstanding these examples, support to multilateral bodies by these three donors is essentially limited.

It is only Sweden that demonstrates a commitment to widespread support for the work of multilateral organisations in the fields of democracy and human rights. Financial assistance is provided to the activities of a wider range of UN bodies and to other inter-governmental organisations and IFIs. Examples of the many and varied projects supported include:

- UNDP's electoral assistance in Eritrea, Mozambique, El Salvador and Burundi;
- UNICEF activities in the West Bank and Gaza;
- UNHCR work in El Salvador and Peru;
- general financial support to the UN Human Rights Centre;
- specific assistance for the production of a UN handbook on 'Women and Human Rights';
- the ECOWAS peace-keeping force;
- OAS's electoral activities in Honduras.

5.4.4   Donor government organisations as implementers

Sweden, the EU and the US all have a small minority of projects where the implementing agency is itself a donor government-related organisation, or member state public institution in the case of the EU. In some cases this appears to be a misuse of funds that are, after all, aimed at promoting democratisation in developing countries. Such instances are examined below. Preceding this, however, attention is drawn to a favoured method by SIDA of implementing its public administration assistance through Swedish public institutions 'partnering' a counterpart institution in a recipient country, known as institutional co-operation or 'twinning'. One example is the twinning programme between Gothenburg and Beira (Mozambique) City Councils. Such arrangements involve a range of government agencies including, the Swedish National Audit Bureau (with the Office of Auditor General in Botswana, for example), Statistics Sweden (with the Central Statistical Office in Namibia, for example), or the Swedish National Tax Board (with the Ministry of Finance in Zimbabwe, for example). Generally, SIDA's role is limited to financing a long-term programme of capacity building, as negotiated and determined by the co-operating partners themselves (Lindgren 1991, pp. 47–9). Where such an arrangement is not possible with a Swedish public institution, then a private company is sought as an alternative partner. This form of providing public administration assistance has been ongoing since 1983 and considered by SIDA as a most effective method (ibid., p. 48).

Less commendatory are instances where donor government institutions or political parties expend scarce resources on themselves, for example, the women's associations of the Swedish Social Democrat and Liberal parties for pre-election study tours in South Africa.

Summary of findings

Hypotheses regarding implementing agencies anticipated that:

4a.   Political aid will be disbursed predominately to recipient governments to implement, with a much smaller proportion to NGOs.

4b.   Of the proportion to NGOs, the larger part will be channelled to Northern NGOs, with limited aid disbursed direct to Southern NGOs.

To what extent are these hypotheses confirmed or refuted? Strong corroboration of the central hypothesis is only provided by the UK, with its refutation by the other three donors, all channelling a significant proportion of resources to NGOs. In the case of Sweden, the hypothesis is 'turned on its head' with only a small proportion of political aid disbursed directly to recipient governments.[84] The EU appears to have shifted from greater to lesser support for NGOs, but figures are distorted by two large government projects, and the actual change is both less than appears and less than is claimed by the European Commission. A shift to 'mainstreaming' democracy and human rights activities does imply, however, that a smaller proportion of funds could be disbursed to NGOs, even if overall expenditure in this field increases. The inclusion of support to non-state actors is an issue for discussion between the European Commission and recipient governments when negotiating democracy assistance programmes. US D/G programmes do commonly include a non-governmental component, but the proportion of assistance allocated tends to be low compared with government support.

Hypothesis (4b) is confirmed overall. No UK aid is disbursed directly to SNGOs, there is limited assistance from US programmes, and both Sweden and the EU disbursed a lower proportion of resources direct to Southern organisations. There are two qualifications, however. First, in the case of Sweden, the proportion of democracy and human rights funds received by SNGOs is *not* 'limited', amounting to 21 per cent of assistance. Second, although EU assistance to SNGOs declined as a percentage of total aid over the two years, it actually increased in financial terms. In general, however, it would appear that donors do feel more comfortable in channelling their resources to relatively large-scale and well established NGOs based in the North. This has important implications regarding access to donor funds by SNGOs active in political fora. One is that the overall resources *directly* available to SNGOs are limited. Another is that SNGOs will commonly have to rely on gaining access to donor funds through a NNGO as intermediary. While such a relationship may work successfully in many cases, there are potential negative aspects. Having to satisfy both NNGO and donor requirements can be an additional hurdle to jump. Perhaps more fundamentally, there are inherent dangers that elements of a donor–recipient relationship may be reproduced between Northern and Southern NGOs, including issues of conditionality and power asymmetry. In all, SNGOs are most likely to face problems of exclusion from resources, especially those more radical civil society actors. If donor assistance to civil society is to involve more than merely strengthening 'a select group of civil society players' (Ngunyi *et al.* 1996, p. 23), it is vital that channels of funding be increasingly opened up to SNGOs, both directly and through Northern intermediaries.

A further finding was that political aid remains essentially bilateral, with limited use of multilateral implementers. This is disappointing, given the 'comparative advantage' of multilateral organisations, particularly in countries emerging out of conflict. As international bodies, their activities are less likely to be subject to the historical baggage and hidden agendas of some Northern governments, notably the pursuit of economic and political advantage. Further, with membership including the governments of developing countries, their activities are less subject to accusations of imposition or intervention by Northern powers.

Additional findings include SIDA's use of Swedish government agencies as 'partner' institutions in good governance assistance, commended as worthy of replication. This method of delivering development assistance contrasts with another finding, the privatisation and 'marketisation' of US assistance. A distinguishing feature of US programmes is the role of PVOs, quasi-governmental organisations (such as NDI and IRI) and private companies in the provision of services to recipient governments and purchased by USAID. This contrast between Swedish and US delivery mechanisms is one of differing policies and dominant political ideologies. The US rejection of 'big government', influenced by neo-liberalism, has led to the re-structuring of service delivery into a purchaser-provider split between public and private institutions. This contrasts with the Swedish model of greater state provision of public services. One consequence is that while SIDA continues to look primarily to the Swedish public sector to build the capacity of counterpart institutions in developing countries, the privatisation of US foreign aid has spawned a whole industry of PVOs and private consultancy firms, both 'non-profit' and 'for profit', to deliver its aid programme, including D/G assistance. There is an important difference in the situation of such public and private aid implementers. Swedish public institutions perform this service as part of a joint, co-operation agreement, aiming to establish indigenous capacity and then withdraw, with no financial motivation involved. In contrast, some of the US private organisations are themselves extensively *dependent* on finance from USAID.[85] Somewhat ironically, whereas the Swedish state institutions have relative autonomy in pursuing aims agreed with recipient counterparts, the US private organisations are often more tied to the US government's agenda, unwilling to threaten future funding possibilities. While neither the public nor the private nature of institutions guarantees effective service provision, it would seem that the former arrangements offer a better response to the expressed needs of *recipient* organisations.

5.5   Beneficiaries

One theme of the literature examined in Chapter 1 was an expectation of donor promotion of a narrow, procedural model of democracy, focusing on the selection of political leaders through multi-party elections, with limited support to institutions and organisations that seek a broadening and deepening of democratic control over government. A more substantive democracy involves the continuity of popular influence and democratic control between elections, but dependent on the relative strength of bodies both outside and within the state sphere. At governmental level, the legislature and the judiciary play key democratic roles, notably in relation to executive accountability. Elected parliaments not only contribute to ongoing policy debates and approve legislation, they are also responsible for scrutinising the activities of the executive and ensuring its political and financial accountability. An independent judiciary is essential to uphold the rule of law and to ensure the legal accountability of the executive, that is, that both elected and non-elected officials act within the law and the constitution. Outside of government, relative attainment of the democratic principle of popular control requires an active civil society to undertake both 'advocacy' and 'watchdog' roles.

This section examines patterns of donor expenditure to different beneficiary sectors in order to deduce the form of democracy being promoted. It is recalled from the methodology section (5.1) that each project was categorised by the sector that benefited from the political aid received.[86] The subsequent analysis by beneficiary concentrates first on the relative proportions of assistance to state and civil society actors, then examines sub-categories of both governmental and non-governmental sectors.

5.5.1 State : civil society beneficiaries

As Table 5.5 shows, the political aid of three donors benefited state sectors more than non-state, though to differing degrees. The UK was the most pronounced in its concentration of assistance to governments, with 92.9 per cent to state beneficiaries. Although the EU and the US both favoured state over non-state institutions, it was to a lesser degree,

Table 5.5 Distribution of political aid by beneficiary sector (as a percentage of sectoral expenditure, 1992/93–1993/94 combined)[87]

Beneficiary	EU (%)	Sweden (%)	UK (%)	US (1994) %
Central government	53	32.4	86.4	53.4
Local government	1	3.0	6.5	2.3
Human rights groups	31	34.8	0.3	5.1
Pro-democracy groups	11	21.8	2.4	14.1
Interest/pressure groups	4	8.0	4.4	25.1

Sources: Project database (EU, Sweden and UK) and USAID 1994a, Table IV.

54 per cent to government and 46 per cent to non-government in the case of the EU, and 55.7 per cent compared with 44.3 per cent for the US. Sweden alone expended a higher proportion funds on civil society beneficiaries, 64.6 per cent of total expenditure, almost twice as much as that on state beneficiaries.

As regards actual disbursements to non-state beneficiaries, Sweden spent $118.6m, the EU $57.1m, and the UK $3.1m, over the two years examined. The US had by far the largest expenditure, however, with $136.4m committed to non-state projects in 1994 alone.

5.5.2 Government beneficiaries

State beneficiaries are initially divided between central and local government, with the central government 'tree' then divided into five main branches, the constitution, the electoral system, the legislature, the executive and the legal system. The proportion of assistance received by local government is discussed first, followed by a comparative analysis of donor support for the sectors of central government.

Local government

While central government is always going to receive the 'lion's share' of disbursements to government, all donors have emphasised 'decentralisation of government' as a policy objective. Yet, Table 5.5 above, indicates minimal support to local government. Additionally, in terms of projects, only 33 out of 1573 were identified as local government assistance, of which 13 were Swedish, 10 UK, 7 US and 3 EU. As regards expenditure, the US commits most to this area, while the UK and EU spend the least. It is noteworthy that eight of the 13 Swedish local government projects are funded from the public administration budget, involving quite substantial expenditure, but with almost complete neglect of local government within the democracy and human rights programme. Projects aimed at decentralisation in Cape Verde and local elections in Zambia were the only instances of local government support from this budget line over the two years examined.

Why have all donors failed so demonstrably to put policy into practice with regard to support for democratic local government? Two tentative reasons are put forward. One is that bilateral aid channels are overwhelmingly central government to central government, with relatively few links with local government. One exception is the twinning arrangements between Swedish local authorities and those in developing countries, aimed at public administration objectives.[88] The other reason pertains to increased centralisation of power, a common feature of authoritarian regimes, for instance in post-colonial Africa (Tordoff 1997, p. 4). One consequence has been the long-term neglect and underdevelopment of local government structures. While there is a possible counter trend in the 1990s, it is still at a relatively early stage and the significant reversal of such long-term trends of centralisation takes time. This is especially so given that national governments, democratic or otherwise, do not readily devolve their powers to other bodies. Such difficulties, however, suggest the need for greater attention by recipient country actors on strengthening democratic local government, with donor support sought. From a democratic viewpoint, the pertinence of decentralisation of power is that participation is enhanced and routes of democratic accountability are generally more accessible at the local level. From the evidence examined, however, it was a neglected area.

Central government

What are the patterns of donor support to the five sectors of central government? What are the similarities and differences in their efforts to promote democratic government at the national level? Table 5.6 provides a sectoral analysis of expenditure.

Table 5.6 reveals significant variations in the main emphases of donor support, as well as common areas of relative neglect. The EU concentrates its governmental support overwhelmingly on elections, with minimal assistance to other areas. In contrast, almost three-quarters of Swedish assistance to central government is to the executive, that is public administration support. Very limited assistance to governments is provided from the dedicated budget for democracy and human rights, projects with restricted support for the electoral and legal systems. Both US and UK aid similarly prioritise strengthening the executive and the rule of law, in addition to some electoral support. The US is the only donor to provide any significant support to parliaments.

Table 5.6 Political aid to central government beneficiaries (as a percentage of sectoral expenditure, 1992/93–1993/94 combined)

Sector	EU[89] (%)	Sweden (%)	UK (%)	US (1994) (%)
Constitution	0.1	1.1	0.0	N/A[90]
Electoral system	76.0	15.5	15.3	16.6
Legislature	5.1	0.5	0.0	10.1
Executive	3.6	73.1	50.7	42.5
Legal system	10.8	9.5	33.9	30.7

Sources: Project database (EU, Sweden and UK) and USAID 1994a, Table IV.

The most notable areas of overall neglect are the constitution and the legislature. The formulation of constitutions is a precise legal field and not anticipated to attract a large volume of assistance. Nevertheless, the virtual *absence* of assistance is surprising, given that a democratic constitution is the foundation of a democratic polity, with constitutional reforms often crucial to the process of democratisation. At times an entirely new constitution (as in Malawi) may be adopted as an integral element of the democratic transition process. A vital part of ensuring that a suitable form of democracy is chosen for a particular society entails a process of consultation and negotiation on constitutional arrangements to secure, for example, the most appropriate electoral system and effective protection of the rights of minorities. The significance of constitutional matters is highlighted by the example of South Africa, where the all-party talks led to agreement on the Interin Constitution, itself providing the basis for the 1994 elections (Kiloh 1997, pp. 312–19). The relative neglect of support to legislatures is also surprising, with only the US providing any real assistance. The important legislative and accountability functions of parliaments were discussed above. Yet, in new democracies, especially where a change of government has not occurred, the independent role of parliament can be marginalised. This is said to have happened in Kenya, for example, after the multi-party elections of late 1992. In order to ensure that 'democracy' is more than an 'empty shell', it is essential to strengthen ongoing mechanisms of political debate and of holding government to account, with a vibrant parliament crucial in this respect. Unfortunately, it would appear that donors here, except the US, have largely neglected this important task.

Turning to areas of concentrated support, it is the executive that receives the most extensive assistance, the largest central government beneficiary of the three bilateral donors (Table 3.6, above). This focus is somewhat surprising given that the association between strengthening the executive and democratisation is only partial. On the one hand, the enhancement of transparency and accountability mechanisms within the executive is clearly linked to democratisation, yet, on the other, activities to increase the efficiency and effectiveness of public administration are pertinent to any government, whether democratic or not. Moreover, there is a further question concerning executive support, relating to the issue of donor motivation and whether democracy assistance is an end in itself or a means to economic reform. How closely is strengthening the government executive associated with an economic reform agenda?

Table 5.7   Swedish and UK political aid to sectors of central
government executive (1992/93–1993/94 expenditure combined)

Sector	% of total expenditure		$m expenditure	
	Sweden	UK	Sweden	UK
Institution building	10.5	11.0	23.6	6.4
Civil service reform	0.7	8.1	1.6	4.7
accountability	3.0	2.6	6.8	1.5
transparency	3.1	3.5	6.9	2.0

Source: Project database.

Table 5.7 provides a breakdown for Swedish and UK executive assistance, showing a similar pattern of expenditure, with the exception of civil service reform, often a euphemism for downsizing, emphasised more by the UK.[91] Findings indicate a tendency to concentrate on a narrow range of public sector activities related to economic management functions. In this respect, a high proportion of executive assistance dovetails with an economic reform agenda in general and with the implementation of structural adjustment programmes in particular. For both donors, assistance is targeted particularly at institution building, within which financial management is the most common subcategory.[92] Civil service reform itself is frequently a key element of adjustment loans and accompanying conditionality. Even measures to enhance executive accountability and transparency frequently have an economic dimension, with financial accountability and statistical information projects being the most common, and can serve to facilitate donor surveillance of compliance with economic conditionality.[93] At a minimum, it can be stated that measures in this field of executive support often have a dual role of promoting democratisation and economic reform. In some instances, the particular targets of donor assistance suggest that the structural adjustment agenda is central, if not primary, for example, financial management and accountability.

Moving on to the remaining governmental sectors, the electoral and legal systems both receive significant proportions of total central government assistance. More notable are the variations between donors. It was anticipated that electoral assistance would be a key area in the first half of the 1990s, especially with transitional elections in many African countries and the resolution of some long-running conflicts, for example, in Central America. The breakdown of assistance *between* donors, however, reveals an over-concentration on this area by the EU, to the detriment of support for other sectors, and an under-emphasis by Sweden. Similarly, as regards legal system support, the UK and the US both emphasis what they respectively term 'rule of law' and 'administration of justice' programmes. These activities to enhance the protection of individual rights from executive action by strengthening an independent legal and judicial system contrast with the relatively low levels of EU and Swedish assistance to the state sector, both of whom seemingly prefer to pursue similar aims through channelling funds to human rights NGOs.

5.5.3   Civil society beneficiaries

This section considers the different types of organisations favoured by donors not simply to 'strengthen civil society' but to promote democratisation. The initial three-fold classification of non-state organisations is recalled, in which 'human rights groups' and 'pro-democracy groups' can be characterised more as pursuing 'public benefits', whereas 'interest groups' tend to seek self-interests or 'mutual benefits' for their members. The latter's role in democracy building is consequently less guaranteed. Table 5.8 examines support to human rights beneficiaries, while Table 5.9 provides a breakdown of assistance to sub-categories of groups that promote various aspects of human rights, including minority rights and those of vulnerable groups. Pro-democracy beneficiaries are analysed in Table 5.10, with information on US support to non-state beneficiaries given separately in Table 5.11.

Table 5.5, above, showed that support for civil society organisations is substantial for all donors except the UK. Under the former Conservative government in Britain, assistance to the three categories of non-state

Table 5.8   Political aid to human rights non-government beneficiaries (1992/93–1993/94 expenditure combined)

Sector #	Sector	% of total expenditure			% of sectoral expenditure (3.)		
		EU	*Sweden*	*UK*	*EU*	*Sweden*	*UK*
3.	Human rights (general)	2.8	10.3	0.0	11.20	36.2	0.0
3.1	Protecting human rights (violations)	3.9	7.7	0.0	15.6	27.1	0.0
3.2	Promoting human rights	18.1	10.4	0.2	73.2	36.7	100
	Total	24.8	28.4	0.2	100	100	100

Source: Project database.

Table 5.9   Political aid to non-government beneficiaries for the *promotion* of human rights (1992/93–1993/94 expenditure combined)

Sector #	Sector	% of total expenditure			% of sectoral expenditure (3.2)		
		EU	Sweden	UK	EU	Sweden	UK
3.2	Promoting human rights	1.1	1.0	0.0	6.3	9.9	0.0
3.2.1	Human rights education	2.9	0.6	0.0	15.8	6.2	0.0
3.2.2	Women's rights/gender equality	0.4	0.5	0.0	2.3	5.1	0.0
3.2.3	Ethnic minority/indigenous rights	1.9	1.0	0.1	10.7	9.4	61.1
3.2.4	Disability rights	0.0	0.0	0.1	0.0	0.3	38.9
3.2.5	Children's rights	10.7	2.7	0.0	58.9	25.5	0.0
3.2.6	Trade union rights	0.1	2.3	0.0	0.7	22.0	0.0
3.2.7	Advocacy groups	0.3	0.0	0.0	1.9	0.0	0.0
3.2.8	Legal training (lawyers)	0.1	0.1	0.0	0.8	1.0	0.0
3.2.9	Human rights research	0.2	1.1	0.0	1.1	10.9	0.0
3.2.10	Legal advice and assistance	0.3	1.0	0.0	1.4	9.6	0.0
	Total	18.0	10.3	0.2	100	100	100

Source: Project database.

Table 5.10   Political aid to pro-democracy non-government beneficiaries (1992/93–1993/94 expenditure combined)

Sector #	Sector	% of total expenditure			% of sectoral expenditure (4)		
		EU	Sweden	UK	EU	Sweden	UK
4.	Pro-democracy groups	0.1	0.7	0.0	1.4	3.7	0.0
4.1	Political parties	0.0	3.4	0.0	0.0	19.1	0.0
4.2	Independent media	3.8	0.9	0.0	44.4	5.2	0.0
4.3	Local democracy associations	0.3	7.7	0.0	3.3	43.0	0.0
4.5	Role of women in democratisation process	0.0	0.6	0.0	0.0	3.3	0.0
4.6	Civic/democracy education	2.8	0.9	0.0	33.3	5.2	0.0
4.8	Conflict-resolution	1.1	2.8	1.8	12.7	15.5	100.0
4.9	Reconstruction/peace building	0.4	0.9	0.0	4.9	4.9	0.0
	Total	8.5	17.9	1.8	100	100	100

Source: Project database.

beneficiary totalled only 7.1 per cent of overall political aid, most of which was channelled to interest groups (4.4 per cent), with project titles often more suggestive of community development activities, for example, in Tanzania and Zimbabwe. There are indications that the strengthening of civil society is a higher priority under the Labour government since May 1997, but details of support remain unclear.

Table 5.11 US political aid to non-state beneficiaries

Non-state beneficiary	USAID 'activity Code'	Expenditure ($m) (1994)	Expenditure (as % of total political aid (1994)	Number of Projects (1994)
3. Human rights groups	Human rights (DIHR)	15.7	5.1	23
4. Pro-democracy groups	Civic education (DICE)	20.2	6.6	40
	Media (DIME)	12.8	4.2	36
	Leadership Training (DILT)	10.4	3.4	2 (?)[97]
5. Interest groups	Civil Society (DICS)	69.9	22.7	75
	Labour (DILA)	7.4	2.4	9

Sources: USAID (1994a) Table IV; USAID (undated) 'Appendix 1' document, p. 7.

The pattern of EU and Swedish assistance to the three non-state beneficiary sectors is similar, with greatest support to human rights groups, followed by pro-democracy groups and with least funding to interest groups (see Table 5.5, above). Thus, both donors have tended to focus their civil society assistance on democracy-specific organisations, including groups strengthening civil and political rights. Such assistance is examined in greater detail.

Human rights NGOs receive at least a quarter of total political aid from both donors. The EU channels a smaller proportion to the *protection* of human rights in situations of violations, however, indicating less of a focus than Sweden on countries where civil and political rights are repressed by authoritarian regimes (Table 5.8). Regarding the *promotion* of human rights, both donors highlight the rights of minority and vulnerable groups. Most remarkable are the proportions of assistance dedicated to children's rights, perhaps due to the relatively recent adoption of the UN Convention on the Rights of the Child (1990) and to the contemporary focus on the issue of street children (Table 5.9). Both donors have provided significant, though not substantial, support to minority and indigenous groups (Table 5.9). Given the contested role of democracy in divided societies, with views that multi-partyism can fuel conflict, it is essential that minority rights (ethnic, religious and linguistic) are protected, not only the right to participate on equal terms in national affairs, but also the right to participate in decision-making that affects their particular communities (Beetham and Boyle 1995, pp. 104–5). Hence, this is an area that could be given more emphasis, especially with reference to the 1992 UN Declaration on Minorities.[94] One area of neglect by both donors in the years examined, however, is the cross-cutting issue of gender oppression and the rights of women, including their political participation, (see Tables 5.9 and 5.10).

Regarding support to pro-democracy groups, these receive a higher proportion of assistance from Sweden than any other donor. This is tempered, however, by the fact that the large bulk of such assistance in the years examined went to the ANC in South Africa, no longer characteristic of current practice, with funds now transferred to a country budget.[95] Additionally, the media is one important sector that receives limited assistance from Swedish aid. In contrast, EU support to pro-democracy groups is relatively low, yet concentrated on the media.

Of the three main non-state categories, least assistance is given by both donors to 'interest' groups, less guaranteed to contribute positively to democratic reform. Within this category, it is pertinent that trade unions and church organisations benefit from Swedish support, given their greater potential for undertaking a pro-democracy role, yet hardly feature in EU assistance.[96] Labour rights are also a priority sector in Swedish human rights support (Table 5.9).

Based on USAID's own categorisation of its democracy projects, Table 5.11 shows that 44.3 per cent of US political aid is targeted at non-state beneficiaries, amounting to total expenditure of $136.4 million for 1994 only. This confirms the US as the largest funder of such projects and tends to justify the (self-) perception of USAID as the lead donor agency in civil society work. The specific categories that are directly linked to democracy promotion each receive substantial funds, with the possible exception of human rights, which compares unfavourably with the proportions of total political aid channelled to human rights beneficiaries by both the EU and Sweden (Table 5.8, above).

What is most notable about US assistance, however, is its support to the more general category of 'civil society' beneficiaries, itself accounting for almost a quarter of all assistance and a top priority within US democracy promotion activities. At first sight this would seem to verify that the US has not merely concentrated its democracy assistance on governmental institutions but also taken a bottom-up approach. A closer look at the project data qualifies such presumptions, however. While many of the 75 civil society projects within USAID's democracy inventory for 1993 and 1994 clearly fulfil pro-democracy objectives, a significant number appear to have little or nothing to do with political development. In Sri Lanka, for example, a number of projects are all coded solely as civil society assistance within the democracy initiative, yet are directed at economic, environmental and agricultural objectives, with no apparent democracy element. Project descriptions (USAID undated) include:

- 'to enhance the market orientation of the Sri Lankan economy';
- 'to promote the development of private enterprise';
- 'agricultural and rural development';
- a grant to the Sri Lankan *government* 'to increase the capacity of *public* and private institutions to develop sound environmental policies and programs' (emphasis added).

In Latin America, participatory rural development activities in a number of countries – Bolivia, Ecuador, El Salvador, Guatemala and Peru – are entitled 'Special Development Activities' and categorised as civil society assistance. The Bolivian project states its aim as 'to assist small rural communities and local organisations to undertake self-help projects which have an immediate impact on the community's social and economic welfare' and argues that it contributes to strengthening democracy by 'enhancing the participation of rural communities in decision-making processes' (USAID undated). While participatory development can lead to increased pressure from below on governmental institutions, such activities can also pursue small-scale, self-help aims without recourse to wider political efforts. Examples given of 'typical projects' in El Salvador tend to corroborate this view – construction of primary schools, bridges and even basketball courts!

Such misleading practices are made possible by the broad and loose usage of the term civil society, without clear definition or precise delimitation of which organisations or activities are pertinent to democracy promotion. It is recalled that in a study for USAID, Fox *proposed* a concentration on those 'specialised civic organisations' that serve the public interest and undertake democracy building tasks (Fox 1995, pp. 10–12, cited in M. Robinson 1996, p. 5). Additionally, in an evaluation report on USAID civil society activities, Hansen stated that such 'civic advocacy organisations' were the focus of attention, declaring that civil society 'is defined as nonstate organisations that can (or have the potential to) champion democratic/governance reforms' (Hansen 1996, p. 3). From the evidence examined here, however, it is clear that such thinking had yet to inform practice.

Summary of findings

It is recalled that a number of general hypotheses were proposed regarding the distribution of donor support to various levels of beneficiaries. Taking each in turn, has the evidence corroborated them or not?

5a.   Donors will concentrate on strengthening public authorities, with limited support for civil society.

Beneficiaries of political aid were predominantly government organisations for three out of the four donors, confirming the hypothesis that political aid would focus on strengthening public authorities. An important proviso, however, is that civil society actors *do* receive a substantial *proportion* of EU and US funds. In contrast, the above hypothesis is comprehensibly *refuted* by Swedish assistance, displaying a distinct focus on support to non-state sectors in its democracy and human rights support.

5b.   Despite policy statements stressing 'decentralisation', local government will receive little support in practice.

This hypothesis is emphatically confirmed. The UK provides more assistance proportionally than any other donor, but still very limited. Swedish furnishes some assistance as part of its public administration programme, but local government support is almost absent from its democracy programme.

5c.   Assistance will concentrate on the electoral system and new legislatures, with less support to the executive and judicial branches.

A picture of differential support by donors was revealed, but with no donor confirming the anticipated foci of assistance. Electoral systems did receive considerable attention, to the point of over-emphasis in the case of the EU, but the profile was varied between donors. The strengthening of new legislatures was relatively neglected, apart from by the US. Again in contrast to the hypothesis, the executive received the greatest volume of aid to central government, with the legal system also the focus of more attention than anticipated, with assistance approaching that of electoral support. The concentration of assistance to the executive, combined with the particular targets of donor support, confirmed the centrality of the economic reform agenda in this field of good governance. Many measures aimed at enhancing government accountability and transparency simultaneously facilitate donor surveillance of the implementation of structural adjustment programmes.

5d.   With regard to civil society support, donor assistance will focus on those public benefit organisations that specifically promote democratisation.

This hypothesis is neither confirmed nor refuted overall, with a somewhat variable picture between donors. The proposition is corroborated on the whole by the EU and Sweden, both of whom concentrate their support to human rights and pro-democracy beneficiaries. While the US disbursed a greater volume of assistance to non-state beneficiaries, the activity code of 'civil society' has been used as a 'catch-all' and includes non-state projects that have questionable pertinence to democratisation.

6
Evaluation

This chapter evaluates the political aid programmes of the four donors. As a preliminary point let me make clear that an impact evaluation is *not* attempted here, given that an assessment of the impact of donor policies in terms of modifying, reinforcing or accelerating patterns of political change requires detailed country case-studies. Rather, an evaluation is undertaken of the general contribution to democratic development of each donor's political aid programme. The methodology is first outlined, then the evaluation provided. The findings are then utilised to reflect on outstanding research questions.

Methodology

To provide criteria for an evaluation of democracy promotion measures, Beetham's concept of the democratic pyramid is recalled (Figure 1.1 above), with each element essential to the whole. The implication of the democratic pyramid is that a narrow, procedural model of democracy (or polyarchy) cannot itself be effectively democratic without simultaneous democratisation of both government institutions and society as a whole. It provides an analytical device to assess donor efforts to promote democratisation in aid recipient countries along lines of inclusion and exclusion of each component and to indicate the stages of democratisation where measures are concentrated. Assessment is largely based on the analysis of expenditure by beneficiary sector outlined in the preceding chapter.

6.1 Aid contribution to democratic development

6.1.1 EU political aid

Clearly, the EU has provided substantial assistance to processes of democratic transition, but considerably less to subsequent democratic consolidation. Of the four necessary components of democracy, the EU has concentrated its support on promoting free and fair elections and on civil and political rights, with more limited assistance to promoting open and accountable government and to a democratic society. The neglect of promoting open and accountable government is particularly noticeable. No projects are identified with the aim of encouraging transparent government. There is limited assistance to improving the various line of accountability, confined to relatively low levels of support to parliamentary bodies (responsible for political accountability) and to the legal system (for legal accountability), with one sole project targeted at financial accountability through an independent auditor. Support for civil society is more extensive, yet somewhat incoherent in itself, with a lack of balanced support for the range of non-state organisations often pertinent to democratic consolidation. Trade unions, women's groups, minority groups and church organisations were particular omissions.

Thus, EU assistance is characterised by a strong concentration on the process of democratic transition, but restricted support, both forwards and backwards, to other phases of the democratisation process. In terms of backwards linkage, there is limited assistance to defend and protect civil and political rights in situations of government repression. Yet, such support can be significant in sustaining those very non-governmental organisations that will maintain pressure internally for political liberalisation, often the prelude to democratisation. It is also frequently the sole means by which external actors can encourage the potential for democratic reforms in contexts of non-democratic and obstructive governments.[98] In terms of forward linkages to the process of democratic consolidation, the EU has particularly neglected the institutional components of a functioning democracy, its executive, legislative and judicial systems, as well as some important non-government elements. If new and fragile democracies are to prevail, especially given the pressure from competing anti-democratic tendencies, it is clearly essential to strengthen their institutional frameworks, both state and non-state.

6.1.2 Swedish political aid

Sweden's promotion of respect for civil and political rights is the single outstanding aspect of its political aid. Assistance is also provided to a number of transitional elections. Support to aspects of democratic consolidation is more limited, however, with the exception of strengthening executive capacity.

Swedish concentration on human rights translates into substantial assistance to human rights NGOs, including that to groups engaged in defending civil and political rights in contexts of government violations. Post-democratic transition, the ongoing deepening of a human rights culture, is promoted through the focus on the rights of children, of minorities, and, to a lesser extent, of women. Contributions to free and fair elections are made in a considerable number of instances, although levels of financial assistance are comparatively low. Overall, the process of democratic transition and the ongoing strengthening of civil and political rights receives fairly extensive attention.

Turning to the other two components of democracy, the picture is more varied. The promotion of the different dimensions of open and accountable government is mixed, with some focus on open government and financial accountability, but limited attention to legal accountability and very little to political accountability. Perhaps unsurprisingly, given Sweden's own system of government transparency and freedom of information, there is a notable emphasis within its public administration assistance on the improvement of government information, especially that of statistical services. Similarly, financial accountability is promoted through assistance to accounting and auditing mechanisms as part of support for improved financial management. Yet, legal system support is only significant in a small number of cases, an element of some public administration country programmes. Further, the role of parliamentary bodies in political accountability is almost completely neglected, though support to local government could strengthen accountability mechanisms through the devolution of power to local levels.

In sum, Swedish support for the different elements of democracy is rather uneven. The focus on NGOs perhaps leads to the relative neglect of the state institutional components of a functioning democracy, particularly the legislature and judiciary. Accountability and 'watch-dog' functions are not only fulfilled by non-state actors, with parliamentary and judicial bodies also performing important roles. Regarding support to different phases of democratisation, Sweden has provided more assistance than other donors to strengthening the pressure for political liberalisation in authoritarian societies through its financial support to both local and international human rights NGOs in contexts of repression. Support for transitional elections has been somewhat selective, but it is particularly in the area of democratic consolidation that more comprehensive coverage is needed, focusing on strengthening both democratic government institutions and a democratic civil society.

6.1.3 UK political aid

The UK states an intent to promote 'good government' through support for both governmental and non-governmental sectors, including a specific reference to strengthening civil society British (ODA 1993, para. 4.7). Yet, it is clear that the UK has failed woefully to channel political aid to non-government actors in the period examined. But before outlining the omissions and weaknesses, what are the achievements of UK assistance in this field?

Of the four components of democracy, the UK has focused almost solely on promoting open and accountable government. Open and transparent government has been encouraged in a number of instances, as has financial accountability within the executive (Table 5.7 above). In addition, legal accountability has been bolstered through measures to strengthen the rule of law, yet the overall effectiveness of such efforts is compromised by the astonishing concentration on police assistance, shown in Table 6.1. Political accountability mechanisms through parliament and the public are completely neglected.

As regards the other three components of democracy, the evaluation of UK assistance can only be one of neglect, relatively worse in some areas than others. Electoral assistance is limited both financially and geographically. Protection of civil and political rights is provided by strengthening the rule of law, but again the preponderance of police assistance seriously questions the achievement of this objective. Human rights NGOs are a vital aspect of guaranteeing respect for civil and political rights, yet such support is non-existent. Further, assistance for the type of civil society organisations that are central to democracy promotion is conspicuous by its absence.

Table 6.1 UK political aid to strengthening the rule of law (1992/93–1993/94 expenditure combined)

Legal system beneficiaries (1.5)	Numbers of projects	Expenditure ($000)	Percentage of sectoral expenditure
1.5 General	1	190	1.5
1.5.1 Judiciary	1	930	7.4
1.5.3 Legislation	1	348	2.8
1.5.5 Police	41	11 021	87.8
1.5.6 Prosecution service	1	45	0.4
1.5.7 Courts	1	20	0.2
1.5.8 Prisons	1	4	0.03

Source: Project database.

In sum, the only strength of UK democracy promotion efforts lies in encouraging the transparency and financial accountability of the executive. Even here it could be argued that such measures are driven more by the agenda of economic reform than by that of political reform. All other dimensions of democratic development are characterised by relative deficiency. Additionally, assistance is not limited to countries undergoing democratic transition or consolidation, with good government funds also disbursed to non-democratic governments in the years examined, for instance, to Nigeria, Indonesia and China. Such financial and technical assistance is not directed at political liberalisation, however, since projects have either little direct connection to political reform, such as the large Shanghai Environmental Project in China, or, paradoxically, involve support to the police, the very forces implicated in the repression of pro-democracy movements in Indonesia and Nigeria. Overall, UK good government aid under the former Conservative government had so little success in promoting democratic development that the integrity of such an aim is severely questioned.

6.1.4   US political aid

Of the donors examined, the US provides more comprehensive support to all four components of democracy. One reason is that the relatively higher financial sums involved allow broader coverage, both thematically and geographically. The most significant reason, however, is the incorporation of democracy and governance projects as an integral element of individual country development assistance programmes, in other words, *mainstreaming* democracy promotion. This has required more serious attention to the overall process of democracy building through foreign aid as well as to the development of individual country programmes more appropriate to specific circumstances. This approach contrasts with the relatively *ad hoc* and incoherent disbursal of assistance that characterises democracy promotion efforts through budget line funding, typical of the EU and Sweden.

Promotion of respect for civil and political rights is not the strongest element in US support, although significant assistance is provided to both human rights NGOs and through 'administration of justice' programmes. The former receive considerably less funding, however, despite being more central to rights promotion. Additionally, in contrast to the EU and Sweden, the professional activities of international human rights NGOs are generally excluded from US government assistance. Electoral assistance programmes are widespread, although commonly offered as a package implemented by US private voluntary organisations (PVOs), (for example, the National Endowment for Democracy, the Africa–America Institute, the International Foundation for Electoral Systems), with less sensitivity perhaps to local needs.

Turning to attempts to assist democratic consolidation, there is evidence of both top-down and bottom-up measures. Support for open and accountable government clearly involves the former, with assistance primarily, but not exclusively, directed to a range of state-related institutions. The three dimensions of accountable government all receive considerable support, with the US notably giving more attention to political accountability through its focus on strengthening democratic representation, specifically its assistance to legislatures, to decentralisation and to the media. One area lacking evidence of support is the encouragement of open and transparent government. Bottom-up support through promoting the development of civil society is also very apparent. This is a prominent feature of US democracy assistance and regarded as an integral element of most country programmes. Such commendation is tempered, however, by recalling that expenditure figures for civil society are augmented by inappropriately classified projects, for instance, rural development projects, and generally civil society support is insufficiently focused on pertinent pro-democracy organisations.

Various criticisms of US democracy assistance would doubtless arise from more detailed country case-studies. One condemnation of past 'democracy assistance' has been its misuse as partisan support to anti-leftist elements in recipient countries. A comparatively recent example was the assistance provided to the opposition UNO (National Opposition Union) party in the 1990 Nicaraguan elections, with defeat for the leftist Sandinista government (Carothers 1995, p. 66). Attention can also be drawn to the support by USAID's Administration of Justice programme in Colombia for the controversial Public Order courts, ostensibly introduced for trials of guerrilla members but criticised for violation of due process norms and their misuse against legal political actors (Human Rights Watch 1992, pp. 92–3). Further, country case-studies may reveal the inclusion or exclusion of civil society organisations for financial assistance along lines of political orientation, referred to in Ngunyi *et al.*'s study of Kenya as a process of 'fraternalism' and 'donor capture' (1996, p. 23).[99] In addition, US foreign policy may at times appear at odds with its democracy assistance, continuing to provide very substantial economic and military assistance to authoritarian rulers where economic or strategic interests are predominant, thus making a mockery of the relatively diminutive sums of democracy aid – for instance, in Egypt. Nevertheless, such qualifications aside, the evidence here does indicate the broad coverage within US democracy assistance, both top-down and bottom-up, of the various components of a functioning democracy.

6.1.5   Evaluation summary

In sum, the US and Sweden have been most successful in their overall promotion of democratic development, with no areas of complete neglect, although each concentrates on different dimensions. Indeed, Sweden's main focus, its support for civil and political rights, is the weakest aspect of US assistance and its major qualification. The EU was also successful in its support for democratic transitions, but with processes of democratic consolidation requiring greater attention. In contrast, the UK is notably unsuccessful in democracy promotion efforts, providing assistance to strengthen the government executive only.

6.2   Political aid findings

A number of the questions that arose from the initial discussion of the 'new policy agenda' (Chapter 1) remain outstanding:

- Do donors restrict their concerns to civil and political rights and is this valid?
- Is democracy promotion restricted to a formal, procedural version, concentrating on multi-party elections?
- Is there concentration of support in particular phases of the democratisation process? Is there evidence of long-term support or merely short-term projects?
- Is a Western model of democracy imposed?
- Will donors focus on a broad or narrow interpretation of good governance? Is there evidence of hidden agendas operating? In particular, do economic considerations predominate?

What answers are suggested by the examination and evaluation of political aid programmes?

First, with regard to human rights, political aid programmes have clearly focused on civil and political rights and on the rights of oppressed and vulnerable social groups, but not on the promotion of economic, social and cultural rights. Does this entail the continued selectivity and promotion by Western governments of a sub-set of rights as human rights, in contradiction of the indivisibility of human rights? Donors retort that economic and social rights are promoted through the aid programme as a whole, thus justifying their attention to civil and political rights within this particular field of *political* aid. The distinct nature of the two main sets of rights plus the particular significance of civil and political rights to overall political reform objectives does provide some weight to this argument. Yet, two problematic issues remain outstanding. One is the continued conflation of the term human rights with civil and political rights, something for which Western governments (and non-governmental organisations) have been criticised historically. This usage is evident throughout policy discussions in this field, and indeed is reflected in this volume. It is strongly suggested that the term 'civil and political rights' is substituted as being more accurate and more appropriate. The other issue is the contested nature of the assertion that economic and social rights are promoted through aid programmes as a whole. Clearly such debates are outside the boundaries of the present study, but suffice it to say that assessment of the donors' claim depends primarily on the overall poverty alleviation focus of development aid, itself subject to considerable doubt (Cassen *et al.* 1994, p. 54; Burnell 1997, pp. 31–3). Thus, the validity of donor delimitations to civil and political rights is supported as germane to the field of *political* reform. Nevertheless, this is not coterminous with promoting *human rights* through development aid. The introduction of a 'human rights approach to development' (Häusermann 1998) would require not only maintenance of the increased attention to civil and political rights, but also greater emphasis on the realisation of economic, social and cultural rights and the progressive diminishment of the inequalities highlighted in the anti-discrimination conventions, for instance, between women and men.

Second, to some extent Northern governments have confounded those critics who anticipated that their interest in democracy promotion in developing countries would be limited to the establishment of multi-partyism and competitive elections, or to 'low intensity democracy'. While donor support is targeted at elections more than any other component, the focus on electoral assistance is far from exclusive, and significant support *is* provided to other dimensions of democratic development. The sceptical attitude to donor interest in democracy questioned in particular whether assistance would be provided to civil society organisations, that is to a strengthening of democracy from the bottom-up. It was confirmed that aggregate support for a democratic society was probably the least of the four components, yet the level of assistance was *not negligible* for any donor except the UK, with the role of an independent media, trade unions and civic education all prominent,

although coverage varied between donors.[100] Additionally, the significant support for the other two dimensions, civil and political rights and
open and accountable government, provides further evidence that
donor measures have been broader than some critics foresaw. Respect
for civil and political rights has been encouraged, especially by Sweden
and the EU, with assistance channelled to human rights NGOs, also part
of civil society. Such rights are of particular significance given that freedoms of expression, association and assembly constitute the building
blocks of the democratic process in any country. Societal participation
in democratic processes and 'keeping an eye' on government are also
enhanced by measures to increase the transparency and accountability
of governments, although such support is limited and the focus on
financial accountability tends to confirm suspicions that measures
synonymous with an economic reform agenda are prioritised. These
general comments are qualified somewhat by the variations between
donors. The US and Sweden display a more comprehensive approach,
inclusive of different components, while the EU's state sector support
confirms an electoral emphasis, with the UK seemingly more focused on
the effectiveness of government than its democratic nature. Overall,
however, there is evidence of support to a wider concept of democracy
than anticipated by some commentators, including both top-down
institution building and bottom-up strengthening of civil society.

This leads to the third and fourth questions. If democracy assistance
initially concentrated on support for democratic transitions, there is
clear evidence of increasing donor attention to the process of democratic consolidation, both the democratisation of state institutions and
civil society strengthening, with the partial exception of the EU. Nevertheless, supporting democratic consolidation introduces particular challenges concerning both its long-term nature and its relative complexity,
not least the potential for stagnation and back-sliding. To what extent
are donors re-orientating their assistance to meet such challenges? The
evidence here is less persuasive. Many programmes remain lacking in
coherence, largely due to the re-active and *ad hoc* nature of budget line
funding (US excepted). To support democratic consolidation requires
'mainstreaming', that is, the integration of political aid into mainstream
development co-operation. Of the donors examined, only USAID had
established 'democracy building' as an increasingly standard element of
their individual country programmes. 'Mainstreaming' enables a more
pro-active approach, based on assessments of the opportunities for and
constraints on democratic development in specific country contexts,
and facilitates greater coherence in the design, implementation and

evaluation of democracy assistance activities. It also provides the opportunity for variations in strategy from the 'natural sequence model' outlined by Carothers (1997, p. 124), with strategies tempered to the individual country context and its particular democratisation trajectory, including democratic stalling or reversal. Additionally, the programming process (by which aid programmes are determined) itself requires democratising by extending participation to include civil society actors, an example by which the reciprocity of policy standards could be respected. These improvements in strategy and in programming are especially important in post-conflict situations where the careful crafting of democratic institutions and procedures, including the safeguarding of minority rights, is an essential element of sustaining peace, particularly in ethnically-divided societies. Findings here indicated, however, limited attention to conflict resolution and peace building activities through non-state actors (Table 5.10, above).

Fifth, a related criticism of political aid programmes concerned the imposition of a Western model of democracy as a universal one. Has the evidence supported this? One cogent finding is that the variations in patterns of donor assistance for democratic development tend to reflect the differences in their political cultures, with respective priorities within assistance emanating from the nature of their own political system. Hence, the emphasis within Britain on an efficient civil service gives rise to a concentration on strengthening the executive arm, with less focus on democratic representation or political accountability. The US, with its self-image of a mission to promote democracy abroad, however hypocritical in practice, focuses not only on *democracy* assistance as distinct from human rights and good governance, but also on a form of democracy that reflects its own model of the separation of powers and the accountability of the executive. Sweden's internationalism, especially its history of support for liberation movements in the third world, is reflected in its focus on civil and political rights. EU member states have found agreement on foreign policy more difficult than economic co- operation, but a less contentious common denominator has been the promotion of human rights and democracy, with European Commission measures consequently focusing on electoral assistance and civil and political rights, as the least controversial and most straightforward to implement. Hence, the evidence suggests not so much the imposition of a Western model of democracy, but more that each donor is promoting its own particular approach to democracy, though unconsciously so. Carothers (1997, pp. 120–2) has commented similarly on the problem of 'overspecificity' of US democracy assistance, demonstrating how perceived universalistic components of democracy are in fact very US-specific. The finding here is that this phenomenon is not restricted to US assistance, but widespread amongst the donors examined, with the unintended consequence of promoting country-specific forms of democracy as universal. This is clearly unsatisfactory, contradicting the nature of democracy as an internally-driven process, *per se*. The notion of 'national democratic dialogue' is discussed in the concluding chapter of this book as a mechanism for resolving this contradiction.

Finally, turning to questions concerning the nature of good governance assistance, to what extent is it promoting *democratic* governance and/or how closely is it associated with an economic reform agenda?

It is evident that there is greatest divergence between donors in this sub-field and that good governance remains an imprecise concept. The problems associated with a broad interpretation are illustrated most clearly by USAID. Its programmes are entitled 'Democracy and Governance', yet the lack of a clear distinction between the two concepts means that measures directed at the executive branch are merely one of a number of dimensions, all subsumed under the umbrella of democracy assistance. In contrast, both Sweden and the UK support a more discrete set of activities that correspond with public administration management. Such measures certainly involve significant overlap with a democratisation agenda. Most notably, they include the promotion of accountability and transparency, core values of democratic rule – for instance, improvements to financial accountability and to statistical services. Yet, two points remain pertinent. One is that the strengthening of executive *capacity* can be outside of democracy promotion, relevant irrespective of the nature of the political regime. The other is the extent of overlap with an economic reform agenda, with findings indicating how such activities often dovetail with structural adjustment programmes (Table 5.7, above). Ostensibly promoting the open and accountable nature of the executive branch, they can also enhance the 'policing' of structural adjustment programmes by donor institutions. Evidence of a 'hidden agenda', that is of democracy promotion as a *means* to economic reform, may not be conclusive. Nevertheless, it can be asserted with confidence that good governance support simultaneously promotes a dual agenda of economic liberalisation alongside that of political reform.

Critical issues that arise from these findings, as well as a series of suggestions for policy action, are discussed in the concluding chapter (Part IV).

Part III
Aid Sanctions

Part III explores the implementation of political conditionality as narrowly defined: that is, the imposition of aid sanctions as an attempt to leverage political reforms in recipient countries in the direction of improved respect for civil and political rights and democratic principles. A global survey was conducted into the application of aid sanctions by the four selected donors in the first half of the 1990s, searching for country cases where at least one donor had imposed (or threatened to impose) aid restrictive measures. Chapter 7 presents the empirical findings of 29 country cases and conducts a comparative analysis of the similarities and differences in the donors' responses. The empirical material is then used to assess donor practices along two wider lines of enquiry: effectiveness and consistency. It is recalled that both these issues were matters of key concern in the political conditionality literature examined in Chapter 1. Chapter 8 addresses the instrumental question of effectiveness, that is, 'can political conditionality work', can donors' aid and foreign policy objectives be achieved through conditionality? Effectiveness is determined by appraising, first, the improvement in the democracy and human rights situation in each country between 1990 and 1995, and, second, the contribution, if any, of aid sanctions. A main finding is of the *in*effectiveness of aid sanctions. In many instances, however, this is accounted for more by the weakness of measures imposed than by the strength of recipient governments to resist them, querying the seriousness of donor intent in many cases. This indicates the inadequacy of merely exploring the instrumental issue of whether aid sanctions work. There are wider processes in operation and one of these is explored through an examination of the consistency of policy application, examined in Chapter 9. Have aid restrictions been implemented in a manner that treats all nations fairly and equally, as required by the Final Declaration of the 1993 UN Vienna Conference?[101] Alternatively, has donor practice been characterised by inconsistency, punishing some countries for political misdemeanours, but not others? If so, what is the basis for selectivity and has it changed in the post-cold war period? Findings are of overall *in*consistency, with the subordination of human rights and democracy to other dominant foreign policy concerns, especially economic self-interest and geo-political interests, itself undermining the credibility and legitimacy of political conditionality.

7
Sanctions Imposed

This chapter presents the findings of the global survey of the aid restrictions taken by the four selected donors in the first half of the 1990s. It is presented in four main sections. First, a preliminary section provides background information on the institutional procedures and key actors involved in decision-making processes for each donor. The second section then presents the empirical findings of 29 country cases where one or more donors have implemented aid restrictions, including the grounds on which sanctions have been imposed. Third, a comparative analysis is carried out, highlighting the similarities and differences in the practices of the four donors. Finally, a summary of the empirical findings is provided.

7.1 Institutional procedures and actors

Prior to the investigation of the aid restrictive measures taken by the selected donors, it is necessary to clarify who is involved in decision-making and what the institutional processes are. More detailed coverage is required of the EU and the US due to the greater complexity of foreign aid programmes, of legislative provisions and of institutional procedures. Additionally, in the case of the EU, a detailed examination is included of the innovation of human rights and democracy clauses, introduced into development co-operation agreements as a legal instrument by which aid suspension would be administered if breached.

7.1.1 European Union

The Maastricht Treaty on European Union (TEU) introduced the implementation of a 'Common Foreign and Security Policy' (CFSP) as a 'second pillar' of the Western European integration process, remaining essentially inter-governmental in character.[102] This is pursued through three main instruments: declarations on international political events issued by the Presidency; 'common positions' as agreed and defined by the Council of Ministers, with which member states' national policies must conform; and 'joint actions' as decided by the Council, for instance, support for a peacekeeping force or for a transition election.[103] Aid suspension is one possible element of a 'common position', as in the case of Nigeria in November 1995 (see Table 7.1 below), and one mechanism through which aid restrictive measures could be taken.

More generally, who has the competence and jurisdiction, and in what circumstances, to impose aid sanctions? Three procedures were outlined by a legal adviser of the Commission, at an European Parliament (EP) Public Hearing in November 1995 (Pipkorn 1995, pp. 43–4). First, the *cancellation* of an agreement is decided by the Council, following a proposal from the Commission, and, depending on the case, after the assent of the EP. Cancellation would only occur in the most extreme circumstances, however, and is unprecedented. Second, the *total suspension* of an agreement follows the same procedure, except that, in the legal adviser's view, the assent of the EP is not required, only that it be informed. Third, regarding *partial suspension* of co-operation, his *opinion* is that the Commission has the competence to do so: the power accorded to the Commission to execute a programme also extends to decision-making on measures to partially suspend programme activities (ibid.). The lack of institutional clarity is noteworthy. Nevertheless, in practice, as *political* decisions, questions of aid suspension remain primarily within the remit of the Council, and are determined through CFSP processes.

The role of the European Parliament in CFSP processes is limited to being 'consulted', largely an advisory capacity. Hence, as regards *ongoing* agreements with third parties, it can merely make its views known through passing resolutions, but with no right to initiate proposals.[104] The EP's control over budgetary matters does accord it greater authority concerning *new* agreements, however, with the power to refuse its assent on human rights grounds, for example.[105]

It is recalled that both development co-operation agreements between the EU and 'third countries' benefit from having a firm contractual basis and that a November 1991 Council Resolution stated the intention to introduce human rights and democracy clauses into future agreements. Indeed, without such a clause there is in fact no legal basis for aid suspension on human rights or democracy grounds, although in practice this did not impede both the Council and the Commission from doing so in the early 1990s.[106] Nevertheless, the introduction of a human rights and democracy clause became a 'standard component' in new co-operation agreements by the mid-1990s, crucial in establishing a legal instrument for their potential suspension on political grounds (European Commission 1995a). Although initially variant in character, a common formula for such clauses was established by 1995, inclusive of respect for human rights, the rule of law and democratic principles as an essential element of an agreement, with an associated suspension or non-performance clause (ibid.).[107] Questions remain, however, regarding the consistency and the evenness by which human rights and democracy clauses are included and enforced in agreements with third countries.

7.1.2 Sweden

For many years Swedish aid has had a relatively small number of 'programme countries', 19 in recent years, selected for long-term co-operation and to whom resources are concentrated. Many other developing countries also receive Swedish assistance, but generally less significant amounts, comprised of technical co-operation and concessionary credits, aid to non-government bodies, research co-operation or emergency aid.

In the Swedish political system, policy determinations are by government, the Foreign Ministry and Cabinet in this instance, with policy implementation by the aid agency, SIDA, relatively autonomous in the Swedish tradition. Within the Ministry for Foreign Affairs, there is a specific Department for International Development Co-operation, with a policy-making role, headed by a cabinet minister of the same title, junior only to the Foreign Secretary.

Determinations of country aid budgets are approved annually by Parliament as part of the overall Budget Bill. A strong Parliamentary tradition ensures that government aid policy and financial decision-making is subject to scrutiny, questioning and lively debate.[108] Any subsequent decisions to reduce or suspend aid would be made by the Foreign Ministry, although discussed and co-ordinated with SIDA. Since its entry into the EU in 1995, the Swedish government also has obligations associated with the CFSP process.

7.1.3 United Kingdom

The UK provides some aid to the large majority of developing countries. However, although without a formal system of selected countries like

Sweden, it does concentrate its resources amongst a relatively small number of major recipients, mainly ex-colonies and current Commonwealth members, and frequently only has small programmes of technical co-operation with minor recipients. In 1994/95, 69 per cent of British aid went to the top twenty recipients (Chalker, 14 February, 1996).

Annual aid allocations by country are formally approved by parliament, but within the context of the budget for all public expenditure, and therefore subject to little specific scrutiny at that point. Parliamentary questions provide a limited forum for examination of government policy in both the House of Commons and the House of Lords, with additional scrutiny through Parliamentary Committees, notably the Commons' Foreign Affairs and Public Accounts Committees, and, since 1997, the Select Committee on International Development.

Decisions on aid sanctions on political grounds are generally taken by the Foreign Office, though involving collaboration with the Department for International Development (DfID). In addition the UK government is legally bound to implement 'common positions' determined at EU level and 'honour bound' to implement other CFSP declarations.

7.1.4   United States

An investigation into US foreign aid sanctions requires preliminary clarification of the different programmes of assistance as a precursor to an examination of the range of legislative prohibitions.

Foreign aid programmes

The annual International Affairs Budget presented to Congress by the US government contains four different types of foreign aid programmes, only some of which would classify as official development assistance (ODA) as defined by the DAC.[109] The four categories are as follows:

- *Development assistance.* This is bilateral or multilateral economic aid for the purposes of promoting development, most of which would come under the DAC's definition, and is mainly administered by USAID.
- *Economic support funds* (ESF). These are fast-disbursing, cash transfers direct to the recipient government. They are similar in kind to the balance-of-payments support (or structural adjustment support) provided by other donors. However, the policy objectives and the

targeted beneficiaries of ESF are quite distinct. ESF is extended only to countries on the basis of perceived US special economic, political and security interests. The main beneficiary governments are Israel, Egypt and Turkey. Therefore these funds are not strictly *economic* support to economies in distress, undergoing stabilisation or adjustment measures. Rather they are financial support disbursed on criteria pertaining to US geo-political objectives.

- *Military assistance.* This consists of grants (or credits) provided to 'eligible' countries, (see below for Congressional prohibitions), for purchase of US military equipment and training.
- *Food aid* (known as P.L.480). This is food commodities given or sold to developing countries. Governments are often able to re-sell such commodities, hence raising cash for their own purposes.

In making a distinction between 'development aid', comprised of development assistance and food aid, and 'security aid', comprised of ESF and military assistance, security aid made up 61 per cent in 1990 and 59 per cent in 1991 of the total foreign aid budget (Overseas Development Council 1990).[110] This study concentrates on development aid only, as defined by the DAC, but in cases of sanctions, there is frequent overlap between the different types of foreign aid.

Legislative prohibitions

In contrast to other donors, a number of legislative prohibitions of a political nature largely *pre-existed* the shift to political conditionality in the 1990s, even if characterised by uneven application. Such prohibitions have stemmed less from government policy and more from Congressional-driven legislation, particularly true of the human rights conditionality enacted in the mid-1970s. The Foreign Assistance Act (FAA) of 1961 (as amended), still the current legislation, contains the following prohibitions, though often with exemptions.

1. *Ineligible countries.* There is a general prohibition on assistance to communist countries and to military regimes that have overthrown a civilian government. Exemptions, however, to this restriction are as follows: the national interest of the US (as determined by the President, according him wide discretionary powers); disaster relief; and humanitarian assistance.
2. *Human Rights Conditionality.* Congress made foreign assistance conditional on respect for human rights in three pieces of general legislation:

(a) Section 116 of the FAA, known as the Harkin Amendment after its sponsor and passed in 1975, prohibited all development assistance to 'the government of any country which engages in a consistent pattern of gross violations of internationally recognised human rights'. The only exemption was 'unless such assistance will directly benefit the needy people in such country'.

(b) Section 502B of the FAA was amended in 1978 with the same wording to prohibit all security assistance.

(c) A human rights provision was also enacted in the International Financial Assistance Act of 1977, which governed multilateral aid through such institutions as the World Bank and the IMF. This instructed the US government, by means of its voice and its vote in the IFIs, to oppose loans to governments that are gross violators of human rights.

The reporting requirement attached to this Congressional legislation invoked the establishment of the annual Department of State *Country Reports on Human Rights Practices*, global in coverage.

3. *Terrorism.* The Export Administration Act of 1979 contained the Fenwick Amendment, after its sponsor, requiring the State Department to identify countries that have 'repeatedly provided support for acts of international terrorism', and prohibiting all development and military assistance, as well as trade sanctions, to listed countries. This is the most severe restriction and currently applies to seven countries.[111]

4. *Drug trade.* In 1986 Congress passed legislation conditioning economic and military assistance on co-operation with US anti-drug efforts. All governments of countries listed by the US Drug Enforcement Agency (DEA) as involved in narcotics production or trafficking have to be certified annually as co-operating with US authorities. Decertification involves a legal prohibition on all foreign assistance, and applied notably to Nigeria from 1994 onwards.

5. *Country-specific legislation.* This was passed when Congress felt that the executive was ignoring the intent of general legislation. Forsythe (1988, p. 6) lists 14 examples by 1984, though commenting that some provisions were 'quite weak and only of temporary significance' (ibid., p. 14). El Salvador is regarded as the case that provoked the most friction between the legislature and the Reagan Administration.

Institutional actors

The main actors are elements of the executive and the legislature. In contrast to the parliamentary systems of Sweden and the UK, the greater separation of powers integral to the US presidential system, combined with weaker party political identities, generally bestows the legislature with a greater and more independent role both in policy determinations and in their implementation, as well as budgetary powers. In particular, the annual detailed scrutiny of the International Affairs Budget by the Appropriations Committees of both the Senate and House of Representatives furnishes the opportunity to make amendments to country aid allocations, and to attach country-specific conditions, including earmarks on how assistance is to be spent or not spent. Within the executive, in addition to White House staff, the most important actors are the Department of State (DoS), responsible for disbursement of ESF and for foreign policy generally, and USAID. Decisions on aid sanctions are generally taken by the DoS, though in consultation with USAID. Decertification on narcotics grounds is determined by the President, as advised by the DEA.

7.2 Implementation of sanctions

This section presents the findings of the global survey into aid sanctions. From information in the public domain, the instances of aid restrictive measures taken from 1990 to early 1996 were compiled.[112] Four types of restrictive measures, plus a catch-all category, were distinguished, in descending order of severity:[113]

- full suspension (of all aid, except humanitarian assistance);
- programme aid (or balance-of-payments support) suspended;
- new project aid suspended (including technical co-operation);[114]
- overall reduction of aid allocation or aid disbursements on political grounds;
- 'other related measures', for example, political statements, threats to take restrictive action, and non-aid measures (such as arms embargoes).

A total of 29 country cases were identified where aid disbursements were restricted, or threatened with curtailment, by at least one of the donors. A summary of the cases is presented in comparative form in Table 7.1 below.[115] Countries are presented in alphabetical order by region: Africa, Asia, Latin America and the Caribbean, and the Middle East.

Table 7.1 Aid sanctions – January 1990 to January 1996

Country	EU	Sweden	UK	US	Grounds
Burundi	*De facto* full suspension from October 1993 to October 1994, except humanitarian aid. Willingness to assist reconstruction efforts stated in October 1994. The 'common position' adopted in March 1995 specified support to reconstruct democracy and the rule of law. Disbursements were adversely affected, however, by a perceived lack of representative government. Aid suspended again in April 1996.	No government programme. Emergency aid only.	Small programme of technical country-operation (TC) only before 1993. Emergency aid only from late 1993.	Full suspension from October 1993, except humanitarian aid. Aid gradually restored to coalition government, but then increasingly questioned for same reasons as EU, and aid jointly suspended with EU in April 1996.	Oct. 1993: democratic reversal; ethnic violence; political instability. April 1996: unrepresentative government. (Subsequently, military coup in July 1996).
Cameroon	Statement on 4 November 1992 welcoming elections, but noting irregularities. Intention stated to follow developments closely. But no measures taken then or subsequently.	No government programme, with exception of substantial import support in 1994/95.	Small programme of technical country-operation only. No restrictions.	New project aid suspended from November 1992, with closure of programme announced in October 1993, implemented in FY1995.	Lack of democratisation (US).
Equatorial Guinea	Not officially suspended but described as 'put on	No programme	No core aid programme	No programme 1993 and 1994. Small programme	Violation of civil and political rights and

Country					
	ice' in 1994 owing to repeated human rights violations and repression of opposition parties.			in 1995. No activities subsequently.	general lack of democratisation.
The Gambia	From October 1994 to date new projects reviewed on a case-by-case basis, with approval only for those that help needy people.	No government programme. Support to NGOs only.	New project aid suspended from October 1994 to date.	New project aid suspended from October 1994 to date. A return to democracy within 12 months was demanded.	Military coup against elected government.
Guinea	No aid restrictions	No government programme. Emergency aid and support to NGOs only.	Emergency aid and small amounts of technical co-operation only.	Programme aid and food aid suspended from December 1993, plus re-channelling to NGOs.	'Flawed' presidential elections (US).
Lesotho	Threat to suspend aid in August 1994 after military-backed coup by monarch.	Aid frozen immediately after the coup. Co-operation resumed after civilian government restored.	Statement that development assistance programme was being 'reconsidered'.	Aid suspended for duration of coup. Phase-out of programme commenced in 1994, before coup, due to small size of country.	Short-lived coup (by monarch and military) against democratically elected government.
Liberia	De facto full suspension from 1990 to date, except humanitarian assistance.	Emergency aid only.	Emergency aid only.	Full suspension of development aid since 1990, except emergency assistance.	Civil war and collapse of central government institutions.
Kenya	Programme aid suspended since 1990. Slow disbursement of EDF allocation.	Programme aid frozen since FY1990/91. Consecutive reductions in annual budget.	Programme aid suspended from November 1991 to November 1993.	Programme aid suspended since November 1991. Project aid Straight-lined.	Economic mismanagement predominantly; lack of democratisation.
Malawi	New project aid suspended from May 1992 to November 1993.	No core programme. No TC. Unrestricted participation on international training programmes.	New project aid suspended from April 1992 to June 1993. No disbursements of programme aid in FY 1992/93.	New project aid and programme aid suspended from April 1992 to June 1993.	Abuse of civil and political rights; failure to democratise.

Table 7.1 Continued

Country	EU	Sweden	UK	US	Grounds
Niger	New project aid suspended from January 1996, except assistance benefiting the poor.	No government programme. Support to NGOs only.	Small amounts of TC only.	Full suspension of all assistance to government following coup. Programme closure during 1997.	Military coup against elected government.
Nigeria	From July 1993, review of new project aid on a case-by-case basis. In November 1995, a 'common position' adopted, including total suspension of development co-operation.	No core programme. No TC. Unrestricted participation on international training programmes. Support to NGOs.	From July 1993, review of new project aid on a case-by-case basis. Compliance with 'common position' from November 1995.	Limited aid programme, mainly in child and maternal health. In April 1994, decertification for non-co-operation with US anti-narcotics efforts, with penalties including full suspension of aid to government. Decertification repeated in 1995 and 1996.	Democratic reversal (EU, UK); drugs (US).
Rwanda	Full suspension from April 1994 until late October 1994. Subsequent disbursements delayed by lack of representativeness and power-sharing within government. Short-term suspension in May/June 1995 after Kibeho refugee massacre.	No government programme. Emergency aid provided.	Pre-1994, some TC only. Post-1994, rehabilitation assistance only.	*De facto* suspension from April 1994. Rehabilitation assistance from late 1994, with no explicit political conditions attached.	Genocidal civil war; later, perceived lack of power-sharing.
Sierra Leone	Statement of concern after internal military	No government programme.	Fairly small and declining programme of	Small programme of food aid and peace corps only.	To ensure democratic transition (EU).

	coup in January 1996. Threat to 'reassess support' if planned democratic elections adversely affected.	Support to NGOs only.	TC only, though with programme aid re-commencing in 1993/94. TC increased since 1996 elections.		
Somalia	De facto full suspension from end of 1991 to date. Humanitarian assistance provided.	No government programme. Emergency aid provided.	Full suspension from late 1991, except humanitarian assistance. From 1996, rehabilitation aid through UN agencies and NGOs.	Full suspension since late 1991, after sacking of US embassy. Humanitarian assistance provided.	Civil war, collapse of national government.
Sudan	Full suspension from 1990 to date. Discussions on co-operation under Lomé IV abandoned.	No government programme. Emergency aid provided since 1991.	Full suspension of aid since January 1991, except humanitarian assistance.	Full suspension since 1991. In 1993, Sudan declared as sponsor of international terrorism, carrying legal prohibition on aid.	Human rights; civil war; support for terrorism (US, UK).
Togo	New project aid suspended from 1992, with partial resumption from March 1995 'to encourage efforts at democratisation'.	No government programme. Some support to NGOs.	No core aid programme. Small 'heads of mission scheme' only.	New project aid suspended from January 1992 until 'free and honest elections held'. Programme closure in 1994.	Lack of progress in democratisation.
Zaire	New project aid suspended from early 1992 to date.	No government programme. Some support to NGOs plus emergency aid.	Small programme of TC only. No restrictions.	Congressional restrictions from 1991. Programme closure in 1994.	Lack of democratisation, human rights
Zambia	No restrictions.	Programme country. No explicit political conditionality.	Threat to withhold aid made in December 1993. (See US).	Initiated allegations of high-level corruption in December 1993, with threats to cut aid if appropriate action not taken.	Corruption, lack of good governance.
Burma	No co-operation programme. Unwilling	No government programme.	New project aid suspended since	New project aid suspended since	Military rule; repression of pro-democracy

Table 7.1 Continued

Country	EU	Sweden	UK	US	Grounds
	to enter into agreement with military junta.	Very limited support to NGOs.	November 1988.	November 1988.	opposition
China	New project aid suspended from June 1989 to October 1990, when restrictions lifted Subsequently 'gradual acceleration' of aid.	New project aid suspended from June 1989 until April 1991, when Social Democratic government announced resumption of development assistance.	New project aid suspended from June 1989 to October 1990, when restrictions lifted in common with EU decision.	No foreign assistance programme.	Repression of pro-democracy opposition
Thailand	No restrictive measures taken. Part of EU – ASEAN agreement.	No country budget, but significant aid programme, mainly TC. No restrictions on political grounds.	Significant programme of TC and ATP. No restrictions on political grounds.	New project aid suspended in February 1991 after military coup, resumed in October 1992 after relatively fair elections held	Military coup against civilian government (US).
Vietnam	No restrictions. Increasing amounts of aid in 1990s. New co-operation agreement (1995) contains human rights and democracy clause.	Programme country. Consecutive cuts in country budget on democracy and human rights grounds from FY 1992/93 to FY 1994/95.	No restrictions. Small, but increasing, TC since 1990.	No foreign assistance programme.	Democracy and human rights (Sweden).
Cuba	Currently, no programme. But negotiations on a co-operation agreement suspended by EU in May 1996, citing Cuban inflexibility on political reforms.	All development aid terminated in November 1991 by centre-right government on democracy and human rights grounds.	No programme	No programme. Total economic blockade for over 35 years.	Democracy and human rights (Sweden).

El Salvador	Political statements issued twice in 1993 expressing concerns regarding an amnesty for perpetrators of human rights abuses and renewed political violence, but no aid restrictions.	No government programme, but considerable assistance to NGOs, especially human rights organisations.	No bilateral programme.	Disbursements of ESF in FY 1993 made conditional on implementation of 1992 Peace Accords.	To promote Peace Accords (US).
Guatemala	New project aid suspended in May 1993 after President Serrano's 'self-coup'.	No government programme, but considerable assistance to NGOs, particularly human rights and refugee organisations.	No bilateral programme.	Full suspension of all government aid in May 1993.	Presidential coup against democratic institutions.
Haiti	Full suspension from October 1991 to October 1994, until reinstatement of President Aristide, except humanitarian aid.	No government programme, pre-1991. Import support after reinstatement of Aristide.	No programme.	Full suspension from October 1991 to September 1994, except humanitarian aid.	Military coup against elected government.
Peru	New project aid suspended from April 1992 to March 1993.	No government programme, with exception of import support in 1992. Support to NGOs.	New project aid suspended from April 1992 to March 1993.	Full suspension from April 1992 of project and programme aid, excepting anti-narcotics activities and humanitarian aid. Development assistance resumed in November 1992; ESF remained suspended in 1993.	Presidential coup against democratic institutions.
Syria	Aid suspended from 1986 until October 1990, when restrictions lifted.	Zero programme	Small scale TC only.	No foreign aid programme, due to listing of Syria as	Human rights (EP); terrorism (US).

Table 7.1 Continued

Country	EU	Sweden	UK	US	Grounds
	European Parliament blocked new agreements during 1992 and 1993, finally giving its approval.			sponsor of international terrorism.	
Turkey	Full suspension on human rights grounds from 1980. Lifted in December 1995 when European Parliament approval finally gained.	No government programme. Small scale support to human rights NGOs.	Small amounts of TC. Large amounts of ATP from 1991/92 to 1993/94. No restrictions.	No restrictions. Turkey is third largest recipient of US foreign aid, though almost all security assistance.	Human rights (EU/EP).

7.3   Comparative analysis

What are the similarities and differences between the four donors in how they have implemented political conditionality? Do some donors have a greater propensity to impose punitive measures for political misdemeanours? Is there co-ordination and coherence between donors?

One obvious difference would appear to be the number of cases in which aid sanctions have been implemented. The EU and the US took restrictive measures in the greatest number of cases, both in 22 countries, with the UK taking such measures in 11 cases and Sweden only in five instances. However, this contrast between donors arises less from a significant difference in their propensity to take punitive action, and more from the different nature of their respective aid programmes. The higher number of restrictive measures taken by the EU and the US stems mainly from their distribution of development assistance to a larger number of countries world-wide, perhaps reflecting the wider international role they perceive for themselves. Although the UK also provides some aid to the large majority of developing countries, it concentrates its resources amongst a smaller number of major recipients. Swedish development assistance is concentrated in its 19 'programme countries', generally not those associated with gross violations of human rights, although Sri Lanka (with no restrictions on aid) would seem to be an exception here.[116] Thus, in many cases, aid restrictions are not taken by some donors simply because they do not have a programme to suspend in the first place. However, cases are also noted where the EU and/or the US have taken restrictive measures, yet the Swedish and UK governments appear less inclined to reduce or suspend programmes of technical co-operation to minor aid recipients [for example, Thailand and the former Zaïre (UK only)]. Yet, the provision of such specialist personnel and training could be of direct benefit to governments.

At times, however, there is notable difference between governments *within* a particular donor country. Changes in government have been a significant factor in both the US and Sweden regarding the number of instances of political conditionality. The Clinton administration in the US has shown a far greater propensity to impose aid sanctions than its predecessor under President Bush. One factor that fostered negative measures under Clinton was the budgetary pressures faced by his administration, with closures of 21 country programmes. Significantly, these closures included countries recently subjected to aid reductions on democracy grounds, indicating policy-based selection criteria. In Sweden a clear difference in policy orientation has been noted between the Social Democrats and the Conservative-dominated coalition government. The Social Democratic government is the only one examined here to have stated reservations about political conditionality and expressed a preference for promoting democracy through dialogue.[117]

What is the pattern of consistency *between* donors? Is policy implementation relatively coherent or are there examples where one or more donors have taken punitive action whilst others have continued to provide assistance?

The principal finding is a preponderance of cases where there is overall consistency between donors, particularly the EU and the US. Twenty out of 29 cases (69 per cent) can be characterised as displaying consistency rather than inconsistency, in so far as there is *not* another donor who continues to provide a *significant* aid programme to the recipient government.[118] Some cases show a high degree of donor co-ordination, notably where decisions are taken through World Bank-chaired Consultative Group meetings (for example, Kenya and Malawi), and in instances of military coups (for example, The Gambia). However, some provisos are required. First, in a number of country cases, the only significant donors were the EU and the US, with neither Sweden nor the UK having a core aid programme – for example, in Niger, Togo, the former Zaïre, Guatemala and Haiti. Thus, in these cases, the finding of consistency appertains only to restrictive measures taken by the EU and the US, with Sweden and the UK excluded from consideration. Second, some minor inconsistencies may be hidden within this overall finding. For example, in Rwanda, the US and the UK – unlike the EU – appear not to have attached explicit political conditions to their rehabilitation assistance. Third, a consistent approach between donors does not necessarily imply robustness. Post-Tiananmen China provides one example where the communality of approach was consistently followed up by the weak and short-lived nature of the measures taken.

The remaining nine cases (31 per cent), however, are characterised by more significant differences in donor practices, where punitive measures taken by at least one of the donors studied contrasts with the lack of action taken by others.

In sub-Saharan Africa, the US has displayed a greater propensity to take action than the EU in situations where progress in democratisation has stalled or reversed. For example, in Cameroon, the US suspended new project aid in 1992 on account of flawed elections and subsequently closed their entire programme, whereas the EU, in a political statement, made veiled threats but took no action. Similarly, in Guinea, the US reduced aid after unsatisfactory elections in 1993, whereas the EU took no measures. In Zambia, in differing circumstances focusing on governance issues, the US and the UK were the most vocal donors concerning the drug-trafficking allegations against government Ministers, while the EU and Sweden took no explicit measures on the basis that they had insufficient information.[119] Two explanations can account for such differences in EU and US policy in Africa. One is the closer and contractual relationship entered into by the EU with African states through the Lomé Convention, making reduction or suspension of aid a somewhat more difficult and weighty decision. The other is the influential role of the French government in EU decision-making on Francophone African countries, and its reluctance to impose aid sanctions on governments with which it has had long and close ties. In contrast, the US government has felt less constrained in implementing its policy emphasis on 'democracy', especially in situations of allegations of flawed elections, and particularly against small, poor, aid-dependent countries where there are few US interests.

In the Middle East, Turkey and Syria provide contrasting evidence of discrepancies between donors. Turkey is one of the few examples where the European Parliament has blocked successfully a co-operation agreement on human rights grounds, maintained from 1980 until late 1995. This contrasts starkly with the very considerable amounts of foreign assistance received by Turkey from the US, on geo-strategic grounds, unopposed by Congress. The inconsistency, however, is not only between the EU and the US. Within the EU, contradictory messages have been given to the Turkish authorities by the European Parliament and by the Council of Ministers and the Commission. In Syria, conversely, US foreign aid remains prohibited due to the listing of Syria as a sponsor of international terrorism, whereas EU sanctions were lifted in late 1993. Success in achieving the latter is hailed in a Commission report, stating that 'the European Parliament approved *at last* the financial protocol of Syria at the end of 1993' (European Commission 1994c, p. 12, emphasis added). This indicates the priority accorded to strengthening relations with neighbouring southern Mediterranean states, described as issues of 'security' and 'stability', apparently irrespective of the nature of the regime in power. An alternative argument is that enhanced security will come from the strengthening of democratic governments, generally more respectful of and accountable to their citizens.

In East Asia, contradictions between donor practices are most evident in Thailand and Vietnam. In Thailand, the US was the only donor to take action in response to the military coup in February 1991, as required by legislative mandate. All other donors examined, including Sweden, chose to ignore such anti-democratic developments, including the subsequent repression of pro-democracy protesters in May 1992, presumably prioritising trade and investment opportunities in the rapidly growing Thai economy. As regards Vietnam, Sweden reduced its assistance, ostensibly on democracy and human rights grounds, precisely at the time when other Western countries were re-establishing aid and trade relations, particularly to take advantage of economic liberalisation. This has a more particular explanation, however, situated within Swedish domestic politics. Under the Social Democrats in the 1980s, Sweden was by far the largest provider of development assistance to the Vietnamese government during its isolation by the West, contributing 49.9 per cent of all bilateral aid to Vietnam in 1990 (SIDA 1993c, Table 37). The reduction in 1991 of aid to Vietnam by the Conservative-dominated government was very much a symbolic, domestically-orientated measure, as discussed above.

Two other instances of differences in donor practice remain. In Sierra Leone, the implicit EU threat to the new military rulers to suspend aid should the planned democratic transition not go ahead in early 1996 would appear not to have been reinforced by the UK, whose support has included balance-of-payments assistance since 1994. In El Salvador, the limited conditionality on US assistance, linked by Congress to the implementation of the 1992 Peace Accords, was not replicated by the EU, another major donor. In this case, however, the main difference remains the nature of the EU and US programmes of assistance. The EU's, since its inception in 1985, has focused on regional dialogue and conflict resolution, which contrasts with the latter's massive, historical support for the military-backed, right-wing regimes, responsible for gross human rights violations.

A number of issues were raised in the political conditionality literature concerning the *manner* of donor implementation of aid sanctions. What further comments can be made on the basis of the empirical findings?

First, the discussions on sovereignty affirmed the legitimacy of human rights conditionality, though noted that there was not the same legal justification for democracy or good governance conditionality. The question was posed whether aid restrictive measures would be limited to human rights grounds or extended to democracy and good governance? An initial point notes the delimitation of human rights conditionality to civil and political rights. No donor has taken aid restrictive measures on grounds of violations of economic, social and cultural rights, confirming that this is essentially a *political* agenda. The main point, however, is that *democratic* conditionality was most prevalent. The most common ground for implementation of sanctions was lack of respect for democratic principles, in at least 17 cases, with measures taken more specifically due to civil and political rights' abuses in seven instances, and on good governance grounds in two instances only. In particular, the Clinton administration has emphasised multi-party democracy almost as a pre-requisite for development assistance. While acknowledging the difficulties of differentiating between democracy and human rights, given that civil and political rights are an essential element of democracy, aid restrictions were imposed predominantly in situations of the stalling or reversal of the democratisation process, as in the seventeen instances identified. Clearly, such contexts entail violations of human rights, but it is the issue of democratic transition or reversion to authoritarian rule that remains paramount.

This brings us, secondly, to Tomasevski's criticisms. While supporting international pressure being brought to bear against human rights abusive governments, she reproached Northern governments for invoking human rights in an arbitrary and discretionary way, without recourse to the established inter – governmental human rights bodies. Do the findings confirm her assertions? Indeed, there is considerable evidence to support both aspects of her criticisms. As regards the *discretionary* nature of donor decision-making, donors may co-ordinate the implementation of aid restrictions amongst themselves, but there are no indications of consultation with independent human rights bodies, in particular the UN and regional systems. Essentially, donors do act unilaterally to suspend aid disbursements and do not perceive this as problematic. As regards the *arbitrary* basis of decision-making, no donor has specified the exact criteria against which recipient performance is evaluated, with consequent aid suspension if deemed to be breached.

Finally, support has been expressed by this author for the principle that international human rights law transcends national sovereignty, whilst noting that this does not provide a justification for particular donor practices. Specifically, the question was posed, are donors sensitive to issues of recipient sovereignty? Overall, in the practice of political conditionality, it would appear that donor governments act in a manner that reflects the customary and unproblematised exercise of power over those nations that are relatively powerless.

8
Effectiveness

The imposition of political conditionality by donor governments has the stated intention of exerting pressure on recipient governments to implement political reforms broadly along the lines of democratisation and greater respect for civil and political rights. Economic sanctions of various types have been used on many occasions during the twentieth century as an instrument of foreign policy, especially by the more powerful nations.[120] Opinions vary as to their worth, but there has long existed a degree of scepticism regarding their effectiveness. Such scepticism may be particularly appropriate for aid sanctions, less likely to have as much impact as trade sanctions, and this was reflected in the literature reviewed in Chapter 1. This chapter assesses how effective political conditionality has been as an instrument of policy reform in the first half of the 1990s.

It is fortunate that a number of hypotheses regarding effectiveness have already been generated by Olav Stokke (1995), and these have been used as a basis for this enquiry. Stokke put forward the following general propositions on the likely impact of aid sanctions (Stokke 1995, pp. 42–5). In his words, the factors that may affect the impact of conditionality are:

1. The domestic position of the recipient government and its power basis – weak or strong.
2. The recipient government's ability to use the occasion of external intervention to strengthen its position domestically, at least in the short run.
3. The extent of dependency on aid of the recipient country and, in particular, the importance of the aid at stake, in relation to the total aid package and to the GNP.

4. The magnitude and importance of the bilateral relations.
5. The probability that a unilateral action may have a snowball effect.
6. An internationally co-ordinated action by donors stands a better chance of success than a unilateral action in terms of attaining the policy reforms pursued.

The limited evidence from the cases examined in the edited volume by Stokke and his collaborators was considered insufficient to prove or disprove these propositions (ibid., p. 55). The global survey of aid sanctions undertaken in this research is used in an attempt to evaluate more comprehensively the effectiveness of political conditionality, including verification, or otherwise, of Stokke's hypotheses.

In four parts, this chapter will discuss: first, the lessons to be drawn from evaluations of the effectiveness of *economic* conditionality; second, the methodology adopted here to evaluate the effectiveness of *political* conditionality; third, the evaluation of the 29 country cases is presented in tabular form, with textual discussion of the key findings; finally, the extent to which the evidence confirms or refutes Stokke's hypotheses is considered.

8.1   Lessons from economic conditionality

It is recalled that some commentators, notably M. Robinson (1993b, p. 93) and Uvin (1993, pp. 74–5), make the comparison with the effectiveness of economic conditionality. Noting the frequently high degree of slippage in the implementation of rigorously defined economic conditions, doubts are expressed about the likely effectiveness of political conditionality, given its less specific nature. This issue is examined in greater detail here.

Economic conditionality, associated with structural adjustment programmes, has dominated donor–recipient relationships since the early 1980s. It links donor assistance, particularly programme aid and World Bank loans, to an agreed package of economic policy reforms. How effective has economic conditionality been? To what extent have the conditions attached been implemented by recipient governments? Conversely, what has been the degree of non-compliance or 'slippage'?

Two studies, both on World Bank lending, have produced similar results. The Bank's own research, published in late 1988, found an implementation rate of 'about 60 per cent' of the agreed policy changes (World Bank 1988, cited in Mosley *et al.* 1991, pp. 135–6). Research by Mosley *et al.* into nine country case-studies produced an average compliance rate of 54 per cent, though with wide dispersion from a high of 95 per cent to a low of 15 per cent implementation (Mosley *et al.* 1991 p. 136 and pp. 300–1). What has been the donor response to this failure to implement reforms? Somewhat surprisingly, aid restrictions have rarely been instituted, at least by the World Bank. Two devices to enforce implementation exist. One is the refusal to release the second tranche of a loan. Both studies report that, despite delays, all tranches are eventually released (ibid., pp. 165–6). The second mechanism is to refuse further lending. Mosley *et al.* state that where slippage is below 50 per cent, further loans are virtually assured. In cases of higher slippage, renewal is less certain, but characterised by inconsistency – some high slippage cases are condoned (for example, Ecuador), others are punished by withdrawal of lending (as in Guyana and Bolivia) (ibid., pp. 170–1). One explanation of such inconsistency is the 'reverse leverage' of countries with greater countervailing advantages, for example, strong geopolitical links or larger-scale Bank investments (ibid.). Hence, evaluated by its own criteria of the specific conditions attached, the effectiveness of economic conditionality as an instrument of economic policy reform can be described, at most, as 'partial'.

What lessons can be drawn from this experience? The first lesson is that, in the bargaining game intrinsic to conditionality, recipients may (be forced to) agree to specified reforms, yet remain reluctant to implement them. There is likely to be at least as great a resistance to implement donors' *political* demands, given that incumbent governments generally do not readily agree to the wider dispersal of power in society that democratisation involves. Second, a recipient government will have learnt, in Mosley *et al.*'s words, 'that it can always get away with shortfalls of this magnitude' (i.e. up to 50 per cent slippage), and more if it holds a countervailing card (ibid.). Third, inconsistency in aid restrictive practice provides comparative evidence to support the arguments of 'non-complying' governments that they are being unfairly selected for punishment, as well as generally undermining donor policy. Each of these lessons signals potential negative impacts on the effectiveness of political conditionality.

The differences between economic and political conditionality must also be recognised, with further negative implications for effectiveness. Economic conditionality involves the stipulation of very specific policy reform measures, including particular targets and deadlines, formally agreed between both parties as a condition of the aid being granted. Aid restrictions, when uncommonly taken, are imposed due to a failure to implement the agreed policy reforms. In contrast, political conditionality does not involve such specific, contractual commitments, preceding aid disbursement. The only prior political condition for aid provision is, typically, a minimum threshold of respect for civil and political rights and democratic practices, remaining unspecified at the level of general aid policy. Restrictive measures on political grounds largely involve an interruption of ongoing aid programmes if this threshold is breached, typically occurring as a response to deteriorating situations of human rights abuses and/or democratic reversals. Somewhat more exact conditions maybe declared for their restoration, for example, the holding of free and fair elections. But, in general, there appears more hesitation by donors in prescribing specific political reform measures to be undertaken, in contrast to economic reform where there are no such qualms. This is perhaps due to some sensitivity to accusations of interference in internal affairs. In sum, both forms of conditionality aim to leverage reforms, but in somewhat different ways. Economic conditionality is characterised by the very precise stipulations attached to a development co-operation agreement, rather than by aid restrictions. Political conditionality is characterised more by the exertion of pressure through aid sanctions, or their threat, when a minimum threshold is breached. Taking into account these differences, particularly political conditionality's lack of specificity, commentators have anticipated an even lower rate of effectiveness than that for economic conditionality.

8.2 Methodology

To what extent have aid recipient countries undertaken political reforms they would not have taken without donor pressure? To evaluate effectiveness, instances of political conditionality are assessed according to two criteria. The first is the extent to which the donor objective was in fact achieved. This objective is defined here in broad terms as the promotion of democratisation and of respect for civil and political liberties.[121] The second criterion is the contribution made by the aid sanctions to the achievement of this objective.

These are difficult assessments to make and two provisos are required. The first is that such an impact evaluation can be undertaken most successfully and most thoroughly through detailed country case-studies, and the lack of depth of the global survey provided here is acknowledged. Yet, in contrast to a narrower set of case-studies, the approach does furnish a broader picture of the (in)effectiveness of political conditionality, and the circumstances that may contribute to increased effectiveness.[122] The other proviso is the methodological problem of counterfactuality. The second criterion (above) involves an attempt to isolate the effect of donor pressure on a complex process of political change, influenced by a number of factors, notably internal opposition movements as well as the incumbent government itself. In other words, the question of the extent to which the process of reform would have been different if external pressure had *not* been brought to bear is a counterfactual one, and must at best be a matter of informed judgement.

Further cautionary words regarding any assessment of the effectiveness of external pressure involves the acknowledgement that outcomes depend on the interactions between all actors involved, both internal and external. Political conditionality generally involves a conflict of interest between donor and recipient governments, with many recipient governments reluctant to conform to donors' aims, given that these entail some dispersal of the political power they currently hold. The greater the degree of recipient resistance, the less the likelihood of effectiveness. Even where governments 'sign up' to joint human rights and democracy objectives, as EU clauses entail, examples of 'overt evasion' or 'covert avoidance' are anticipated, in common with economic conditionality.[123] Hence, in the face of such resistance, the effectiveness of donor measures is likely to require rigorous application alongside a high degree of correspondence with internal pressure. Effectiveness in each country case is the outcome of the relative strength and the political guile displayed by all actors. Investigation at a global level, unfortunately, does not allow analysis at such a nuanced level. Nevertheless, in situations of incumbent government resistance, it can be confidently asserted that 'soft' or 'partial' application of aid sanctions is unlikely to be effective.

The 29 identified country cases of political conditionality have been assessed according to the above two criteria.[124] First, the trend towards improvements or regression regarding democratisation and increased respect for civil liberties since 1990 must be established in order to determine the extent to which the general donor objective was achieved. Two classifications have been used. One is the annual Freedom House rating of political rights and of civil liberties for every country in the world, based on a seven-category scale, in which 'one' represents the highest degree of 'freedom' and 'seven' the least.[125] The other is an assessment, based on a four-point scale, of the improvements (or not) in the democracy and human rights situation in each country between 1990 and 1995, as follows:

0 – no improvement or negative trend;
1 – possible improvement but unclear;
2 – modest improvement;
3 – significant improvement.[126]

Second, to assess the contribution of aid sanctions to any general improvement in democracy and civil and political rights, or to effecting more specific political changes, a similar four-point scale is used, as follows:

0 – zero (or negative) contribution;
1 – possible contribution but unclear;
2 – modest contribution;
3 – significant contribution;

The ratings for political rights (PR) and civil liberties (CL) for each of the 29 countries are shown on Table 8.1.

8.3 Key findings

This section refers throughout to the data contained in Table 8.1. (For more detailed information on each particular country case, see Appendix in Crawford 1997.)

Effectiveness

In 13 out of the 29 countries a progressive trend is perceived towards democratisation and greater protection of civil and political liberties, with partial attribution of this to donor pressure in nine of the 13 cases.[127] In only two cases, however, have sanctions made a *significant* contribution. In Malawi the suspension of aid provided a clear signal to Banda's regime that he could not hold out indefinitely in the face of both national and international opposition.[128] In Guatemala the immediate implementation of aid sanctions in May 1993, in the specific circumstances of a presidential 'self-coup', was critical in the rapid dissipation of military support.

In three cases, those of Haiti, Kenya and Zambia, sanctions made a *modest* contribution. In Haiti, aid measures, as part of a broader sanctions package, played a role in the eventual surrender of the military junta and the reinstatement of President Aristide. In Kenya, it is generally recognised that Western donors were important actors in effecting the democratic transition. Here, donor conditionality was

Table 8.1 Effectiveness of aid sanctions 1990–95

Country and sanctions taken by EU, UK, US and Sweden	Freedom House rating										Human rights and democratisation trend 1990–95	Aid sanctions contribution	Comments
	1990–91 PR	CL	1991–92 PR	CL	1992–93 PR	CL	1993–94 PR	CL	1994–95 PR	CL			
Burundi *De facto* suspension from October 1993 to October 1994, except humanitarian aid. Aid suspended again from April 1996.	7	6	7	6	6	5	7	7	6	7	0	0	At best the watchful eye of the international community, especially after the Rwanda genocide in 1994, and its propensity to suspend aid, has had a preventative role in checking army-led ethnically based violence.
Cameroon Partial suspension (new projects) by US only from November 1992, followed by programme closure during 1995.	6	6	6	6	6	5	6	5	6	5	1	0	Punitive action by US only limited efficacy, and any leverage lost by programme closure.
Equatorial Guinea No official suspension, but EU aid 'put on ice' by European Commission in 1994 on human rights grounds.	7	7	7	7	7	6	7	7	7	7	0	0	Lack of official EU sanctions limited impact of measures taken by European Commission.
The Gambia New project aid	2	2	2	2	2	1	2	2	7	6	0	0	Partial aid suspension has had little influence on military

suspended by all donors in October 1994, shortly after military coup.											government to return to civilian rule more immediately.
Guinea Aid reduced by US only following 'flawed' presidential elections in December 1993.	6	5	6	5	6	5	6	5	1	0	Lack of EU sanctions diminished potential for aid conditionality.
Kenya Programme aid suspended from November 1991 by all donors. Restored by UK government only in November 1993.	6	6	6	4	5	5	6	6	1/2	2	Donor role in initial transition to multipartyism, although their emphasis was on economic conditionality. Limited focus on political issues subsequently, except by a minority of donors (e.g. the Scandinavians), despite a rise in political violence and government disregard for the role of opposition political parties and parliament.
Lesotho Aid suspension (US and Sweden) and threatened suspension (EU and UK) in August 1994 after military-backed coup by monarch.	6	5	4	6	4	3	4	4	2/3	1	Aid suspension helped to swiftly re-instate the elected government in 1994. The main influence, however, was the governments of neighbouring states.

Table 8.1 Continued

Country and sanctions taken by EU, UK, US and Sweden	Freedom house rating										Human rights and democratisation trend 1990–95	Aid sanctions contribution	Comments
	1990–91		1991–92		1992–93		1993–94		1994–95				
	PR	CL	PR	CL	PR	CL	PR	CL	PR	CL			
Liberia Full suspension (*de facto*) from 1990 to date, except humanitarian assistance.	7	7	7	6	7	6	6	6	7	6	0	0	Neither *de facto* aid suspension, nor the potential of future support for reconstruction, has had much influence on the warring factions to reach a negotiated settlement.
Malawi New project aid suspended from April 1992 to June 1993 by all donors.	7	6	7	6	6	7	6	5	2	3	3	3	Donor action, together with internal movements, an important influence in forcing President Banda to hold a referendum, leading to the transition to democracy.
Niger New project aid suspended by EU from January 1996 following military coup.	6	5	6	5	5	4	3	4	3	5	3 → 0	0	Political reform in the early 1990s was mainly an internal process, with no aid conditionality. Suspension of EU aid in early 1996, following the military coup, had little impact on bringing an immediate return to civilian rule.
Nigeria EU partial freeze from July 1993, then full suspension from	5	5	5	4	5	4	7	5	7	6	0	0	Aid sanctions, at first partial, had negligible impact on pressurising the military regime under Abacha

November 1995. Total suspension by US from April 1994 due to lack of anti-narcotics co-operation. [...] to adopt a timetable for a transition to civilian democratic rule.

Country										
Rwanda — Full suspension from April – October 1994. Gradual restoration of aid, but brief suspension again by EU in May 1995 following refugee camp massacre.	6	6	6	6	6	5	7	7	0/1 (post-1994)	0/1 (post-1994)
Sierra Leone — EU threat in January 1996 if planned democratic elections affected by internal coup within military regime.	6	5	7	6	7	6	7	6	1	1
Somalia — *De facto* suspension from 1991 to date by all donors.	7	7	7	7	7	7	7	7	0	0
Sudan — Full suspension from 1990/91 to date by all donors.	7	7	7	7	7	7	7	7	0	0

Comments:

Rwanda: Conditioning of assistance for reconstruction on power-sharing may restrict trend to reduced Hutu representation in new government. Outcome unknown.

Sierra Leone: Donor threats may have had positive effect in ensuring completion of transition to democratic, civilian rule following the internal military coup in January 1996.

Somalia: As with Liberia, the international community appears to have had little success in pushing the warring factions to the negotiating table.

Sudan: Co-ordinated aid sanctions have had negligible impact, to date, on entrenched Islamic fundamentalist, military regime.

Table 8.1 Continued

Country and sanctions taken by EU, UK, US and Sweden	Freedom house rating										Human rights and democratisation trend 1990–95	Aid sanctions contribution	Comments
	1990–91		1991–92		1992–93		1993–94		1994–95				
	PR	CL	PR	CL	PR	CL	PR	CL	PR	CL			
Togo New project aid suspended by EU and US following breakdown of democratisation in January 1992. Partial restoration by EU in March 1995. Programme closure by US during 1994.	6	6	6	5	6	5	7	5	6	5	0/1	0	Partial sanctions did little to assist the strong internal movement for democracy, which was ultimately outmanoeuvred by the incumbent dictator. French position most influential, yet characterised by ambivalence.
Zaïre Partial suspension from early 1992 by EU and US. Programme closure by US during 1994.	6	6	6	5	6	5	7	6	7	6	0/1	0	Aid sanctions had little effect on unsettling the personal rule of the hugely wealthy President Mobutu.
Zambia Threats to withhold aid by US and UK in December 1993 due to allegations of high-level corruption (drug-trafficking) leading to ministerial resignations.	6	5	2	3	2	3	3	4	3	4	2	1	Successful democratic transition in 1991 achieved without donor pressure. Threat of aid conditionality used effectively in relation to specific allegation of government corruption in late 1993/early 1994.

													Comment
Burma From September 1988 to date by all donors after crushing of pro-democracy protests.	7.	7	7	7	7	7	7	7	7	7	0	0	Total aid suspension has had no apparent impression on intransigence of the ruling SLORC towards political liberalisation.
China Partial suspension (new projects) by all donors post-Tiananmen Square massacre for 15–22 months.	7	7	7	7	7	7	7	7	7	7	0	0	Limited and short-term sanctions in 1989/90 had no impact on the powerful Chinese regime.
Thailand New project aid suspended by US only in February 1991 after military overthrow of elected government. Aid restored in October 1992 after elections.	2	3	6	4	4	3	3	5	3	5	2	1	Internal pro-democracy movements most influential, but international pressure a contributory factor to the relinquishment of power by military led forces and more genuine elections in September 1992.
Vietnam Swedish aid cut from 1992/93 onwards by Conservative-led government on democracy and human rights grounds.	7	7	7	7	7	7	7	7?	7	7	1	0	Sweden an influential donor, but punitive measures aimed more at domestic audience, plus the reverse of the trend by other Western governments towards improved trade and diplomatic relations.

Table 8.1 Continued

Country and sanctions taken by EU, UK, US and Sweden	Freedom house rating										Human rights and democratisation trend 1990–95	Aid sanctions contribution	Comments
	1990–91		1991–92		1992–93		1993–94		1994–95				
	PR	CL	PR	CL	PR	CL	PR	CL	PR	CL			
Cuba No aid programmes except Sweden, terminated in November 1991 by Conservative-led government.	7	7	7	7	7	7	7	7	7	7	1	0	An example of the limitations of sanctions, with the US blockade of over 35 years having conspicuously failed to depose Castro's government.
El Salvador Annual attempts by US Congress from 1990 to 1992 to link assistance to successful progress in peace negotiations, but evaded somewhat by Bush administration.	3	4	3	4	3	3	3	3	3	3	3	1	Example of some success both in making a specific linkage to the achievement of a transition to peace and a democratic polity, and in attempts by a legislature (US Congress) to restrict the activities of the executive.
Guatemala Suspension of aid by US and EU following President Serrano's 'self-coup' in May 1993, dissolving congress and the Supreme Court.	3	4	3	5	4	5	4	5	4	5	2	3[1]	Immediate implementation of aid sanctions, particularly by the US and EU, in opposition to Serrano's 'self-coup' in May 1993, was undoubtedly a factor in his loss of military support and consequent resignation.

Country	Description											Assessment
Haiti	Full suspension by all donors from October 1991 to September 1994 except humanitarian aid.	4	4	7	7	7	7	7	5	5	3	2	Could be viewed as example of eventual success of economic sanctions, including aid. However, OAS and UN embargoes also characterised by widespread evasion.
Peru	Aid suspension by US, UK and EU from April 1992, following President Fujimori's army-backed 'self-coup', dissolving Congress and suspending the judiciary. Restoration after Congressional election in November 1992, despite opposition boycott.	3	4	3	5	6	5	5	5	4	0^2	1^3	International pressure contributed to a 'return to democracy' following Fujimori's 'self-coup'. But Fujimori's outmanoeuvring of both the internal opposition and the international community limited the efficacy of the sanctions imposed during 1992.
Syria	EU programme subject to blockage by EP from 1986 to 1993. No programmes by other donors.	7	7	7	7	7	7	7	7		0	0	Aid sanctions unlikely to make much impression on the entrenched regime under al-Assad. However, the EU has ceased to impose aid restrictions, with the assent of the EP.

Table 8.1 Continued

Country and sanctions taken by EU, UK, US and Sweden	Freedom house rating										Human rights and democratisation trend 1990–95	Aid sanctions contribution	Comments
	1990–91		1991–92		1992–93		1993–94		1994–95				
	PR	CL	PR	CL	PR	CL	PR	CL	PR	CL			
Turkey EU programme suspended from 1980 to late 1995, when EP finally approved a customs union. Third largest recipient of US assistance.	2	4	2	4	2	4	4	4	5	5	0	0	Despite deteriorating human rights record in the 1990s, the EP rescinded its opposition to aid in late 1995, and no human rights conditionality imposed by the US government.

[1] May 1993
[2] Polity less democratic after Fujimori's 'self-coup'
[3] To restoration of constitutional rule during 1992

more explicitly economic, but there was certainly a perception by the Kenyan government that political liberalisation would assuage donor dissatisfactions.[129] In Zambia, an exception to the high level of support furnished to the MMD government was the threat to withhold aid in relation to a very specific allegation of high-level corruption, leading to the departure from government of the individuals concerned.

In four other cases, those of Thailand, Lesotho, Sierra Leone and El Salvador, aid sanctions or the threat of, made a *likely* though less tangible contribution, using aid or the threat of its withdrawal to influence political developments in the direction of democratisation and the stemming of military power.

Peru is a tenth case where aid sanctions were effective, seen as exerting pressure on President Fujimori to make an early return to constitutional rule following his military-backed 'self-coup' (*autogolpe*) in April 1992. This case is unusual, however, in that Fujimori's political guile in achieving constitutional amendments resulted in a less democratic polity than before his coup.

This minority of cases (10 out of 29) where political conditionality has arguably had some impact on political developments can be divided into two types. The first is where sanctions denote opposition to the wholesale nature of the particular regime and are employed with the aim of exerting pressure to secure a major transition in a country's polity. Examples are Malawi, Haiti and perhaps Kenya. One factor determining success will be the strength of donor political will to achieve such objectives (that is, whether sanctions are applied robustly or half-heartedly). The other type involves a response to more specific circumstances, often to deter or reverse negative developments. This does not necessarily involve the same systemic opposition by donor governments or the objective of structural change. Examples are Guatemala, Zambia and Lesotho. Success in the latter type is more common. However, such specific instances of political conditionality may serve to obscure the overall support provided to a particular regime. Guatemala illustrates this well. The US government, the most influential donor, had been the mainstay of military regimes and military-backed civilian governments in Guatemala during the 1970s and 1980s, providing considerable foreign aid, including military assistance, despite the Guatemalan government's repeated responsibility for human rights atrocities.[130]

Overall, the findings demonstrate that aid sanctions are most likely to be effective in two quite distinct circumstances. The first is in situations where donor measures 'tip the balance', combining with internal opposition movements and a set of contingent circumstances, and provide the extra push necessary to induce a systemic political transition, (for example, Kenya, Malawi). The second is where sanctions are imposed (or threatened) in immediate response to particular events, with specific reforms required for aid to be maintained or resumed (for example, Guatemala, Zambia).

Ineffectiveness

The main finding, however, from this evaluation of the impact of donor restrictive measures is their *failure* to contribute to political change in 18 out of 29 cases (62 per cent).[131] How is this lack of effectiveness to be accounted for? Reasons can be explored along two dimensions. One proposition is the relatively partial and weak nature of the measures imposed by the donors. The other is the relative strength of the recipient country government to resist the privations involved and/or its political shrewdness in avoiding implementation of reforms. Of course, many country cases will be explained by a combination of the two factors.

Weakness of sanctions?

Regarding the first proposition, what does the empirical evidence show concerning the relatively robust or weak nature of the measures imposed? Full suspension only occurs in a minority of cases, with a partial aid freeze on new projects, and/or suspension of programme aid, much more common.[132] A number of reasons could account for the adoption of partial measures, some more genuine than others. First, donors may strategically choose a 'soft' approach as a means of giving a message to the recipient government while simultaneously maintaining dialogue (as in The Gambia). Second, there may be opposition to full suspension from aid agency officials, averse to the disruption of ongoing developmental efforts for political transgressions. Yet it is also true that partial measures are likely to involve less privation and hence less economic leverage. Third, 'soft' measures can also be accounted for by overriding donor concern for economic interests or geo-political relations, while taking sufficient action to appease domestic public or parliamentary opinion. China provides such an example, with the partial, short-term nature of the sanctions imposed after the Tiananmen Square massacre being little more than symbolic and never likely to be effective. A similar scenario is where the punitive measures taken by a donor government are aimed more at mobilising domestic public support for their policies. An example is provided by the cuts in aid to Vietnam made by the Swedish Conservative-led coalition government, where, despite Sweden's position as the main donor, pressure on the Vietnamese government to liberalise politically was never seriously on the agenda.

A further category of relatively weak donor measures is cases characterised by a lack of donor co-ordination, with punitive action taken by some but not by others. For example, in both Cameroon and Guinea the potential for leverage through aid conditionality was limited when punitive measures were taken by the US alone, while EU programmes remained unaffected. Unilateral action to suspend aid is unlikely ever to be effective even by a major donor, as the example of the Dutch in Indonesia in 1991 clearly illustrated.[133]

Strong recipient governments?

Secondly, what evidence is there concerning the other line of explanation – that aid sanctions have remained ineffective, despite being robustly imposed, due to the relative strength of the recipient government? The lack of economic crisis, a relatively weak opposition, and a high degree of control over the means of coercion, would all tend to heighten the degree of political stability and increase the durability of a non-democratic government. However, some doubt is cast on the pertinence to date of this proposition by an initial look at the seven country cases where full suspension of aid has been imposed but without effect: Burundi, Liberia, Nigeria, Rwanda, Somalia, Sudan and Burma.[134] Only the governments in Burma and Nigeria could be described as relatively strong and immune to aid sanctions, due mainly to a firm grip on power through military control and severe political repression, as well as less economic vulnerability. The Nigerian regime in particular benefits from its access to large oil revenues. In addition, the Sudanese regime has withstood Western pressure largely due to its access to alternative sources of external financial support from other Islamic states, notably Libya, Iraq and Iran, enabling it to maintain its hold on power.

In the other four cases, all in sub-Saharan Africa, strength of government is not a relevant factor. Rather, total suspension of aid has been largely a *de facto* measure in situations where development co-operation becomes impossible, due to extreme civil strife and political upheaval, characterised in Liberia and Somalia by the collapse of national government, and in Rwanda and Burundi by military-manipulated genocidal conflict. Aid sanctions are generally of little consequence to the main actors in such conflicts, although the conditional re-establishment of aid can sometimes be an incentive to bring warring parties to the negotiating table, as attempted (though unsuccessfully) on several occasions in Liberia.

The failure of aid sanctions in contributing to political change in Nigeria and Burma also raises the issue of countervailing trade interests. In both cases any economic leverage from aid sanctions is undermined by the maintenance of trade relations. Regarding Nigeria, both the US government and EU member states decided against the imposition of an oil embargo. In Burma, most Western countries have banned aid since the 1988 crackdown on pro-democracy demonstrators, but trade continued relatively unimpeded.[135] Aid restrictions against repressive regimes with access to sizeable export revenues will remain largely symbolic unless part of a broader sanctions package, including trade measures.[136]

Of the other 11 cases where aid sanctions, partially imposed, have been ineffective, only Syria and Turkey stand out as relatively strong regimes economically, hence able to withstand more easily any punitive measures. All the sub-Saharan Africa countries are Low Income Countries, mostly with GNPs *per capita* well below the $750 threshold.

Summary

In many cases, the explanation for the ineffectiveness of aid sanctions is doubtless a combination of the two propositions. However, there is less evidence to support the proposition that ineffectiveness is due to the relative strength of the recipient government to resist aid conditionality, and there are more examples to support the thesis that ineffectiveness is better explained by the weak and partial nature of the measures imposed. This conclusion questions how seriously sanctions have been applied by donors in many cases.

8.4   Stokke's propositions – confirmed or refuted?

To what extent does the evidence presented here prove or disprove Stokke's six hypotheses governing the effectiveness of aid conditionality?

1.   The domestic position of the recipient government and its power basis – weak of strong

The relative weakness or strength of a recipient government is regarded by Stokke as dependent on a number of factors: the state of the economy and the degree of economic crisis; control over the means of coercive powers; the strength of the political opposition and pressure groups like trade unions (Stokke 1995, p. 43).

There is a certain self-evidence about this proposition in that aid sanctions on their own are likely to be ineffective against economically stronger developing countries, an example being Syria. It is also clear that military-backed governments, often characterised by a ruthless suppression of internal dissent, are generally more able to resist external pressure, a fact that includes economically weaker regimes, such as Sudan and Burma. Further, external intervention is more successful when it combines with the internal pressure exerted by an active political opposition, for example, in Malawi and Kenya. In comparison, in Peru, President Fujimori, strengthened by the high levels of public support for his actions, was able to outmanoeuvre international pressure and reduce the power of existing democratic institutions.

Nevertheless, some cases do add qualification to this hypothesis. Some lower middle income countries have been susceptible to leverage – for example, Guatemala and El Salvador – where relations with the US government are important to both. Conversely, aid sanctions have proved ineffective in a number of economically weaker states. Two types have been identified. One is where governments have a strong sense of self-preservation, assisted by the means to achieve this, either the riches of personal rulers (for example, Mobutu in the former Zaïre) and/or control of state resources (for example, Togo and Equatorial Guinea). The other is countries immersed in civil strife (some to the extent of state collapse), where government and non-government forces seek to preserve or capture power through violent combat, and are unlikely to be swayed from their purposes by the withdrawal of aid or the promise of its restoration (as in Liberia, Somalia and Burundi). Both types of regime would appear relatively indifferent to economic pressure.

This hypothesis requires some elaboration to recognise more fully that it is not only the power base of the recipient government that may affect its readiness to comply with donor conditionality, but a broader range of economic and political characteristics. In particular, the degree of governmental control over the economy and its access to revenues, through 'rent-seeking' activities as well as taxation, needs to be considered. In addition, what has been strongly confirmed is the extent to which the effectiveness of external pressure increases in proportion to the level of internal support for reform measures. This suggests that donors, in formulating political conditions, pay close attention to the reforms called for by local groups. This also has implications for the legitimacy of external intervention, something that is discussed further in the next section.

*2. The recipient government's ability to use the occasion of external
intervention to strengthen its position domestically*

This proposition refers to donor conditionality having opposite effects
to those intended. A recipient government may be able to exploit the
infringement of sovereignty inherent in conditionality to arouse
national feelings against external interference, thus diverting attention
from domestic problems (ibid.).

It is true that a few ruling parties in Africa have actually emerged
as stronger from the pressures to democratise, retaining power and
even consolidating it through 'electoral coups d'état', and, although
still aid dependent, become more able to resist external pressure.[137]
Such examples are Togo, Cameroon, Guinea, all in Francophone West
Africa. However, the ambivalent role of the French government,
often maintaining support for authoritarian ruling parties and reluctant
democratisers, has contributed more to such an outcome than aid
conditionality.[138]

Cuba is one possible example where the government has aroused anti-
imperialist sentiment against the US economic blockade in its own
defence. The fundamentalist Islamic regime in Sudan also attempted
to intensify domestic anti-Western feeling through its opposition to the
imposition of aid sanctions.[139]

Yet, these examples notwithstanding, there is little evidence to support such perverse outcomes from the level of analysis conducted
here.[140]

3. The extent of aid dependency

There is some overlap here with Stokke's first hypothesis. Again, it is
somewhat self-evident that the degree of effectiveness of political conditionality will be in direct proportion to the degree of aid dependency.
A key finding here is that, predominantly, aid sanctions have been taken
against the poorest, economically weakest countries, particularly in sub-
Saharan Africa. This is doubtless due partly to the greater likelihood
of effective leverage. However, Table 8.1 shows three other findings.
First, aid dependency is not a sufficient condition to achieve donor
objectives. Sanctions have not been successful in contributing to
improvements in human rights and democracy in many aid-dependent
countries. The reasons are both endogenous (see the first proposition
above) and donor-related (an example being lack of donor co-ordination). Second, and conversely, aid dependency is not a necessary condition of effectiveness and aid restrictions have contributed to the

leverage of political changes in less poor countries. Four out of the ten 'successful' cases are in lower middle income countries, namely Thailand, El Salvador, Guatemala and Peru. Third, the notion of 'reverse dependency' also requires consideration. Donor governments are unwilling to impose rigorous aid sanctions in some larger and more powerful developing countries, hence threatening trade and investment opportunities. China is a prime example. This is explored further in the next proposition.

4. The magnitude and importance of the bilateral relations

This hypothesis examines how the nature of the relationship between donor and recipient parties affects both the likelihood of conditionality being applied, its degree of robustness and its likely success. There are two aspects of this proposition. Where the relationship is closer and more broad-based, including economic and strategic interests, the likelihood of restrictive measures is diminished. Conversely, when sanctions are applied in such circumstances, the impact is likely to be greater (Stokke 1995, p. 44). Historical ties are important here, especially former colonial links.

Does the evidence assembled here support these propositions? There is certainly substantial evidence of countervailing economic and strategic interests subordinating human rights concerns and resulting in the weak application of sanctions (as in China and Nigeria). Similarly, Turkey's membership of the North Atlantic Treaty Organisation (NATO) has insulated it from aid restrictions despite the extremely poor human rights record of successive Turkish governments, with the sole EU action coming from the European Parliament. There is also evidence of historical or political links resulting in sanctions being reluctantly or weakly imposed. Regarding historical ties, the clearest example is the ambivalence of the French government in its African 'sphere of influence' to take negative measures against incumbent regimes it has had a long association with, and its success in influencing EU policy. This is shown by the lack of accord between EU and US policy in relation to Francophone Africa, for example, in Cameroon and Guinea. In addition, the example of the UK and Kenya provides a case of aid restrictions being taken by the former colonial power, yet with measures somewhat milder and a tone less abrasive and critical than those adopted by other donor governments, notably the US and some Scandinavian countries.[141] Regarding political ties, very limited aid restrictions have been taken against those Central American governments closely allied to the US, despite widespread evidence of their involvement in gross human rights abuses. In fact, measures taken have been due mainly to US Congressional action, not to the executive.

Is there evidence of greater impact when measures are taken by donor nations with whom ties are strong? In Guatemala, the loss of support of the powerful and closely allied US government was certainly a very significant factor in the outcome of events following President Serrano's 'self-coup'. But such examples are rare and there is insufficient evidence to substantiate this part of the proposition.

The evidence is considerably stronger in support of the first part of this hypothesis: where bilateral relations are close, tied up with donors' own strategic or economic interests, then the effectiveness of aid conditionality is compromised by the weakness of measures implemented, or by their total absence. Action taken is often due to pressure from legislatures.

5.   The probability that a unilateral action may have a snowball effect

This proposition refers to the greater likelihood of unilateral action by a major power snowballing and being supported by others – and thus having more impact – in comparison with unilateral measures by a small or middle power, which are likely to be less effective (Stokke 1995, pp. 44–5).

Have the US- or EU-led measures been more effective than those initiated by the smaller powers of the UK and Sweden? While it is quite possible that action taken by the most powerful nations or groups of nations will be more successful in assembling support from other donors, the evidence here does not lend itself well to assessing this proposition. First, it is difficult to disentangle the time sequence of different aid restrictions taken in the case of individual countries, including the identification of who initiates and who follows. Second, neither the UK nor Sweden provide a good comparison with the more major powers. As a member state, UK policy is generally in line with that of the EU as a whole, and although Sweden remained outside the EU until 1995, it has only taken aid sanctions in few cases. The restrictive measures taken by Sweden against Vietnam can be seen as an example of a smaller power failing to be influential, but other factors are more significant in this case – economic liberalisation in Vietnam and the (then) Swedish centre-right government aiming to appeal to a domestic audience.

However, the evidence here does demonstrate the ineffectiveness of any unilateral action (see below), and thus the risks, from a donor's point of view, of relying on a snowball effect.

6. An internationally co-ordinated action by donors stands a better chance of success than a unilateral action in terms of attaining the policy reforms pursued

There is considerable evidence to support this hypothesis. The large majority of effective cases were characterised by donor co-ordination. Of particular note are the instances of Kenya and Malawi, where donor pressure was co-ordinated through the mechanism of the World Bank-chaired Consultative Group, most commonly associated with economic conditionality. In both cases, the united front presented by donor governments was a significant factor in the decisions of established regimes to institute political reforms. In Lesotho, co-ordinated action was led by neighbouring states and supported by donor governments. In Guatemala, the US and the EU were united in their opposition to Serrano's 'self-coup'. In Haiti, international opposition to the ousting of Aristide was led initially by the Organisation of American States (OAS), and later by the UN.[142]

In addition, in those cases characterised by unilateral action and a lack of common purpose amongst donors, the impact is largely ineffectual. This is found to be particularly so in cases where the two major powers, the US and the EU, have acted in contradiction to each other – for example, in Cameroon and Guinea (US but not EU sanctions), in Turkey (EU but not US), and in Syria (US but not EU). Indonesia is another oft-cited example of unilateral action proving futile; the Dutch alone implemented aid sanctions following the 1991 massacre in East Timor, but were then themselves ordered to leave the country by the Indonesian government.

Additional propositions

Stokke's six propositions are confirmed on the whole, although with some qualifications and minor refutations, particularly regarding 'perverse' outcomes and 'snowball' effects of unilateral actions. Yet, the evidence also points to their deficiency as a complete framework for the evaluation of effectiveness. Two comments arise. First, Stokke's hypotheses tend to focus on the static contexts within which political conditionality occurs. It is necessary, however, to consider a more dynamic process, involving a range of practices enacted by both donor and recipient governments as active agents. Second, Stokke's hypotheses tend to assume the 'good faith' of donor objectives to promote political reform. Examples have clearly demonstrated how this must be questioned in many cases. Thus, the evidence here itself generates four

further propositions concerning the effectiveness of political conditionality, as outlined below.

*7.   The degree of shrewdness of recipient governments to evade political
conditionality*

From the experience of economic conditionality, it is evident that recipients may (reluctantly) agree to political reforms, but evade putting
them into effect through slowness of pace or by engaging in formal or
rhetorical implementation only. A typical pattern is to allow multi-
partyism, but not a democratic civil society, and to manipulate the
electoral process, occasionally reverting to repression. Kenya is one
example where donor pressure contributed to the initial transition to
multi-partyism, yet this pressure was not maintained after transitional
elections, allowing the government to harass and undermine opposition, with rising violations of civil and political liberties, something
noted both by the annual Freedom House survey and human rights
organisations. In such situations, donor efforts are likely to have greater
success when linked to internal pressures for reform. In the Kenyan case,
however, the opposition has been characterised by division.

8.   The preciseness of reform required

Effectiveness increases the greater is the specificity of the political
reform(s) to be undertaken in order for aid to be resumed.

Of the nine cases characterised by a degree of effectiveness, the majority
involved relatively precise donor demands (for example, Zambia and
Lesotho). The distinction has been made between the application of
political conditionality in situations of systemic opposition to regime
type (the one-party state in Malawi being an example), and in more
particular circumstances as they arise (such as the allegations of high-
level ministerial corruption in Zambia). While it may be easier to specify
the required changes in the latter type of cases (the dismissal of the
ministers involved), it is not impossible to do so in the former type, and
hence increase effectiveness. For example, in Rwanda, where greater
power-sharing is called for, donors could be more precise about the various
means to achieve this, without being unduly prescriptive. Such specificity
itself also creates a criterion against which effectiveness can be evaluated.

9.   The degree of countervailing economic and strategic interests

The greater a donors economic and strategic interests in a particular
country, the less likely that aid sanctions on human rights and democracy grounds will be implemented effectively.

Stokke incorporates this into his discussion of the closeness of bilateral relations (the fourth proposition above). Its significance is such, however, that it requires emphasis in its own right. It highlights how human rights and democracy concerns regarding a particular country can be subordinated to other competing foreign policy objectives, including trade. This proposition, however, questions the genuineness of donor intent in leveraging political change. This issue is explored in detail in the discussion of 'consistency' in the next section.

10. The degree of political will of the donor

Aid sanctions will be effective only to the extent that donor governments have the political will to implement them rigorously.

This proposition closely relates to the preceding one. Political will is clearly compromised in cases where aid restrictions are partial and weak due to countervailing interests. Yet, even in the absence of such interests, the determination of donors is required if sanctions are to be implemented with effect. The lack of such political will is apparent in three differing scenarios. One is where restrictive measures are initiated by the donor legislature but not implemented whole-heartedly by the executive. Examples include El Salvador, where US Congressional action was undermined by the Bush administration, and Syria and Turkey, where repeated attempts were made to remove the European Parliament blocks on new financial packages. A second is where limited sanctions are taken, but for reasons related primarily to donor domestic politics, with governments needing to be seen to be taking action. In consequence, there is little other than symbolic impact on the country in question. Examples include the Swedish government measures against Vietnam, and the initial British government response to the reversal of democratisation and the consolidation of military rule in Nigeria. A third possible scenario is where the rigorous implementation of aid restrictions are thwarted by aid ministry officials less enthusiastic about long-term development programmes being disrupted on political grounds. This may appear more defensible, motivated by a perception that development efforts are undermined due to the political transgressions of a country's rulers. However, the 'fungibility rule' must be recalled. In Mosley's words (1987, p. 235), 'All aid to a government that pursues the policy of violating human rights contributes (directly or indirectly) to repression'. This is because tying aid to a specific project 'cannot stop the recipient reshuffling the rest of his spending pattern in response to a donation: aid is fungible' (ibid.). No examples of the undermining of effectiveness in this way were revealed, however, by the level of research conducted here.

These last two propositions question the extent to which aid restrictions can be taken at face-value in a number of cases, and their effectiveness assessed as if they constituted a serious attempt to press for political change.

9
Consistency

One outcome from the discussion of the effectiveness of aid intervention is to query how seriously aid sanctions have been applied in many
instances. This links strongly to the major issue regarding donor application of aid sanctions, that of consistency. As discussed in Chapter 1
(section 1.4.1), a number of commentators have queried whether
donors would implement aid restrictions in an objective and equal
manner, pointing to the precedent of selective and uneven application
of human rights conditionality by the Carter administration in the late
1970s (Forsythe 1988, pp. 51–60; Nelson and Eglinton 1992, p. 28). The
issue of consistency in application has also been a main concern of
representatives of recipient governments, (for example, Greenidge in
The Courier No.155, 1996). What does the empirical evidence suggest?
Has the practice of Northern governments improved in the post-cold
war period? Alternatively, has inconsistency continued to prevail?

The argument advanced here is that inconsistency in the treatment of
aid recipient countries will have an adverse impact on policy legitimacy
and on the credibility of donor motivations. It is noteworthy that the
damaging effect of inconsistency is explicitly acknowledged by the
British government, stating:

> It is important that the FCO [Foreign and Commonwealth Office]
> should take and be seen to be taking a positive and consistent interest
> in the promotion of human rights worldwide. The charge of incon-
> sistency is damaging to the potential success of our representations
> abroad'. (British Foreign and Commonwealth Office 1991, para. 29)

Consistency is assessed here along three lines of enquiry. The first two
make further use of the evidence from the 29 country cases, analysing

the regional distribution of cases, and then the level of measures taken relative to the degree of human rights abuses. The third line of investigation involved a search for 'non-cases' where aid sanctions have *not* been applied by any of the selected donors despite a recipient government's record of gross human rights violations and lack of respect for democratic principles. This resulted in five further country cases – Indonesia, Sri Lanka, Algeria, Egypt and Colombia – with mini case-studies of each presented below.

9.1   Regional breakdown

What stands out is the overwhelming extent to which aid sanctions have been taken in sub-Saharan Africa – in 18 out of 29 country cases – in marked contrast to other regions (see Table 9.1, below). The non-democratic practices and human rights abuses of authoritarian regimes in other developing regions, particularly in Asia, North Africa and the Middle East, would appear to be subject to less scrutiny. Why is this and why has sub-Saharan Africa been selected for attention in this way?

Three reasons can account for this finding, the first more or less defensible, the others much less so. First, political conditionality policies have arisen in the post-cold war context of the global emphasis on democratisation. Yet, it is particularly in sub-Saharan Africa in the first half of the 1990s that movements for democracy challenged the one-party states and military regimes throughout the continent, opening up situations where external leverage could be exerted in an attempt to influence the outcome in favour of the reformers. Second, as countries in sub-Saharan Africa are amongst the poorest and the most aid-dependent in the world, it is here that donors are likely to regard aid sanctions as being most effective. Third, Northern donors generally have the least to lose in sub-Saharan Africa by applying sanctions. There are fewer countervailing pressures either in terms of economic interests (such as trade and investment) or in geo-strategic interests, since these have faded since the end of the cold war.

Table 9.1   Regional breakdown of aid sanctions (donors combined)

Sub-Saharan Africa	Asia	Latin America and Caribbean	Middle East
18	4	5	2

Thus, the evidence indicates the extent to which political condition-ality has been applied against the poorest countries, particularly in Africa, in contrast to other countries with authoritarian polities, yet with more rapidly growing economies. This initial evidence tends to confirm the suspicions of sceptics of political aid policies that economic self-interest would predominate in relations with the latter group of countries. In addition, strategic concerns remain dominant in other parts of the world, notably in the Middle East.

9.2 Level of sanctions

How have the level of sanctions been selected and what criteria have determined their relative robustness? Is it the degree of infringements of human rights and democratic processes? Alternatively, is the relative strength and weakness of measures more related to the presence of extraneous, countervailing factors? There is little correlation between the level of sanctions imposed and the degree of human rights viola-tions. There is more evidence, however, of less robust measures taken in countries where Northern governments have greater economic and political interests. A more detailed examination is undertaken of three examples where relatively weak sanctions were taken in response to gross human rights abuses and democratic reversals. In each case self-interest would appear to prevail over policy principle.

9.2.1 China

In China, after the Tiananmen Square massacre of June 1989, all the donors examined here, in common with other Western nations, imposed some form of economic sanction, as well as suspending diplomatic relations. The mildest response was from the US gov-ernment, in banning arms exports but President Bush also vetoed Congressional legislation linking 'Most Favoured Nation' trading status to human rights improvements. The sanctions, including aid restric-tions, were maintained only for a short duration, however, and were generally relaxed within 18 months. Yet no improvement in the politi-cal situation had occurred. On the contrary, the 'relentless repression' of pro-democracy activists continued throughout 1990 and 1991 (Human Rights Watch 1992, p. 359), and with no ease-off by the mid-1990s. Reports at this time stated not only was there 'no fundamental change in the government's human rights policy' (Amnesty International 1994a, p. 3), but that 'in 1995 the authorities stepped up repression of dissent' (US Department of State 1996, China Country Report p. 2).

Yet, development assistance to China is not insignificant. Only shortly after the events of June 1989, China was the twelfth highest recipient of Swedish aid in 1991/92 and the tenth highest in 1992/93 (SIDA 1993c). British aid has increased substantially during the first half of the 1990s, with China becoming the sixth highest recipient in 1992/93 and 1993/94 with development assistance of £35m and £34m respectively (British ODA 1994, p. 14). This largely consists of Aid and Trade Provision, £26m and £25m respectively, specifically designed to support British firms gain overseas contracts (ibid., p. 39).

Aid sanctions against China can be seen as no more than a token gesture, implemented in order to be seen to be taking some action to appease domestic constituencies. The trade and investment opportunities available to Northern nations in the rapidly expanding Chinese economy required the expeditious abandonment of human rights policies and the speedy resumption of 'business as usual'. Yet it must not be forgotten that the revenue gained from export earnings is one important means through which the Chinese government maintains its grip on power.

9.2.2   Nigeria

Nigeria was a clear-cut case for total aid suspension on human rights and democracy grounds. The protracted military-led transition to democracy in the early 1990s was aborted at the final stage with the annulment of the presidential elections in June 1993. Formal return to military rule followed in November 1993 when General Abacha declared himself head of a new military government, dissolving the National Assembly and other regional and local democratic structures, and banning political parties and political activities. Subsequent events confirmed not only the anti-democratic but also the brutal nature of the military regime, with repression of the pro-democracy opposition and labour activists, as well as the detention of senior political figures, most notably the acknowledged winner of the presidential election, Moshood Abiola, and the former head of state, Olusegun Obasanjo.[143]

Yet, aid and diplomatic measures taken by the European Union and its member states were relatively weak for a period of over two years.[144] From July 1993 partial measures involved the review of all new aid projects, with other associated measures including suspension of military co-operation and visa restrictions. It was not until November 1995, following the international outrage over the execution of Ken Saro-Wiwa and eight other Ogoni environmental activists, that a total freeze on development co-operation was adopted by the EU Council of Ministers as a 'common position', thus applying to both multilateral and bilateral aid. Full suspension of US assistance occurred from April 1994, but this was due to decertification for non-cooperation with anti-narcotics efforts.

The partial nature of EU measures for over two years must have sent a mixed message to the Nigerian military authorities, indicating a degree of concern and opposition to the turn of events, but not the unequivocal condemnation and tough punitive action one might have anticipated. The ambiguous and compromised nature of the EU's stance to the Nigerian military regime was most evident from the continued export of arms by some member states. The UK government was amongst those most culpable, responsible for issuing 20 new licences for arms exports in 1994 (*The Guardian*, 21 July 1995 and 28 August 1995).[145] Such equipment is obviously sought by the Nigerian authorities for their continued 'ruthless suppression of dissent', as described by the US Department of State (1996, Overview p. 4).

Why were more vigorous aid sanctions not imposed earlier? Nigeria is one of the very few sub-Saharan African countries where Western nations have significant economic interests, notably the oil extraction activities of Shell, the Anglo-Dutch multinational, and other oil companies. Britain especially has extensive commercial interests, with exports of £480 million in 1994 and investments worth over £500 million (Chalker 1995). In adopting its 'common position', the EU continued to eschew harder hitting sanctions, for example, an oil embargo and the freezing of military bank accounts held in member states. It is reported that the British and Dutch governments vetoed such measures (*The Guardian*, 21 November 1995). The Nigerian military regime benefits from and maintains its power through its access to substantial oil revenues. In this context, aid sanctions have to be combined with trade restrictions if effective leverage is to be achieved. Yet, the serious intent of Western donors, particularly the EU, in promoting democracy and human rights in Nigeria is questioned by its lack of preparedness to impose measures that conflict with its own trade interests.

9.2.3 Turkey

The Turkish government has enjoyed the uninterrupted support of the US government for many years as the third largest recipient, after Israel and Egypt, of US foreign assistance. In contrast, European Community aid to Turkey was suspended from 1980 until late 1995, when the

European Parliament finally gave its consent to a customs union, paving the way for new aid and trade deals. EC suspension originally followed the military coup in 1980 and the subsequent systematic violation of human rights, including the crushing of trade unions and leftist groups. Yet, in more recent years, the continued suspension of assistance to Turkey on human rights grounds has been due largely to the European Parliament's persistence in refusing to give its assent to a new aid and trade agreement, despite repeated pressure from both the Council and the Commission. Parliament's concern in particular has been the repression of the Kurdish minority in Turkey and the violation of international humanitarian law by the Turkish army in their actions against the guerrillas of the separatist Kurdish Workers' Party (the PKK), in which Kurdish villages have been evacuated, bombed and destroyed in operations described as 'savage' (Human Rights Watch 1994, p. 244).

In contrast, inter-governmental wishes to re-establish an aid and trade package since 1986 appear to be influenced more by Turkey's strategic position and the desire not to disrupt the NATO military alliance, with human rights issues pushed aside. As a lower middle-income state, Turkey is not aid-dependent, and aid sanctions will have limited *economic* impact. Nevertheless, given the strong desire of most recent Turkish governments to join the EU, aid sanctions confer a powerful symbolic message, with the potential to leverage improvements in the human rights situation, notably the treatment of the Kurds.[146] Any such potential was lost, however, by the lack of a coherent and consistent human rights policy, with contradictory messages received by the Turkish authorities from the parliament and from the other EU institutions. pressure on the European Parliament to drop its opposition was finally successful in December 1995.[147]

9.3   The non-cases

This pattern of inconsistent application of policy is highlighted by the further evidence of five country cases where political conditionality has *not* been applied, despite government records of gross and persistent abuses of human rights.[148] Five mini country case-studies are presented of these 'non-cases', notably all in regions other than sub-Saharan Africa, where no such case could be found. Each of these outlines the human rights and democracy situation, provides a brief aid profile, and analyses the reasons why aid sanctions have not been applied.[149]

9.3.1 Indonesia[150]

Indonesia: political profile

The example of Indonesia provides some of the most compelling evidence of the inconsistency and double standards of Northern governments in their non-implementation of human rights and democracy policies. Two human rights issues remain prominent. First, the indisputable evidence of continuing 'serious human rights abuses' committed by the government in the context of a 'strongly authoritarian' political system, as reported by the US Department of State (1996, Indonesia Country Report p. 1). Second, the continuing occupation of East Timor, invaded and annexed in 1975, in which up to one-third of the indigenous population is estimated to have been killed.[151] The Dili massacre in November 1991 re-focused world attention on East Timor, with smuggled film showing an estimated 200 unarmed mourners killed by the Indonesian army at the funeral of a young independence supporter.

Human rights abuses by the Indonesian government have been worst in areas where its sovereignty is most contested, not only East Timor, but also in Irian Jaya and Aceh (Sumatra), where secessionist movements face 'harsh repression' (US Department of State 1996, Indonesia Country Report p. 1). Yet, violations of civil and political rights are not limited to these territories. Human Rights Watch (1994, p. 157) perceives a pattern of abuse 'characterised by military intervention in virtually all aspects of public life and by the arbitrary exercise of authority by President Suharto', while the Department of State (1996, Indonesia Country Report p. 2) reports 'severe limitations on freedoms of speech, press, assembly, and association'. The armed forces have sizeable representation in the legislature, allocated 100 (out of 500) seats, appointed directly by the President. Specific mechanisms of political control include: the banning of political parties, with the Communist Party remaining outlawed since 1965; press censorship, with three publications closed in June 1994 in a clampdown prior to the Asia Pacific Economic Co-operation Forum (APEC) Summit in November in Jakarta; the denial of workers' rights, notably the ability to form independent trade unions; and the violent dispersal of peaceful demonstrations (Human Rights Watch 1994, p. 158).

Indonesia: aid profile

What is the aid record? Although having recently graduated to classification as a lower middle income country, Indonesia continues to receive a substantial amount of bilateral aid, with gross disbursements of over $2 billion each year since 1990, and as much as $2.6 billion in 1992 and 1993. Despite the reports of its own State Department, the US government remains a major donor, including the provision of Economic Support Funds and military training.[152] British aid is both substantial and rose considerably in the 1990s. It more than doubled in the first half of the 1990s, increasing from £25.4 million in 1990/91 to £57 million in 1995/96, making Indonesia the third largest recipient of British aid (World Development Movement 1995, Table 1, p. 2, and January 1997, p. 6).[153] Despite condemnation of the Dili massacre, EU assistance has continued unrestricted as part of its agreement with the ASEAN member states.[154] Sweden has relatively small programmes of technical co-operation in Indonesia, but which have remained unrestricted. Other major bilateral donors are Japan – by far the largest – as well as Germany and France.

On human rights grounds, the Indonesian government was a clear candidate for the application of aid sanctions as a means of pressurising the government to implement quite specific reforms, for example, the protection of workers' rights or press freedom, as well as to enter UN-brokered negotiations to resolve the status of East Timor. Yet, with the exception of the Dutch after the Dili massacre, no aid sanctions have been imposed on Indonesia.

On the contrary, the annual World Bank-chaired Consultative Group meetings have been characterised by praise of Indonesia's economic achievements, with virtually no mention of human rights or good governance concerns and no human rights conditionality imposed. At the Consultative Group meeting in July 1992, the first after the November 1991 massacre, the US government alone publicly raised human rights issues, although Canada registered its protest by not attending. At the June 1996 meeting, not only did the 'donors reaffirm strong support for Indonesia', but their commendations extended to extolling the relationship with Indonesia as 'one of the best models of productive partnership between a developing country and the donor community' (*World Bank News*, June 27 1996, p. 8).

Indonesia: why no conditionality?

How do we explain the absence of aid conditionality in this case? It is evident that trading and investment interests take priority. Indonesia's sustained economic growth, combined with its large population, make it an increasingly important trading partner and an attractive market, as well as a prominent location of foreign direct investment, with the latter reaching record levels in 1995. Northern governments, themselves influenced by powerful business interests, wish to use their development assistance to improve their own 'market position' within Indonesia, and to enhance the financial opportunities available. It is difficult to explain the remarkable rise in British aid in terms other than the promotion of British commercial interests. With regard to East Timor, Indonesia's interests in the area's mineral riches are shared by the industrialised nations. In 1991, the Indonesian and the Australian governments signed a contract with 12 companies to extract a billion barrels of oil from Timorese waters, the consortium being led by Royal Dutch Shell (joint British and Dutch) and Chevron (US), along with six Australian companies (Instituto del Tercer Mundo 1995, p. 222).

In such a context, any human rights concerns are swiftly overwhelmed, and the likelihood of aid sanctions becomes highly improbable.

The picture gets worse, however, when arms sales are brought into consideration. Whereas other trade and investment may not in itself have a deleterious effect on the human rights situation, arms and muni-tions sold to a repressive regime are likely to be used against the internal opposition rather than an external threat. The US and the UK are the biggest arms exporters to Indonesia; indeed, since 1992, the UK has supplanted the US in first place, with Indonesia the fourth largest buyer of British arms in the developing world (World Development Movement, 1995, p. 58). Portugal and Italy have both banned arms sales to Indonesia, though other EU states, Germany, for example, are also willing to supply weapons. UK exports include the notorious Hawk jets, used in low-flight attacks in East Timor (ibid.). Alarmingly, the World Development Movement, a UK NGO, has drawn up evidence to link British aid to Indonesia with the promotion of arms sales, in total contra-diction to official policy. Peaks of aid to Indonesia, between 1983 and 1985 and again in 1993 and 1995/96, coincide with the negotiations of major arms deals (ibid. pp. 51–2 and World Development Movement 1997, p. 6). This, of course, is similar to the allegations made against the UK govern-ment, though denied by them, of a link between aid and arms deals with Malaysia, being part of the whole Pergau Dam affair.

Turning to the geo-strategic arena, President Suharto's regime was valued by the US government in particular as a cold war ally in the regional struggle against communism.[155] While communism is no longer a political threat, Indonesia doubtless remains valued as some counterweight to the regional muscle beginning to be flexed by China.

The example of Indonesia has shown how the policy of the promotion of human rights and democracy through development aid can be turned completely on its head in three clear stages. First, the non-implementation of aid sanctions as an instrument to promote human rights, subordinate to the promotion of donor country business interests. Second, the maintenance of arms sales to the very forces responsible for serious human rights abuses. Third, the somersault in policy is complete when aid itself is misused as a mechanism to promote arms sales.

9.3.2   Sri Lanka

Sri Lanka: political profile

Despite having a multi-party democratic polity, Sri Lankan politics and society have been dominated since the 1980s by armed conflict on two fronts. First, Tamil secessionists, the Liberation Tigers of Tamil Eelam (LTTE), have fought with government forces since 1983 for a separate state in the north-east of the island, with almost 20 000 killed. Second, in the south, Marxist opposition led by the *Janatha Vimukthi Peramuna* (JVP), the People's Liberation Front, engaged in an armed insurgency against the government, most intense between 1987 and 1990, with a further five-figure death toll before their defeat by the security forces.[156] Undoubtedly, gross human rights violations (including civilian massacre) have been committed by all sides, with ample evidence documented by international human rights organisations. Guerrilla groups, however, do not receive official development aid, and the concern here is that government atrocities have not been the subject of any condemnation or sanctions. Government forces were responsible for detentions, 'disappearances' and extrajudicial executions on a massive scale in both the north-east and the south.[157] A trend in decreased human rights abuses from 1992 was reversed with the cessation of a brief cease-fire by the LTTE in April 1995 and the resumption of fighting. Human rights abuses by both sides in the renewed conflict have included hundreds of civilian deaths in government air bombings (Human Rights Watch 1995, pp. 172–3).

Sri Lanka: aid profile

Bilateral aid to Sri Lanka had remained fairly constant for the five years up to 1994, with gross disbursements averaging about $425 million per annum. The US is the second largest aid donor to Sri Lanka, after Japan, with UK aid also significant. US assistance also includes military training, of which an element is stated to be human rights training. Sri Lanka is one of Sweden's 19 programme countries to whom aid is concentrated. There is no evidence of aid restrictions. A new trade and co-operation agreement between the EU and the Sri Lankan government came into effect in April 1995 and included a human rights and democracy clause as an essential element. The upsurge of human rights abuses since then, including by the government, has not led so far to the invoking of that clause by the EU.

Sri Lanka: why no conditionality?

Why has there been no linkage of aid to improvements in the Sri Lankan government's human rights record, either at the height of the civil conflicts in the late 1980s and early 1990s or since mid-1995? Three reasons are explored.

First, an up-turn in the human rights picture in Sri Lanka is discernible from 1991 onwards, and the lack of donor conditionality could be attributed to this progressive trend, despite it bottoming-out from an abysmal level of human rights performance. Such an explanation is inadequate, however. Quite specific improvements could have been required of the Sri Lankan government, for example: the investigation of extrajudicial killings and disappearances linked to the security forces. Such conditionality measures would have been particularly appropriate given the situation of human rights reforms being undertaken not by a new government but by the old regime, itself responsible for the abuses. This opportunity was not taken by the donors.

Second, any inclination to criticise the Sri Lankan government's appalling human rights record was probably tempered by the ideological sympathy felt towards the regime, given its formal democratic credentials and the violent opposition it faced from both separatist and Marxist guerrillas. This could account for a disposition to turn a 'blind eye' to the counterinsurgency methods used by government forces.

Third, trade is also a significant determinant, and it would appear that trading relations with Sri Lanka have generally been accorded a greater priority than human rights. During the 1980s, the Sri Lankan government introduced economic liberalisation policies, offering new prospects for direct foreign investment, especially in 'export-processing zones'. Consequentially, trade has grown in importance with many Northern countries.

9.3.3 Algeria

Algeria: political profile

Since the cancellation of the parliamentary elections in January 1992, Algeria has degenerated into a bloody civil war between the military-led government and radical Islamic armed groups, with unofficial estimates of up to 50 000 Algerians killed by late 1995, including many unarmed civilians. Gross human rights violations have been committed by both sides. The Islamist extremists, notably the *Groupe Islamique Armée* (GIA – Armed Islamic Group), have waged a campaign of terror and intimidation, responsible for countless atrocities since January 1992. For its part the government has engaged in torture, 'disappearances' and arbitrary killings against both the armed Islamist groups and unarmed civilians.[158] The issue of the abuse of women is a highly disturbing aspect of the war, with women subject to attacks by both sides.

Algeria: aid profile

As a lower middle income country, Algeria receives a modest amount of development assistance, with gross bilateral disbursements averaging $349.4 million per annum between 1990 and 1994. It is an undeniable example of where an abrupt halt to the democratisation process through military intervention, with subsequent gross human rights violations by state forces, has not entailed aid sanctions. On the contrary, development assistance from the European Commission to the Algerian government has increased dramatically from approximately $10 million in the early 1990s to $46m and $37m in 1993 and 1994, as has French assistance, the biggest donor, with grant aid of over $100m each year since 1991. The EU and its member states together provide over 80 per cent of all bilateral aid. The UK is a very minor donor and Sweden contributes only emergency aid and assistance to NGOs. The US provides no economic assistance but it does furnish an annual grant for military training.[159]

The EU has prioritised the strengthening of its relations with the countries of North Africa and the Middle East, culminating with the Barcelona Declaration of the Euro-Mediterranean partnership, agreed in November 1995. This involves a large increase in aid to the region generally and the negotiation of a new Association Agreement with each country. It is stated that these will all include a human rights and democracy clause as an essential element with an associated suspension clause.[160] In the case of Algeria, it is anticipated that it will be subject to a circle-squaring exercise in order to avoid the implementation of aid restrictive measures.[161]

Algeria: why no conditionality?

The treatment of the Algerian military-led authorities provides a sharp contrast to the punitive measures taken against other countries by both the EU and the US where a breakdown in democratisation has occurred, notably in sub-Saharan Africa.[162] Why were such measures not taken in the case of Algeria? Why have different standards of human rights and democratic practices apparently been applied to Algeria? The key factor would seem to be opposition to Islamic fundamentalism, with human rights policy abandoned.

There is a somewhat weak, pro-democracy justification for the cancellation of the January 1992 elections, arguing that the Islamist movement, after gaining power by democratic means, would then have abolished democracy. Whether such arguments were right or wrong, they became increasingly superfluous as the subsequent political violence unfolded, and neither side displayed any commitment to human rights or democratic practices. What is instructive, however, is the one-sided approach of Western governments and their failure to be even-handed, with condemnation of Islamist atrocities contrasted with uncritical support for the Algerian authorities. Within the EU, the French government is the key player, providing active and unconditional support to the military-led Algerian government in their attempts to crush the radical Islamist opposition. This support has not been publicly contested by any other member state or by the US. EU policy is driven by the strong motivation to stem the rise of Islamic fundamentalism. Radical Islam is seen as a threat to political stability in the region, with an Islamist victory in Algeria resulting in a domino effect in neighbouring countries and a wave of migration to southern Europe, especially France. Like the defeat of communism before it, there are no objections to the means used, including violations of human rights and the basic tenets of humanitarian law. In the conflict between principles and self-interests, the latter wins handsomely. The priority is the defeat of an ideological opponent in Europe's 'backyard' and the protection of 'fortress Europe'.

9.3.4 Egypt

Egypt: political profile
The constitution of the republic of Egypt describes it as a multi-party democracy in which human rights are guaranteed. Egyptian politics and society have long been characterised, however, by the suppression of internal dissent by the government, involving restrictions on democratic processes and abuses of civil and political rights. The primary mechanism is the state of emergency in force without interruption since October 1981, with broad powers of detention resulting in tens of thousands of arbitrary arrests of 'political suspects' without charge or trial, and related torture (Human Rights Watch 1991,

p. 630).[163] The elections in 1995 were characterized by the jailing of leading opposition candidates and campaigners (Human Rights Watch 1995, p. 269). Such undemocratic practices have resulted in a political system so dominated by the ruling National Democratic Party that the US Department of State, hardly an antagonist of the Egyptian government, recognises that 'the people do not have a meaningful ability to change their government' (US Department of State 1996, Egypt Country Report p. 1).

Moreover, the overall human rights situation has deteriorated considerably with the escalation from 1992 of armed opposition to the Egyptian government from radical Islamist groups, with both sides culpable of serious abuses. The response of the Egyptian government to the armed opposition has been two-fold. The first is the intensification of pre-existing practices of violent repression. Such methods are primarily directed against the Islamist militants, but with 'frequent victimisation of non-combatants as well' (US Department of State 1996, Egypt Country Report, p. 2). Allegations of extrajudicial killings by the security forces have become common in an environment of impunity (US Department of State 1995b and 1996, Egypt Country Reports; Human Rights Watch 1994, p. 264 and 1995, p. 270). The second response has been to generalise the state clampdown with significant restrictions on the civil and political liberties of non-violent opponents and other dissenting voices, including the curtailment of press freedoms.

Egypt: aid profile

Egypt receives very substantial official aid, with gross bilateral assistance of between $2.5 billion and $4 billion each year between 1990 and 1994. The US is by far the biggest donor, contributing over $2 billion per annum in foreign aid, though the majority of this is military assistance. The European Commission also provides very considerable assistance, with net average disbursements of $121.8 per annum in the same period. This makes Egypt one of the largest recipients of aid from the EU. As with Algeria, Egypt comes under the strengthened Euro-Mediterranean partnership, with the new Association Agreement to include a human rights and democracy clause, likewise anticipated to be the subject of a circle-squaring exercise. The UK is a minor donor and the Swedish programme is also very small. Other major donors are France, Germany, Italy and Japan, with Canada, Denmark and the Netherlands providing not insubstantial sums when compared with their programmes for other countries. German and French assistance, including debt write-offs, has averaged $424m and $265m respectively per annum between 1990–94.

Egypt: why no conditionality?

The failure to link economic aid to human rights and democracy conditions replicates some features in common with Algeria, though with the US as the key player here to whom the EU states tend to defer. Human rights abuses and undemocratic practices are again consciously ignored in the context of overriding foreign policy considerations.

Egypt occupies an important geo-strategic location in relation to the Middle East, North Africa and the Horn of Africa. A friendly government in Egypt fulfils a number of important roles in the achievement of a number of Western foreign policy objectives. First, Egypt continues to be an essential ally for the success of the Arab–Israeli peace process. Second, a friendly Egypt plays a key role in mobilising the support of moderate Arab states as circumstances arise, most notably in the Gulf War of 1991 after the Iraqi invasion of Kuwait. Quite explicitly, the US has a cold war-type understanding with the Egyptian government – aid in return for political support. Third, the retention of a pro-Western government in Egypt is a requisite for the wider objective of fostering a wider alliance of moderate forces that share the goals of free markets and secular, liberal states. Fourth, related to this last point, is the struggle against Islamic fundamentalism, perceived as the foremost threat to such an objective and to future stability in the Middle East.

In reviewing the importance of an allied Egyptian government to Western foreign policy objectives, it becomes evident that the silence on human rights abuses and undemocratic practices is not merely due to such considerations taking priority. The repression of the opposition and the restrictions on democratic processes in themselves serve Western governments' interests in maintaining the ruling élite in power. In contrast, an active, multi-party polity would raise the potential for undesired changes in the power-holders, particular when the main opposition is the Muslim Brotherhood. It is a silence by the US and by the EU which condones and approves the actions of the Egyptian government as necessary for their own objectives.

9.3.5   Colombia[164]

Colombia: political profile

A democracy in name, Colombia is one of the most violent societies in the world, with approximately 30 000 Colombians murdered each year, including about 10 political killings each day. Colombia is most well known for violence related to drug-trafficking, but the rate of political murders has been the highest in the Americas for almost the past decade, matched only by Peru at the height of the *Sendero Luminoso* insurgency. Political killings stem mainly from the armed conflict between leftist guerrilla groups and government security forces allied with paramilitary groups. The latter also target non-violent political parties and economic and social groups in death squad activities. Human rights violations are committed by all sides. Yet it is the role of government security forces and the allied paramilitary groups that stands out, responsible for the majority of the 3000 to 4000 political murders each year.[165]

The impunity with which the armed forces and the paramilitary groups can operate is a principal cause of the continuing gross abuse of human rights in Colombia. A fundamental flaw in the Colombian judicial system is the jurisdiction of military tribunals over cases involving members of the armed forces, as well as over civilians on public order offences (for example, leftist groups). Human Rights Watch (1995, p. 81) reports how 'Military tribunals continued systematically to cover up crimes and absolve the military and police officers involved'. The Colombian government has repeatedly failed to reform this judicial defect, and there has been no attempt by Northern governments to leverage such a change through aid conditionality. Indeed, there is no indication of any aid restrictions.

Colombia: aid profile

As a lower middle-income country, Colombia receives a moderate amount of bilateral aid, with gross average disbursements of $231.6 million between 1990 and 1994. The biggest provider of foreign assistance is the US, though the development assistance component of this is relatively small, eclipsed by the substantial sums provided in ESF, military aid and counter-narcotics assistance, all of direct benefit to the Colombian state. The largest official aid donor in recent years has been Germany. European Commission aid has risen in the first half of the 1990s from a modest $5.2m (net) in 1990 to $12–14m in 1993 and 1994. EU aid to the Colombian government is part of the agreement with Andean Pact countries, signed in 1993 with a human rights and democracy clause as an essential element. The UK provides a small amount of assistance, with Sweden contributing small sums to NGOs and in technical assistance. Between them, the EU and its member states provided approximately 70 per cent of Colombia's official aid between 1990 and 1994.[166]

Colombia: why no conditionality?

Despite the overwhelming evidence of Colombian government forces' involvement in gross human rights abuses, there is no indication of any aid restrictions. Why has the Colombian government escaped criticism? Three reasons are put forward.

First, Northern donors are less disposed to impose conditionality on a democratically elected civilian government with a rhetorical commitment to human rights. Yet, the example of Colombia vividly demonstrates how a formal democracy far from guarantees the protection of civil and political liberties. A government must be judged on the determination it expresses and the effectiveness it displays in combating and preventing abuses; and the efforts of the Colombian government in this respect can be judged to be woefully inadequate.

Second, there is deference by European governments to the US as the most influential external actor. US policy in Colombia is dominated by its 'war on drugs' in the Andean countries. This entails the provision of counter-narcotics assistance in the form of financial aid, equipment and training to the very police and military forces that are responsible for gross human rights abuses, making it difficult to square this with human rights concerns.

A third factor is an ideological leftover from the cold war. There remains a predilection towards support for governments engaged in 'counter-insurgency' activities to defeat leftist guerrillas and to play down the human rights abuses committed in doing so. This is particularly characteristic of US policy, given their provision of military assistance and training.

9.4 Summary of findings: inconsistency and legitimacy

The findings from all three lines of investigation in this section reveal a pattern of selective and inconsistent application of policy.

First, the regional analysis of the 29 country cases displayed the overwhelming extent to which aid sanctions have been taken in sub-Saharan Africa, where Northern governments have little to lose. In comparison, restrictive measures are much less common in other regions where Northern economic and political interests are more prevalent.

Second, the general lack of correlation between the degree of human rights violations and the level of sanctions imposed indicate a failure to implement human rights policy on the basis of objective criteria. This is illustrated in particular by the evidence from the three country cases, China, Nigeria and Turkey; all demonstrate how the level of response to human rights abuses is muted and ambiguous where countervailing interests are held to be more manifest. In China, there was a token response to the Tiananmen Square massacre. The degree of international condemnation of the actions of the Abacha regime in Nigeria was not matched by robust practical measures, with aid restrictions as part of a wider package of military, trade and diplomatic sanctions. The closeness of bilateral relations between Turkey and both the US and the EU provide the chance for significant leverage towards human rights improvements, but such opportunities have largely been foregone.

Third, the evidence of the five 'non-cases', where aid sanctions are conspicuous by their absence, provides further confirmation of the subordination of human rights and democracy policies to other dominant foreign policy concerns. In the cold war period this was mainly attributable to geo-strategic considerations. These remain evident, especially in the Middle East, where EU and US security interests take priority over human rights issues – for example, in Algeria and Egypt. After the end of the cold war, however, other factors start to carry more weight. Foremost of these is the pursuit of economic self-interest by Northern donors, with trade and investment considerations prioritised – for example, in East Asia. In addition, old and new elements of ideology continue to result in selective condemnations. In continuity with cold war practices, human rights violations by governments engaged in civil wars against left-wing guerrillas tend to be overlooked, as the examples of Colombia and Sri Lanka show. New Western fears concerning the rise of Islamic fundamentalism in Algeria and Egypt have led to fresh examples of government abuses of human rights in counterinsurgency campaigns being tolerated and condoned.

Instances of civil war, encountered in four out of the five non-cases, undoubtedly present aid donors with complex political situations. While not ignoring these complexities, including the difficulties of governments faced by insurgent groups, it remains paramount that objective judgements on alleged human rights abuses must be based on the nature of the acts perpetrated and not the identity of the perpetrators. Failure to conduct counterinsurgency within the framework of international humanitarian law and with full respect for human rights must remain subject to condemnation. These cases of civil wars also indicate a tendency by donors to overlook the roots of violent opposition in the undemocratic practices of incumbent regimes, for example, in Algeria and Egypt, and a failure to condition development assistance on specific political reforms, for example, reform of the flawed justice system in Colombia or the investigation of extrajudicial killings in

Sri Lanka. It is worth recalling that such precise conditionality has been shown to be relatively more effective in leveraging reforms.

The evidence from all three lines of enquiry demonstrate conclusively that the post-cold war shift in aid policy rhetoric has not been matched by a change in practice. There is continuity from the cold war period in the selective manner in which Northern governments approach issues of human rights and democracy. A greater propensity to implement aid sanctions has been observed only in countries where Northern economic or political interests are absent or have declined, notably in sub-Saharan Africa. Elsewhere, human rights criteria remain subordinate to other competing foreign policy concerns. Notwithstanding, there has been some evolution in practice in the 1990s, and two developments are notable. First, the anti-communism of the cold war years has been succeeded by anti-Islamic fundamentalism. Second, the geo-strategic concerns have been replaced by trade and investment as the primary countervailing factors. Such developments, however, merely represent 'continuity in change'.

What is the impact of this inconsistency on policy legitimacy? The UK has explicitly recognised the significance of a consistent approach to human rights, and the damaging effect of inconsistency. Yet the British government itself, in common with the other donors examined here, has manifestly failed to apply human rights criteria in an objective manner. The implications are self-evident. Donor credibility in implementing its new policy agenda is undermined. The inherent legitimacy of the policy, derived from international human rights law, becomes corrupted.

The implications of these findings are discussed further in the Conclusion in Part IV, with proposals made on strengthening the normative framework of policy implementation.

Part IV
Conclusion

10
Conclusion

External actors seek to, and indeed do, play a role in the democratisation process in other countries. Since, the 1990s, aid policy has been one new means by which such influence has been attempted by Northern governments. As democratisation is essentially an internal process, it is recognized that impact can only be modest, limited mainly to supporting internal pro-democracy elements and to applying pressure on governments in conjunction with local actors.

Looking at political aid programmes and aid sanctions in turn, this conclusion focuses on critical issues that have an adverse impact on both policy effectiveness and legitimacy. A series of concluding proposals are made for each instrument, aiming to strengthening its normative basis as well as its effectiveness.

10.1 Political aid programmes

10.1.1 Critical issues

To what extent can political aid effectively influence the process of democratisation in aid recipient countries? What limitations and constraints were discovered, both in practical and normative terms?

Although Northern governments have confounded some critics' expectations that democracy promotion would be restricted to a narrow, procedural model, political aid has been found wanting in a number of respects, nonetheless. In these concluding discussions, the problems and constraints associated with both governmental and non-governmental assistance are explored, followed by a series of proposals suggesting improvements to donor practices.

Strengthening democratic government

Regarding political aid to government beneficiaries, a key constraint pertains to the degree of political commitment towards democratisation shown by both recipient and donor governments. This relates to questions of political will, power relations and self-interests. Generally speaking, progress in democratisation occurs largely through the actions of political leaders, either acting in accordance with their own agendas or under pressure from societal actors. Whether pro-democracy influences predominate in a country depends on the outcome of struggles between competing political actors and social classes, with commitment to democratic political reform varying between different actors at different historical moments, often dependent on whether such reforms are perceived as congruent with self-interests. Such considerations seem largely absent from the political aid agenda, however. Indeed, there is more evidence of the effectiveness of political aid being undermined by the lack of political commitment on the part of both recipient and donor governments. Such findings are most stark in those country cases where, in the context of government abuses of human rights, not only are aid restrictions *not* imposed, but also overall aid programmes contain a political aid component directed to government beneficiaries. Examples include US assistance to Egypt and Colombia and UK assistance to Indonesia under President Suharto.

Why are political aid resources disbursed to governments where efficacy is so unlikely? One explanation pertains to what Carothers (1997, p. 122) calls the 'missing link of power', precisely involving a failure to address power relations in a society and ignoring the resistance of powerful actors to a democratisation agenda. In this way, democracy assistance providers presume that it is possible to reduce the democratic deficit of key government institutions, 'without grappling with the deep-seated interests of the actors involved' (ibid.). Democracy assistance thus becomes a technical exercise, with the underlying reasons for the democratic failings of institutions left unaddressed. For example, in judicial reform, it is not asked 'why the judiciary is in such a lamentable state, whose interests it serves in its current form, and whose interests would be threatened by reforms to the system' (ibid.), with clear adverse implications for effectiveness. Another explanation offered here focuses on donors' commitment to democratisation being compromised by the operation of other agendas. As discussed, the selection of countries for US and UK political aid programmes was driven in a number of instances by donor governments seeking political influence in order to further their own commercial and strategic interests. Therefore, however unconducive the prevailing conditions for democratic reform and however resistant the actors involved, support is extended to the 'administration of justice' in Colombia (by the US) and for 'police training' in Indonesia (by the UK), as part of a package of assistance to governments favoured for reasons of geo-political (as in the former) or economic interests (as in the latter). This analysis questions not only the naïvety of strategy (as Carothers) but also questions the genuineness and seriousness of donor intent and motivation.

To influence the process of democratisation more effectively, there is a need for greater discrimination in the type of governments and governmental institutions that are strengthened and for recognition of circumstances where democratising the state is best pursued through support for non-government actors. Of the donors examined, only Sweden makes an explicit distinction between regime types, respectful or not of civil and political rights, with implications for the measures undertaken and type of organisations assisted. While such a distinction has been commended, the need for a variety of strategies can be extended much beyond a mere authoritarian/democratic divide (something that is examined further below). Indeed, the fact that a government has been *voted* into power does not guarantee a commitment to democracy. As Carothers (1995, p. 67) points out, it is 'perfectly possible for a newly elected government to represent the apparent triumph of democracy but not to be genuinely interested in strengthening either the independence of the judiciary, the autonomy of the parliament or the power of local administrators'. Such outcomes are most likely where democratic transition has not resulted in a change of government, with the ruling party retaining power. Analyses of democratic transition processes indicate that they are frequently initiated from above by incumbent authoritarian governments in an attempt to maintain and legitimate their hold on power, albeit in contexts of internal pressure and threats to their legitimacy. It is also quite possible that a new party in power may be less enthusiastic in office about implementing the democratic reforms they advocated in opposition. Indeed, one can assert with confidence that governments in general are more concerned about power and how to retain it, while it is the populace (or society) who advocate democratic controls.

There are two inferences from this problematisation of government institution building and the need for greater discrimination in the contexts where support is provided. First, it is incumbent on both recipient *and* donor governments to demonstrate a commitment to democratic reforms, with outside observers encouraged to adopt a watchful eye on their seriousness and genuineness. Supporting democratisation is far more complex than merely providing resources and the technical capacity that are lacking in a given context, that is, the tasks donors can do most simply. Part of the required analysis is an ongoing assessment of the potential for, and obstacles to, democratic reform, with a focus on identifying the pro-reform actors, both within and without government. Second, following on from this, it is clear that the aim of democratising state institutions itself involves more than a top-down exercise. It is somewhat naïve to expect governments to take action of their own accord that will limit their power. In all societies, the role of non-government actors is essential in applying pressure for democratic reform and in ensuring democratic sustainability by maintaining vigilance over the performance and nature of state institutions. For example, the transformation of a politicised judiciary into one characterised by greater independence is likely to require pressure from those outside groups, such as human rights groups and professional legal associations, articulating dissatisfaction with the inadequacies and injustices of legal decision-making processes. Highlighting the significance of such non-government groups moves the argument onto the next issue, the participation of civil society organisations in democracy building.

Strengthening civil society

Donors have extended considerable support to the objective of strengthening civil society. The argument advanced here has been to affirm the significance of civil society to the democratisation process, as a sphere of democratic practice itself and for its role in democratising state institutions. Findings have indicated, however, that donor support to civil society has not been subject to sufficient critical examination, with adverse implications for its effectiveness in enhancing democratisation.

As with support to governments, a key constraint pertains to the lack of discrimination in the type of groups assisted, with a significant proportion of aid to non-state beneficiaries extended to organisations with questionable pertinence to democracy promotion. The origins of this problem stem from the lack of conceptual clarity in the use of the term civil society, with only USAID providing some definitional focus in the period examined, as well as from the prevailing assumption of the state and civil society as separate spheres in which civil society acts as a counterweight to the state. The conceptual confusion, fuelled by a 're-labelling' exercise, led to a range of non-state projects being classified as 'strengthening civil society' as part of political aid, despite many having little apparent relevance to democratisation. Regarding its 'countervailing' influence, it was argued (in Chapter 1) that civil society organisations are frequently not autonomous bodies and can be closely related to the state. Although more difficult to ascertain from project data, it is likely that some civil society organisations are either created by government, especially given the attraction of donor funding, or associated with the ruling party, or 'captured' or 'penetrated' either by government or by donors themselves.

In all, the complexity of the nature of civil society and its relationship with the state requires more thought and analysis by donors. The implication again is of the importance of extensive knowledge of the local political context at individual country level. Two aspects in particular can be highlighted. One is to identify those particular organisations that are most relevant for the defence and promotion of democracy. The other is to explore the degree of overlap and inter-relationship between non-government actors and the state. The inference is that political aid can then be concentrated on those civil society organisations that are specifically pro-democratic and more genuinely autonomous, thus more able to press for political reform. The choice of pertinent organisations will clearly vary, dependent on both the specific country and the stage of the democratisation process.

The issue of strategy

Clearly, the core strategy (outlined in Chapter 3) of a check-list of institutions and a process of institutional modelling is inadequate, with a variety of strategies required. Different strategies are needed for different phases of the democratisation process, for example, from authoritarian contexts, to those where political liberalisation has not resulted in electoral transition, to the range of transitional situations from electoral facade to where regimes are consolidating genuine change. The appropriateness of strategy is also highly dependent on the specific country context, with considerable variation between, for example, conflict-ridden and post-conflict societies, those emerging from military rule, those characterised by weak or collapsed states. The requisite strategy will also change with circumstances, for instance, where democratisation stagnates or backslides. Additionally, a variety of models need to be examined, learning not only from established democracies, but also, and perhaps more pertinently, from the experiences of recent successful transitional cases on a regional or comparative basis. Optimistically, there is the potential for progress along the democratic continuum in most countries globally. Nevertheless, if external agencies are to provide support, it is imperative that coherent and appropriate strategies are devised to promote such democratic potential in widely varying contexts.

Such instrumental discussions of increasing the effectiveness of donor support through attention to strategy, in turn, raise a wider, normative issue pertaining to donor legitimacy. Who determines the appropriate strategy? How is it devised? What gives donors the right to select which state and non-state actors should be the beneficiaries of their munificence? How is non-partisanship maintained? How can the external orientation of domestic politics be reconciled with sovereignty? The encouragement of democratic dialogue at a national level between government and non-state actors is a proposed remedy to such questions.

Strengthening national democratic dialogue

Dialogue is fundamental to democracy, itself a form of political decision-making through discussion and negotiation, without recourse to superior force and violence. The importance of dialogue extends to addressing the asymmetrical power relations between Northern and Southern actors, including within democracy assistance itself. It is suggested that the concept of 'national democratic dialogue' has a dual significance, both in reinforcing internal democratic processes and in providing a more legitimate foundation to donor activities. The notion of national democratic dialogue stems partly from the National Conferences held in Francophone African countries at the beginning of the 1990s as a mechanism for the transition to democratic rule, but proposed as a regular mechanism. Initiated in Benin in February 1990, the National Conference involved dialogue between a range of political representatives and, in this first instance, was successful in achieving a change in political regime through negotiation. The concept of democratic dialogue is currently promoted by the International Institute for Democracy and Electoral Assistance (IDEA) including in the context of ACP–EU relations (International IDEA 1998).

National democratic dialogue involves the encouragement of a formal and structured dialogue on the democratisation process, bringing together key stakeholders, both government and non-state. Dialogue encourages political debate on the state of democracy and democratisation in a given country context, addressing both obstacles to and opportunities for further progress. Clearly, debate involves differences and disagreements, but the aim is to seek consensus on the priorities for democratic development. The process of dialogue stimulates an ongoing political dynamic between elections. Outcomes can be at both organisational and sectoral levels, with the former including the strengthening of pro-reform networks, and the latter involving the identification of key areas of reform. Additionally, donors are provided with opportunities for support through external funding that have emerged out of an internally-driven process.

The concept of national democratic dialogue is potentially a key to a number of outstanding issues in discussions of the role of external agencies in democratisation. First, it reasserts the primacy of democratisation as an internal process to which external assistance is subordinated. The lead role of democratic government is respected, while ensuring the participation of civil society. Second, guidance on appropriate democratisation strategies is provided by the outcomes of national dialogue, a shift from external prescriptions and providing a more legitimate foundation for external support. The integrity of donor efforts is more assured given that they are directed from within the recipient country, rather than influenced by hidden agendas and/or particular self-interest. Third, recipient government commitment to democratisation is enhanced through their engagement in dialogue on democratic consolidation with the range of non-state stakeholders. Fourth, coming full circle, the process of dialogue itself contributes to the fundamental objective of promoting democratisation. By its nature, it reinforces and deepens the democratic process, encouraging the development of a democratic culture and providing a mechanism for conflict prevention and/or resolution. Indeed, donor governments are encouraged to introduce such a model to address the democratic deficits in their own countries.

10.1.2   Towards democratic development: concluding proposals

One aim of this work has been to critically evaluate the implementation of political aid measures by Northern governments. Finally, a series of concluding proposals are offered as a contribution to ongoing discussion on the promotion of democratic development, aimed at strengthening the legitimacy of democracy assistance as well as its effectiveness.

1. An increase in the political aid component of overall aid budgets to at least 10 per cent would be more in line with the prioritisation accorded to this area.

2. 'Mainstreaming' political aid as an integral element of individual country aid programmes enables greater coherence in the design, implementation, monitoring and evaluation of political aid activities. Short-term projects, typical of budget line funding, are inappropriate for support to the long-term and complex process of democratisation.

3. Nonetheless, *human rights and democracy budget lines remain an important mechanism for channelling support to non-governmental organisations where non-democratic regimes retain power.* Support to the organisations that defend and promote civil and political rights in such contexts is frequently crucial to sustaining prospects for future democratisation. Assistance can be disbursed direct to local human rights and pro-democracy groups or through international human rights organisations, whose expertise and comparative advantage in this sphere has been noted.

4. *Country assessments are an important methodological tool* to determine appropriate strategy and to facilitate the design of political aid programmes. Undertaken on a regular basis, assessments examine the evolving nature of the democratisation process, with wide coverage of both governmental institutions and civil society, as well as broader knowledge of the country's political context. Where national democratic dialogue occurs, as proposed above, this *itself* will largely perform the function of a country assessment. Otherwise, it is necessary that country assessment methodology includes consultation and dialogue with the range of local stakeholders. Not only does this ensure greater inclusiveness of opinion, but also that the consequent strategy has local endorsement.

5. *Inclusion of co-operation with local civil society organisations is an essential element* of overall political aid programmes. One dilemma attached to 'mainstreaming' political aid is an inherent tendency towards 'top-down' government institution building, given that recipient governments become the main partner in co-operation programmes, yet it is necessary that a substantial programme of support to pertinent non-state actors is maintained. An unwillingness by recipient governments to countenance donor assistance to non-state actors would question their own commitment to democratisation.

6. *Support to civil society to be more narrowly focused on those organisations that are of particular significance for the defence and promotion of democratic government.* Relevant organisations will vary between countries *and* between phases of the democratisation process, but can most commonly be described as civic advocacy organisations, rather than those pursuing a more sectional or private interest.

7. *Regional imbalances in the distribution of political aid to be addressed.* In particular, more extensive donor support to democratic development in Asia is required, along with greater examination of the potential within the Middle East.

8. A larger proportion of political aid to be disbursed directly to organisations in recipient countries, governmental and non-governmental, with a decreased proportion of funds benefiting donor-based consultancy and training firms. An increase in 'direct funding' of SNGOs is particularly endorsed. The model of using NNGOs as conduits for disbursal of funds to SNGOs also has advantages, benefiting from the close partnerships established between like-minded organisations.

9. Increased utilisation of multilateral organisations as implementers of political aid is suggested, especially UN bodies. Their enhanced legitimacy in situations of conflict resolution and peace building was particularly noted.

10. Good governance measures to encourage open and accountable government require a focus not only on strengthening executive capacity, but also on those institutions, governmental and non-governmental, that have a role in exercising democratic control over executive power, for example, legislatures, national audit bodies, ombudsman institutions, and societal organisations such as the media and research institutes.

11. Support to democratic local government is crucial, valued as a mechanism of enhanced public control and participation in decision-making processes. It must be noted, however, that decentralisation *per se* does not necessarily strengthen democracy.

12. Donor support for economic adjustment programmes should be made conditional on being subjected to democratic decision-making processes, including public scrutiny and parliamentary approval. Incompatibilities have been noted between economic policy sovereignty, an essential element of democracy, and the imposition of structural adjustment programmes by the powerful international financial institutions (IFIs), abetted by Northern governments. Findings here have highlighted the dovetailing between some good governance measures (for example, financial accountability) and donor surveillance of the implementation of economic adjustment programmes. Donors can demonstrate the primacy of national democratic politics and their commitment to economic policy sovereignty by making their support for economic adjustment conditional on it being subjected to the democratic process.

13. Gender equality is a fundamental principle to strive for through increased support for women's rights, for improved access for women to public office, and for women's advocacy groups. The dearth of evidence of such measures is partially accounted for by the poor record of Western democracies on women's representation in government. The Scandinavian countries are an exception and could take a lead role in activities to overcome gender inequalities in political affairs, with lessons to be learnt by donor and recipient countries alike.

14. Donor support be provided for the implementation of the 1992 UN Declaration on Minorities. One test of a democratic society is its protection and promotion of minority rights, one indicator being the implementation of the UN Declaration.

15. The concept of 'do no harm' requires donor vigilance against negative, unintended effects. It is incumbent on donors to ensure that political aid programmes are continually scrutinised in order to identify potentially harmful effects of political intervention, especially the fuelling of conflict. Donor agencies require not only expertise in democracy and good governance matters, but also a thorough knowledge and understanding of local political contexts.

10.2   Aid sanctions

10.2.1   Critical issues

Questions surrounding the effectiveness and legitimacy of aid sanctions have been highlighted as key interconnected issues. In assessing the 29 instances of political conditionality along lines of effectiveness, it was discovered that aid restrictive measures had been successful in only a minority of cases. Investigating the reasons for policy *ineffectiveness* in the majority of cases, it was found that the weakness of the measures taken had more explanatory power than the strength of the recipients. Stokke's six hypotheses regarding effectiveness were generally confirmed, though with the evidence generating additional propositions. Two of these, the degree of countervailing economic and strategic interests and the degree of political will of the donor, strongly questioned how seriously Northern donors had pursued their stated objective of promoting human rights and democracy. This dimension was explored further in the examination of consistency of application, with overwhelming evidence from three lines of investigation that political conditionality had been applied weakly or not at all in circumstances of donor economic and political self-interests. Thus, policy implementation had been characterised by the selective and inconsistent application of human rights and democracy criteria. It was argued that this undermines both policy legitimacy and the credibility of donor motivations, as well as having an adverse impact on effectiveness.

For many commentators, these findings may be not only unsurprising but also anticipated. They will confirm the intuition of those sceptical of the whole political conditionality agenda that it would not be an effective policy instrument and that implementation would be characterised by inconsistency. Others of a more pragmatic or realist viewpoint will point to the underlying flaw in appraising policy application solely on the basis of consistency. Their view is that of course there will be inconsistency given that the promotion of human rights and democracy is only one of a number of foreign policy concerns that impact on development co-operation. How can political conditionality be considered separately from other foreign policy goals? Further, is it not naïve to expect that Northern governments will place human rights and democracy at the centre of their foreign policies, or that such concerns will take precedence over issues of trade or perceived 'security'? Rather, is it not to be expected that donor government positions will be adopted on a country-by-country basis, with human rights concerns often competing with other more compelling interests? This may lead to inconsistency when decisions on aid sanctions are examined in terms of one criterion only, that of human rights, but is this not an inevitable aspect of policy implementation in the real world?

On the other hand, should a normative dimension to foreign and aid policy be abandoned meekly in the face of such realist arguments? What are the counter arguments? First, it is obviously correct that human rights concerns co-exist with and cannot be addressed in isolation from other foreign policy objectives. Yet the evidence presented here demonstrates that when *any* other foreign policy goal comes into conflict with the promotion of human rights and democracy, then it is the latter that is abandoned. In a hierarchy of foreign policy objectives, an element of consistency is that human rights and democracy concerns are at the bottom of the pile. Second, it is itself inappropriate to examine policy implementation in this area solely from a realist or pragmatic perspective. Northern donors have *themselves* chosen to move their foreign and development policy to an arena where they are appealing to certain norms as universally binding – that is, respect for human rights and democratic principles. The implications are that inconsistency in policy implementation cannot easily be dismissed as a function of conflicting foreign policy objectives. Universal norms require both donor and recipient governments to act according to defined standards. If donors, having stipulated the norms themselves, then act more in accordance with self-interests, this not only exposes them to the accusation of double standards but also undermines the credibility and legitimacy of the policy agenda. If donors' commitment to the principles of human rights and democracy is at best partial and dependent on the lack of competing self-interests, they can hardly require development partners to abide by those principles in a manner that commands respect.

10.2.2   Towards a strengthened normative framework: concluding proposals

Initial discussions of the literature on political conditionality established the legitimacy in principle of human rights conditionality. Simultaneously, it was noted how legitimacy in practice depended on the *manner* of policy implementation. Findings have demonstrated the failure of donors to apply human rights policy 'fairly and equally', as undertaken in the Final Declaration of the UN Vienna Conference in 1993. The following suggestions are put forward in the spirit of forging policy instruments in which the values of human rights and democracy are shared and within which the participation and authorship of recipient nations is enhanced. The primary endeavour is to *internationalise* policy implementation.[167]

1.   A human rights clause

A human rights clause be introduced as a standard component in development co-operation agreements. In line with EU practice, this clause would be an essential element of the agreement with an associated 'suspension mechanism'. This provides a firm, legal and contractual basis, agreed by both parties, to respect for human rights as a threshold condition of development assistance, with known consequences if breached.

Two outstanding issues remain, however. First, how are human rights defined? Second, should the clause be extended to include respect for democratic principles, as EU practice has evolved? As a threshold requirement, *it is suggested that human rights be delimited to civil and political rights only*, as defined in the UN International Covenant on Civil and Political Rights and ratified by the majority of the world's states. This suggestion does not contradict the 'indivisibility' of human rights. In contrast to the 'aspirational' nature of economic, social and cultural rights, civil and political rights are appropriate as a threshold condition: they are subject to implementation without delay or deferment, whatsoever the level of economic development of a ratifying state.[168] Further, *it is suggested that the clause is not extended to democratic principles*, due to the current lack of a clear definition of democracy in international law. This is not to deny the importance of democracy. On the contrary, as discussed in Chapter 1, democracy concerns are in fact covered by civil and political rights as an essential element of democracy and as a pre-requisite for meaningful elections.

2.   Assessment criteria and performance indicators

Having achieved definitional clarity, it is then possible to develop *an inventory of criteria by which country performance will be assessed, and of measurable performance indicators.* Tomasevski's (1993) criticisms of the arbitrary and discretionary manner of donor decision-making are recalled. It is suggested that criteria be based on the guidelines provided by international human rights bodies, notably the UN Human Rights Committee, the supervisory body of the ICCPR. A list of measurable performance indicators can similarly be determined in co-ordination with such bodies.

3.   Monitoring performance

Monitoring and evaluation of the political situation in recipient countries for aid allocation purposes appears to occur on a fairly *ad hoc* basis, mainly responding to crisis situations as they arise. A *systematic and regular monitoring of performance is suggested,* based on existing monitoring mechanisms of the UN and regional systems of human rights,[169] as well as those of international human rights NGOs. There are both pragmatic and normative benefits to greater use of UN monitoring bodies. They are well established, with experience both of standard setting and measuring compliance. They are endowed with legitimacy, mutually acceptable to all parties, and can contribute to the development of a 'commonly shared normative framework' (van Boven 1995).

4.   Transparency

It is essential that the whole process is characterised both by agreement between parties and by transparency, including dialogue with recipient countries. Clarity is required regarding which violations will trigger which restrictive measures, enabling recipients to respond to any perceived unfair treatment by donors. Transparency is also necessary to permit donor parliaments and wider publics to fully participate in policy discussions. To this end, *an annual report could be submitted to individual donor legislatures, including the European Parliament,* on the promotion of human rights and democracy through development co-operation, including negative measures taken.

5.   An international body

To facilitate joint Southern and Northern authorship of the aid policy regime, as well as to avoid duplication of effort by individual donor governments, *an international body could be delegated responsibility* for the above tasks. As well as the initial one-off tasks of defining concepts and criteria, the responsibilities of this body could include ongoing country performance monitoring and the investigation of instances of perceived violations as they arise, removing determinations of what constitutes contractual breaches from Northern hands.[170] *The preferred location is within an existing UN agency.*[171] As regards decision-making, this international body would have the competence to make recommendations, including on charges of violations, although individual donor governments would have the choice to accept or disregard its advice.

6.   Legislative mandate

Following the example of the US Congress, in order to circumscribe the discretionary powers of individual donor governments to act in a selective and subjective manner, *donor legislatures could amend aid legislation to mandate a suspension of assistance to governments who engage in gross abuses of civil and political rights and/or take power through a military coup.*

10.2.3   Effectiveness and legitimacy

The compatibility of instrumental and normative issues within political conditionality has been demonstrated, with effectiveness and consistency strongly interlinked. Inconsistent policy application has a detrimental impact not only on policy legitimacy but also on its effectiveness. Similarly, strengthening the normative framework and applying policy objectively and non-selectively both increases legitimacy and has positive implications for effectiveness. Further, an enhanced ethical dimension within foreign policy implies the use of a broader range of instruments, namely trade restrictions, arms embargoes, and diplomatic measures. These are especially relevant in situations where aid sanctions have limited impact on their own. Again, the implications for effectiveness are positive. Additional links between effectiveness and consistency have been demonstrated in this study. The greater the specificity of political reforms required for development assistance to be maintained, the greater the likelihood of effectiveness. Moreover, if donors give due regard to the reforms called for by internal movements, then both legitimacy and effectiveness are augmented.

The relative ineffectiveness of aid conditionality in some circumstances should imply neither its worthlessness nor the maintenance of development assistance to governments culpable of political repression. Rather, aid restrictions need to be implemented with greater integrity by Northern donors and with enhanced Southern participation, entailing the fair and equal treatment of all nations, as part of a larger package of non-co-operation with regimes that show contempt for the rights of their citizens. The alternative is a rhetorical commitment only and a practice that continues to be based on self-interest and characterised by an assertion of power over poorer and weaker nations.

10.3 Democracy promotion and neo-liberal hegemony

Wider critiques of the West's 'putative' promotion of democracy were made by some writers, as discussed in Chapter 1. Before making some final comments, it is useful to briefly recall their arguments.

Gills *et al.* (1993) used the phrase 'low intensity democracy' to describe the West's narrow interest on procedural democracy, a mechanism of intervention to enable the removal of discredited authoritarian rulers, to provide democratic legitimacy for the implementation of harsh adjustment measures, and to pre-empt and co-opt demands for more substantial change. In separate works, Barya (1993), William Robinson (1996), as well as Gills *et al.* (1993), share a view of Western democracy promotion as the political element of a wider project to establish global neo-liberal hegemony, itself operating in the interests of transnational capital. Within such a project, economic concerns are clearly paramount and political restructuring essentially a means to ongoing economic liberalisation. These are propositions which, by their nature, lend themselves less readily to the type of empirical investigation undertaken here. Thus, (dis)agreement with such statements is more a matter of judgement. To what extent does the evidence here enable more informed judgements? The findings are mixed, some tending to support the thrust of radical left arguments, others tending to qualify their statements.

First, are donors merely intent on promoting 'low intensity democracy'? Evidence against such a proposition has indicated the significant support provided to broader dimensions of democratic development, in particular support for civil society organisations, somewhat contrary to Barya's specific expectations (1993, p. 21). Yet, it remains questionable whether donors have explicitly encouraged the 'popular participation of civil society in the decision-making of the state', as seriously doubted by

Barya (ibid., p. 17), with findings here highlighting the often indiscriminate and haphazard nature of civil society assistance. Taking a somewhat distinct tack, W. I. Robinson (1996, p. 319) anticipated the *inclusion* of civil society in democracy promotion, with donor intent to develop allies and co-opt civil society bodies, pre-empting more radical change. Investigation of such claims requires the detail that country case-studies provide, and it is noted that Ngunyi *et al.*'s (1996, p. 23) study of Kenya did affirm a process of donor selection of favoured civil society groups and the exclusion of more radical actors.

Second, to what extent is democracy promotion subordinate to a neoliberal hegemonic project, that is a means to wider ends, primarily economic? Again, the evidence is mixed. On the one hand, the political reform agenda has been shown to be closely interrelated with that of economic liberalisation, especially with regard to executive strengthening measures. For all the bilateral donors, these constitute a substantial proportion of overall political aid and it has been noted how such efforts often dovetail with structural adjustment programmes, for example, measures aimed at financial accountability and the provision of statistical information. Ostensibly promoting open and accountable government, they enhance the 'policing' of structural adjustment programmes by donor institutions. Moreover, it remains questionable whether civil society organisations that pose a challenge to economic orthodoxy have received donor sponsorship, with investigation through country case-studies required. Hearn's findings on civil society support in Ghana, South Africa and Uganda are pertinent, however, with 'civil society organisations committed to promote liberal democracy and economic liberalism [being] the most popular with donors' (Hearn 1999, p. 4).[172] Additionally, there is evidence here that some donors, notably the US and UK, pursue democratisation when it coincides with their economic interests, yet abandon democracy promotion when it contradicts such interests, for example, the 'non-cases' here. Further, hidden agendas surface when political aid programmes are established with governments that are most unlikely proponents of democratisation, for instance, in Egypt, Colombia and Indonesia, the former two supported by the US and the latter by the UK. The democracy building component could be interpreted both as a means to exert political influence and as an attempt to legitimate substantial aid programmes with non-democratic governments, allies for a variety of economic and geo-political reasons.

On the other hand, some findings make it difficult to sustain the idea that the predominant thrust of political aid is as a means to Western global dominance. From the project information gathered here, it is evident that many measures are unequivocally dedicated to promoting various aspects of democratic development, for instance, the human rights projects supported by the EU and Sweden, with support channelled to NGOs with proven track records in such fields. To imply that such organisations can be so easily manipulated by donor agendas and deflected from their own objectives is insulting in itself.

Thus, findings on these broader issues are inconclusive, unsurprisingly, with more detailed country case-study research required. The evidence here has indicated that there is some basis for criticism of a propulsion to democratisation from outside that aims at asserting a political system that reinforces the current restructuring of global economic exploitation. Nevertheless, this is balanced by examples of quite distinct practices, exhibiting commitment to the principles of human rights and democratic development. Yet, perhaps this presentation of diversity does enable us to make a more informed judgement. The differences in practices that have been evident from the comparative examination highlights that the picture of neo-liberal hegemony is less a description of how the world is and more an account of *some* attempts to construct it, albeit those of powerful actors. How is a counter hegemonic strategy developed? One component is precisely through radicalising the democracy promotion activities discussed here. By this means a neo-liberal hegemonic agenda can be unsettled and the effects of its thrust mitigated. It is through addressing the policy deficiencies and radicalising policy implementation that the processes of Western dominance can be undermined. Discussions here are intended to be a contribution to that end.

Appendix: Database Categorisation Codes

Implementers

1 Recipient government
1.1 central
1.2 local
1.3 state-related (e.g. government-established commissions)

2 Northern NGOs (i.e. donor country)
2.1 human rights NNGOs
2.2 development
2.3 humanitarian
2.4 women's groups
2.5 TU/labour
2.6 church
2.7 legal groups
2.8 business/commerce
2.9 professional
2.10 media
2.11 solidarity / campaigning groups
2.12 private institutions and foundations
2.13 conflict-mediation / peace groups
2.14 education / research institutions / universities
2.15 other private organisations
2.16 disability groups
2.17 ethnic minority organisations
2.18 political organisations / electoral assistance
2.19 cultural
2.20 youth / children
2.21 quangos (government-funded)
2.22 private consultants / companies

3 Southern NGOs (i.e. recipient country)
3.1 human rights SNGOs
3.2 development
3.3 humanitarian
3.4 women's groups

3.5   TU/labour
3.6   church
3.7   legal groups
3.8   business/commerce
3.9   professional
3.10   media
3.11   political parties
3.12   private institutions and foundations
3.13   conflict-mediation/peace groups
3.14   education / research institutions
3.15   other private organisations
3.16   disability groups
3.17   ethnic minority/indigenous groups
3.18   pro-democracy groups
3.19   community groups
3.20   universities
3.21   cultural/arts
3.22   children/youth

4   International NGOs
4.1   human rights INGOs
4.2   development
4.3   humanitarian
4.4   women's groups
4.5   TU/labour
4.6   church
4.7   legal groups
4.8   business/commerce
4.9   professional
4.10   media
4.11   lobby/campaigning groups
4.12   private institutions and foundations
4.13   conflict-mediation/peace groups
4.14   education/research institutions
4.15   other private organisations
4.16   disability groups
4.17   electoral assistance/parliamentary groups
4.18   ethnic minority/indigenous peoples' organisations

5   Multilateral and inter-governmental organisations
5.1   UN agencies

5.2   international financial institutions
5.2.1   World Bank
5.2.2   IMF
5.2.3   regional development banks
5.3   inter-governmental
5.3.1   northern
5.3.2   southern

6   Donor institutions
6.1   parliament
6.2   political parties
6.3   executive

Beneficiary by sector

1   Central government
1.1   constitution
1.1.1   constitutional commission
1.1.2   public participation/consultation mechanisms
1.2   electoral system
1.2.1   pre-election activities
1.2.1.1   voter registration
1.2.1.2   voter education
1.2.2   elections
1.2.3   monitoring and observation
1.2.4   referendum
1.3   legislature
1.3.1   infrastructural development (e.g. equipment)
1.3.2   personnel development
1.3.2.1   legislators (elected members)
1.3.2.2   parliamentary officials
1.3.3   legislative capacity
1.3.4   accountability function (executive)
1.3.5   role of opposition
1.3.6   promoting political role of women
1.3.7   public participation mechanisms/consultation
1.4   executive
1.4.1   political leadership
1.4.2   public administration
1.4.2.1   institution building
1.4.2.1.1   policy-making capacity

1.4.2.1.2	financial management (budgeting and resource allocation)
1.4.2.1.3	revenue administration (taxes and custom duties)
1.4.2.1.4	personnel development/human capacity
1.4.2.2	civil service reform
1.4.2.2.1	training
1.4.2.2.2	privatisation
1.4.2.3	accountability
1.4.2.3.1	to parliament
1.4.2.3.2	financial (accounting and audit practices)
1.4.2.3.3	auditor general
1.4.2.4	transparency/open government
1.4.2.4.1	(independent) statistical services
1.4.2.4.2	information systems
1.4.2.4.3	public consultation / representation mechanisms
1.4.2.5	controlling corruption
1.4.2.6	promotion of women in public sector
1.4.3	support of public service provision
1.5	legal system (rule of law)
1.5.1	judiciary
1.5.2	legal drafting
1.5.3	Ministry of Justice
1.5.4	military (including civilian control)
1.5.5	police
1.5.6	prosecution service
1.5.7	courts
1.5.8	prisons
1.5.9	participation of women
1.5.10	participation of minority groups
1.5.11	legal aid/assistance
1.5.12	para-legal services
1.5.13	ombudsman
1.5.14	legal education
1.5.15	legal framework for economic activity
1.5.16	human rights Commission

2	Local government
2.1	electoral system
	same sub-categories as 1.2
2.2	local authorities
2.2.1	local representative bodies (elected councils, etc.)

2.2.1.1	personnel development
2.2.1.2	infrastructural development
2.2.1.3	accountability mechanisms
2.2.1.4	controlling corruption
2.2.1.5	promoting role of women
2.2.2	local government administration
2.2.2.1	institution building
2.2.2.2	accountability
2.2.2.3	transparency/openness
2.2.2.4	public participation mechanisms
2.2.2.5	role of women in public sector
2.3	decentralisation

3   Human rights groups (non-state)
3.1   protecting human rights (violations)
3.1.1   victim-support groups (including legal support)
3.1.2   civilian victims of war/conflict
3.1.3   human rights reporting (information gathering/
           documenting violations)
3.2   promoting human rights
3.2.1   human rights education/awareness raising
3.2.2   women's rights/gender equality
3.2.3   ethnic minority/indigenous rights
3.2.4   disability rights
3.2.5   children's rights
3.2.6   Trade Union rights
3.2.7   legal advocacy groups
3.2.8   legal training (lawyers)
3.2.9   human rights research
3.2.10   legal advice and assistance

4   Pro-democracy groups (non-state)
4.1   political parties
4.2   independent media
4.3   local pro-democracy associations
4.4   participation of ethnic minority organisations
4.5   role of women in democratisation process
4.6   civic/democracy education/information
4.8   conflict-mediation/resolution (peace process)
4.8.1   demobilisation of ex-combatants
4.9   reconstruction/peace building

5   Interest groups
5.1   intermediate organisations (national)
5.1.1   business groups
5.1.2   professional organisations
5.1.3   TU/labour
5.1.4   church/religious groups
5.1.5   ethnic associations
5.1.6   women's groups
5.1.7   advocacy NGOs (charitable organisations)
5.1.8   development NGOs
5.1.9   research institutes/policy think tanks/ universities
5.1.10   personnel development in strategic professions
           (e.g. university training)
5.1.10.1   accountants and auditors
5.1.10.2   lawyers
5.1.10.3   bankers
5.1.10.4   economists
5.1.10.5   management
5.1.11   education
5.1.12   arts/cultural groups
5.2   local groups
5.2.1   self-help groups (specific)
5.2.2   community associations/grassroots groups (more general)
5.3   civic associations (misc.)

6   Donor country support
6.1   donor public
6.2   donor organisation/public authority
6.3   donor political party
6.4   donor administration costs
6.5   donor aid agency
6.6   donor NGOs
7   Multilateral organisations
7.1   UN
7.2   World Bank

Notes

1 The (eventual) re-instatement of President Aristide in Haiti in September 1994 is one recent example of democracy promotion through military intervention.
2 For example, authorisation and support for military coups against elected governments in Guatemala in June 1954 and in Chile in September 1973.
3 A wider literature examines not just the explicit role of external actors, but also the more subtle and often implicit influence of international processes. Such influences take two main forms. One is the impact of changes in international *structures*, for example, the global economy or geo-political relations, dependent on a country's particular location within these. The other is the general influence of international *trends*, both at the level of dominant ideas and of actual events, such as a regional demonstration effect. This literature is not examined here.
4 Economic assistance to countries in Central and Eastern Europe through the European Bank for Reconstruction and Development (EBRD) was made conditional on a commitment to 'multi-party democracy, pluralism and market economics' (EBRD Charter).
5 The broader version of the governance concept is evident in the volume edited by Hydén and Bratton (1992). In Hydén's opening chapter, his theoretical discussion of the concept appears to equate effective or good governance with democratic governance. Similarly, in Bratton and van de Walle's chapter, 'Toward Governance in Africa', discussions are essentially about the process of democratisation, and one is left wondering why they do not simply call it that.
6 Of the multilateral banks, it is recalled that the Inter- American Development Bank (IDB) alone has introduced an emphasis on democracy and advocates the concept of democratic governance (see Introduction).
7 Christian Aid, for instance, provides continuing evidence of declining health and education indicators, e.g. increased female childbirth mortality rates and decreased secondary school enrolments in Zimbabwe, two years after the introduction of a SAP (Madeley *et al.* 1994).
8 The International Bill of Rights is made up of the International Covenant on Civil and Political Rights and the International Covenant on Economic, Social and Cultural Rights, adopted by the UN General Assembly in 1966, with each entering into force in 1976 after ratification by the required number of states.
9 See Lipjhart 1984, for a comprehensive review and comparison of the two contrasting models of democracy, majoritarian and consensual. Mechanisms to foster consensus decision-making include: an electoral system based on proportional representation; executive power-sharing (i.e. guaranteed seats on executive for all main political parties, representing major social groups); power-dispersal through regional autonomy; guaranteed constitutional rights that are immune from majority vote; adequate representation of women. The democratic South African government, which includes many of these features, is a good example of what is *possible* in constructing a consensual model, even in a situation where one party (the ANC) enjoys overwhelming majority

support. Lipjhart's conclusion is that majoritarian democracy works best in homogeneous societies, whereas consensus democracy is more suitable for plural societies (1984, pp. 3–4).

10 Statements by British Foreign Secretary, Douglas Hurd, Development Minister, Baroness Chalker, and European Commission Vice-President and Development Commissioner Manuel Marin are quoted, as well as World Bank officials, Landell-Mills and Serageldin.

11 For example, in Africa, changes in government through the ballot box occurred in 13 countries (Wiseman 1997, p. 285), despite multi-party elections in approximately 35 countries in the early 1990s.

12 Citation from *Codesria Bulletin* No. 2, 1990. Implicit here is the notion that democracy entails social reform, as in Gills *et al.* (1993, p. 5).

13 The term 'polyarchy' was adopted by Dahl in 1971 and used to describe an institutional form of democracy, focused on the selection of government by universal suffrage, but with the subsequent role of governing performed relatively uninterrupted and relatively insulated from popular pressure, in other words with limited accountability and democratic control of government between elections.

14 The former 'European Community' became the 'European Union' on 1 November 1993 with the entry into force of the Maastricht Treaty. In general, the term 'European Union' is used, though at times 'European Community' refers to activities before November 1993.

15 The European Commission is also the second largest multilateral donor, after the World Bank.

16 Aid to the Mediterranean countries has increased considerably, totalling ECU 4.7 billion for the period 1995–99, compared with a total of ECU 4.23 billion for the period 1978–91 (European Commission 1995c, pp. 7 and 19).

17 Declarations were made at the Dublin Summit in June 1990 on human rights and good governance in Africa, at the Rome Summit in December 1990 on the promotion of democracy and human rights in external relations, and at the Luxembourg Summit in June 1991 on human rights.

18 Article 103u, paragraph 2 states that 'Community policy in this area shall contribute to the general objective of developing and consolidating democracy and the rule of law, and to that of respecting human rights and fundamental freedoms'.

19 Resolution on 'Human Rights and Development Policy' adopted by the European Parliament on 22 November 1991, document number PE 155.084.

20 Lomé III (1985–89) did in fact include a reference to human rights in the Preamble. The provision on human rights in Lomé IV was considerably strengthened by its inclusion in the main body of the Convention.

21 The Government Aid Bill of 1962 stated that: 'it seems reasonable to try to direct our aid so that it contributes...to development in the direction of *political democracy* and *social equality* (author's italics). It would contradict both the motives and the aims of Swedish aid, were it to help conserve a reactionary social structure' (Cited in Andersson 1986, p. 39).

22 The four goals were: economic growth; economic and social equality; economic and political independence; the development of democracy in society. A fifth goal, 'environmental quality', was added by the Swedish Parliament in 1988.

23   The review was conducted by the 'Commission for the Review of Sweden's International Development Co-operation', which consisted of members of all five parties represented in Parliament. Its report was submitted to the Government in 1977.

24   For example, Staffan Herrström, Under-Secretary of State in the 1991–94 Coalition Government and Liberal Party MP, stated that 'the democracy goal that was outlined during the sixties had very little practical effects for Swedish development policy until the end of the 1980s' (Interview: 8 September 1993). It could be argued, nevertheless, that the so- called 'humanitarian assistance' given by Sweden since the 1970s contributed to democracy promotion. Such assistance went primarily to liberation movements in Southern Africa and to victims of military dictatorships in Latin America, especially Chile.

25   Aid to Cuba was in fact very minimal by 1991, having been cut under the previous centre-right coalition government of 1976–82.

26   The legislative framework for British aid is the *Overseas Development and Co-operation Act* of 1980. This is a technical piece of legislation, mainly consolidating administrative provisions from a number of other Acts. It is generally bereft of policy, merely a broad-ranging statement that assistance shall promote 'the development... of a country... or the welfare of its people' (Part 1, section 1). Prior to the 1998 White Paper, the previous policy document was the 1975 White Paper 'Help for the Poorest'.

27   This speech, at the Overseas Development Institute, London, was at an international conference on African prospects in the 1990s, organised under the auspices of the UN Africa Recovery Programme.

28   Criticisms of the funding of the Pergau dam in Malaysia, the biggest ever single British aid project, highlighted not only the ineffective use of a very substantial amount of scarce resources on a project with limited benefits, but also the abuse of aid for non-development (and disreputable) purposes by its link, despite government denials, with the securing of military contracts. In an unprecedented move, the British pressure group, the World Development Movement, successfully challenged the government in the High Court over the legality of funding the £234 million project out of the aid programme. The High Court ruled that the project did not promote the development of a country's economy as required by the *Overseas Development and Co-operation Act* of 1980 (*The Guardian* 11 November 1994, p. 1).

29   In countries where aid to governments has been reduced or suspended, it is stated that the provision of humanitarian aid to the population will continue, particularly channelled through NGOs.

30   The other three policy initiatives were: Environment; Business and Development; Family and Development.

31   The NED's four core components are the National Democratic Institute for International Affairs and the International Republican Institute for International Affairs, the international wings of the Democratic and Republican Parties respectively, the Center for International Private Enterprise and the Free Trade Union Institute.

32   Closure of 21 country programmes entailed the concentration of development assistance on fewer so-called 'sustainable development' countries, seen as offering the best prospects for achievement of its objectives. Criteria for

closure were: (a) 'graduated', e.g. Botswana; (b) too small; (c) or 'poor performers' either on economic or on democracy and governance grounds, and therefore deemed a bad investment of scarce development resources, e.g. (former) Zaïre.

33 Personal correspondence from the (then) Head, Government and Institutions Department, ODA 20 January 1995.

34 In a Commission document of March 1998, good governance was defined more narrowly as 'the transparent and accountable management of all a country's human, natural, and internal and external economic and financial resources for the purposes of equitable and sustainable development', following the World Bank definition (European Commission 1998).

35 The World Bank also espouses the cause of decentralisation of government, despite its non-political mandate and avowed concern with economic accountability only.

36 It is of interest that M. Robinson (1996, p. 4) notes different interpretations of civil society *within* USAID. In contrast to the emphasis on civic advocacy organisations adopted by the Global Center for Democracy, the Africa Bureau focused more on local development organisations.

37 Somewhat confusingly, budget line codes are subject to frequent change. Those given here were correct as of mid-1999.

38 The new Commission that came into operation in September 1999 involves a degree of consolidation of administrative structures, although overall fragmentation remains. There is now one amalgamated Directorate of external relations, DGI, and ECHO is integrated into DGVIII, with the number of Commissioners dealing with development issues reduced to three, those for external relations, trade, and development and humanitarian aid.

39 Democracy and human rights projects can also be financed from country budgets, but in practice country desk officers sought funds from the budget line during the period examined.

40 Expenditure where political objectives are secondary is not included, for example, good government expenditure as a significant, but not principal, objective in UK aid. The secondary nature of any human rights or democracy component in such projects is clearly indicated by their titles, for instance: population and family health (Bangladesh); forestry programmes (Belize, India and Indonesia); road maintenance (Nepal); and veterinary services (Zambia and Yemen).

41 Converted into US $ equivalents by using annual average US Dollar Exchange Rates for 1993 and 1994 (*The Reality of Aid 1995* p. 119). Exchange rates as follows:

US $1 = ECU 0.8537 (1993); 0.8402 (1994)
US $1 = Swedish Kroner 7.7854 (1993); 7.7157 (1994)
US $1 = Pounds Sterling 0.6660 (1993); 0.6533 (1994)

42 EU figures are oda to developing countries only. Assistance to Central and Eastern Europe not included.

43 Total Swedish bilateral oda to developing countries only. Assistance to Central and Eastern Europe not included.

44 Bilateral aid includes assistance to Central and Eastern Europe. In British aid statistics this is subdivided into assistance to those countries classified by the

DAC as oda recipients and those that are not. The latter are termed 'countries in transition' by the UK government and received £47 m aid in 1993 and £59 m in 1994.

45   In fact donors' financial years could not have varied more, commencing on the four different quarters of the year. The EU budget runs on the calendar year; Sweden is 1 July–31 June; the UK is 1 April–31 March; and the US is 1 October–31 September, with, for example, FY 1994 commencing on 1 October 1993. Thus the years examined are as follows. EU: 1993 and 1994; Sweden: 1992/93 and 1993/94; UK: 1992/93 and 1993/94; US: FY 1993 and FY 1994.

46   Such projects were entered as 'QU' for query in the database.

47   A fourth type of implementer was donor government-related organisations (e.g. donor country parliament or political parties), but found to have limited application.

48   The beneficiary sector is distinguished from the implementing agency, though potentially it could involve the same organisation, especially where the implementer is the recipient government or a Southern NGO.

49   In addition, a further two types of beneficiary were identified, 'donor country organisation' and 'multilateral organisation', in order to categorise the small minority of projects where the primary beneficiary appeared to be external to a developing country, e.g. a political party or research institute within the donor country.

50   'Query' was entered where project information was insufficient to categorise with certainty.

51   The 11 activity codes were converted into the six 'purpose' codes as follows:

1.1 legal and judicial institutions – DILJ
1.2 human rights NGOs – DIHR
2.1 state institutions – DIEA, DIPI, DIDE
2.2 civil society – DICS, DILA, DICE, DIME, DILT
3.1 public administration – DIFM
3.2 private sector/professional bodies – no equivalent activity code

52   This analysis excludes those projects whose purpose category could not be determined from the information available (i.e. non-classifiable) and those which have been miscategorised by the donors (i.e. they do not support human rights, democracy or good governance). Of the 1573 projects in the database, 369 were either non-classifiable or miscategorised by purpose category, leaving 1204 projects included in this particular analysis.

53   The Swedish figures reflect the different budgetary allocations, with public administration expenditure just over one-third of the democracy and human rights fund. SIDA's own analysis of its support in 1993/94 confirms this ranking order, with highest expenditure on human rights (SEK 370 m), followed by democracy (SEK 274 m) and public administration (SEK 175 m), though with larger gaps between categories, (SIDA 1994a). A later SIDA report, omitting public administration support, gives the breakdown of expenditure as follows: democracy 47%, human rights 41%, and the new category of conflict management as 12% (SIDA 1997, p. 41). This indicates a switch in the order of priorities, with greater support for democratic institutions. This later report does include support for Central and Eastern Europe,

however, which may contribute towards the apparent shift in proportions of expenditure.

54 Based on USAID's own 'activity code' classification, hence 'miscategorised' and 'unknown' categories do not apply.

55 The evaluation of EC positive measures by Heinz *et al.* (1995) had similar findings.

56 It should be noted that the definition of civil society used in category 2.2 is fairly narrow, excluding human rights groups (1.2).

57 For evidence and examples of such miscategorisation and re-labelling, see Crawford 1998b, pp. 114–16.

58 Information provided is based on the donors' own data sets, that is, no exclusions are made of projects judged to be miscategorised.

59 Africa received 37.0 per cent of Swedish aid in 1994/95, compared with 22.05 per cent for Asia and 9.85 per cent for Latin America. Thirteen of the 19 programme countries were in Africa (SIDA 1996, p. 10).

60 In 1993, almost 70 per cent of EU aid disbursements went to sub-Saharan Africa (Crawford 1996 p. 518).

61 For example, 'US assistance to the Salvadoran government's struggle against leftist rebels was a contribution to "the battle for democracy"' the contra war in Nicaragua was a struggle for "true democracy"' (cited in Carothers 1991, p. 3).

62 The annual *Human Rights Watch World Report* in 1995 and 1996 draws attention to human rights abuses in the disputed territory of Kashmir and in the Punjab, for example.

63 Again, information provided is based on the donors' own data sets, that is, no exclusions are made of those projects judged to be miscategorised. Regional programmes, however, have been excluded from this analysis, although some would feature in a top ten of *all* recipients.

64 Of the nine budget headings contributing to EU expenditure on democracy and human rights in 1994, B7–3010 provides the largest sum, Ecu 38.8m., amounting to 40.7 per cent of total funds expended. Yet, it appears that substantial proportion of this is re-labeling of other development activities

65 It should be recalled that this research only examines good government aid to developing countries where it is a primary objective, excluding all assistance to Central and Eastern Europe and as a secondary objective.

66 Uganda and Zambia were the 4th and 5th highest recipients of UK development aid in 1993/94.

67 Notwithstanding this perceived support, President Museveni has criticised the pressure to adopt multi-partyism applied by some international donors in his 1996 autobiography, *Sowing the Mustard Seed*.

68 In 1992/93, for example, six of the top ten good government recipients were simultaneously top ten bilateral recipients, with nine out of ten also top twenty bilateral recipients.

69 Montserrat's population declined by two-thirds to 3500 by late 1997, following the volcanic eruptions that commenced in July 1995.

70 It is noted with some irony that Nicaragua had become the third highest recipient of US democracy assistance, given the clandestine and undemocratic methods used in the 1980s to undermine the leftist Sandinista Front government.

71 One view, in fact, is that the Contras waged a proxy war on behalf of their US sponsors.

72 It is recalled that US figures are for annual commitments, not disbursements. Therefore it is quite possible that committed funds were never fully disbursed, given the violence that ensued from April 1994.

73 A report by the International Commission of Inquiry in January 1993 recommended aid donor pressure on the Rwandan government over human rights abuses, and a UN Special Rapporteur's investigation in April 1993 charged army involvement 'at the highest level' with a damning indictment of the Rwandan government, but no UN action was taken (Klinghoffer 1998, pp. 22–3).

74 This applies in particular to the general 'Democracy and human rights in developing countries' budget, whereas the 'Democratisation in Latin America' budget has partially addressed such shortcomings through establishing multiannual programmes in some countries.

75 Recipient governments *benefit* from Swedish aid to a greater extent than this figure suggests, as much of the public administration programme is *implemented* by Swedish public or private organisations.

76 Such assistance is in the form of 'block grants', with expenditure determined by the NGO. The figure of 13.6 per cent excludes emergency relief and funds from particular budget lines (for example, 'Democracy and Human Rights'), also channelled to NGOs but for more designated purposes.

77 Information from interview with staff member of DIAKONIA, 17 November 1994.

78 This aims to increase aid disbursement by PVOs to 40 per cent of the total budget.

79 TAF is an participant in nine out of eleven country programmes in the first half of the 1990s.

80 This included projects in Bangladesh, Indonesia, the Philippines, Mongolia, Nepal, Sri Lanka, Thailand (USAID Democracy Projects Inventory, undated).

81 Monies disbursed to NDI and IRI to implement USAID democracy projects are separate from and additional to the core grants they each receive from the US government. German political foundations operate in a similar manner. They are closely linked to political parties and, although technically NGOs, receive their funds almost exclusively from the government, endorsed by parliament (Heinz 1995).

82 Grants included: $32,000 to the *Independent Forum for Electoral Education*; $250,000 to the *Independent Mediation Service* for voter education; $319,000 to the *Institute for Multiparty Democracy* for training in electoral monitoring (USAID Democracy Projects Inventory).

83 ONUSAL is the UN Observer Mission in El Salvador.

84 Recipient government beneficiaries of Swedish political aid are somewhat higher than implied by implementer figures, due to the large proportion of public administration assistance implemented by Swedish 'partner' organisations but benefiting host government ministries.

85 Cheru (1998, p. 239) refers to some such organisations as relying on USAID for 60–80 per cent of their budgets.

86 The analysis presented here is based upon the categorisation of each individual project in this manner, with the exception of US projects. Again, the

multiple beneficiaries within each USAID project, with no financial break-down of different activities, prevented such a categorisation. Fortunately, USAID's own financial breakdown of 1994 democracy projects by its eleven activity codes was again utilised (1994a, Table IV) and converted into the five main beneficiary categories as follows:

- Central government included: accountability of the executive (DIFM); legal and judicial development (DILJ); electoral assistance (DIEA); representative political institutions (DIPI) (i.e. legislatures)
- Local government corresponded with decentralization (DIDE)
- Human rights groups corresponded with human rights (DIHR)
- Pro-democracy groups included: civic education (DICE); free flow of information (DIME) (i.e. media); leadership training (DILT) (i.e. political parties)
- Interest groups included: civil society (DICS); labour (DILA)

87 Another four primary level beneficiaries have not been included in Table 5.5, where the beneficiaries are donor country organisations or multilateral organisations, and where the beneficiaries are perceived as 'non-political' or 'unknown'. All these are relatively minor beneficiaries and do not significantly affect overall percentages. For full detail, see Crawford 1998b, Table 14, p. 156.

88 Local government assistance has been a small but intrinsic component of SIDA's public administration programme since its inception in the early 1980s, commencing with help in developing a new local government system in post-Independence Zimbabwe (Lindgren 1991).

89 The EU column is lacking 15.4 per cent of expenditure to central government which could not be further sub-categorised from the information available.

90 There is not a separate US activity code for constitutional support, although 'constitution drafting bodies' are stated to be part of the 1994 democracy project portfolio (USAID undated, p. 2). Such projects are probably subsumed within electoral assistance.

91 Further breakdown of US assistance is not available, but it is noteworthy that executive support is the largest of USAID activity codes, with expenditure of almost $70m in 1994.

92 Financial management accounts for 15 out of 41 Swedish institution building projects and 9 out of 20 UK projects.

93 Eleven out of 17 Swedish accountability projects and three out of five UK projects concern *financial* accountability.

94 UN Declaration on the Rights of Persons Belonging to National or Ethnic, Religious and Linguistic Minorities, adopted by the General Assembly of the United Nations in December 1992.

95 Of the main sub-categories of pro-democracy groups, support to political parties was almost entirely to the central structures of the ANC, while assistance to 'local democracy associations' was largely to various sections of the ANC (for instance, Youth League, Education, Policy Development), though also included funds to Polisario (Western Sahara) and the Zambian Youth Council for a conference on democracy.

96 In Malawi, for example, the activities of churches and religious leaders played a crucial role in pressing for democratisation, while in Zambia, trade unions

were prominent in the Movement for Multi-party Democracy, the main pro-democracy organisation and subsequent ruling party (Wiseman 1997, p. 289).

97 This figure is given in the USAID document, but generally assumed to be erroneous, with perhaps a digit omitted.

98 This shortcoming of EU political aid was also noted in Heinz *et al.* (1995).

99 Ngunyi *et al.* (1996, p. 23) refers to a process whereby donors fund a select group of players in the democracy and governance (DG) sector, while 'uncaptured DG actors have to work extra-hard to be admitted into this donor-NGO fraternity'. Such remarks were about donors in general and not specific to USAID. Also see Hearn 1999.

100 If aid to human rights NGOs was included as civil society support, total volume would be considerably higher.

101 The Final Declaration at the UN World Conference on Human Rights, Vienna, June 1993, stated that: 'The international community must treat human rights globally in a fair and equal manner, on the same footing, and with the same emphasis' (Part II, paragraph 3). It is noteworthy that these principles were initially stressed in the declarations from both the Latin American and Asia and Pacific Regional Preparatory meetings (UN 1993a).

102 The first pillar, and by far the most important, is 'the European Communities', and the third is 'Justice and Home Affairs'. See Nugent 1994, Chapter 3, for more detail.

103 The Amsterdam Treaty of October 1997 (amending the TEU and entering into force on 1 May 1999) introduced 'constructive abstention' into the Council decision-making process on 'common positions' and 'joint actions' (previously unanimous), allowing an abstaining member state not to implement the policy.

104 Resolutions originate most frequently from the European Parliament's Committees on Development Co-operation and on Foreign Affairs, Security and Defence Policy,

105 Such powers of veto do not extend to the Lomé Convention, with the European Development Fund raised separately from member states' contributions, outside of the European Community's budgetary process.

106 For example: Sudan – full suspension in 1990; Haiti – full suspension in Sept 1991; Zaïre – partial freeze in January 1992; Malawi – new projects suspended from May 1992.

107 In legal terms, an 'essential element' clause provides a firm basis for suspending the agreement in cases of serious and persistent human rights violations or interruptions of democratic processes. Additionally, a suspension or non-performance clause establishes the specific rules agreed by the parties in such events. Without the latter, a party alleging breach of an essential element clause would have to seek recourse through the 1969 Vienna Convention on the Law of Treaties (articles 60 and 65), involving a three-month delay and the opportunity for the other party to raise objections. For more detailed discussion, see Crawford 1998a, pp. 134–9.

108 See the annual *Documents on Swedish Foreign Policy* published by the Ministry for Foreign Affairs.

109 To qualify as official development assistance, as defined by the Development Assistance Committee of the OECD, aid must fulfill two main criteria: (1) the

promotion of the economic development and welfare of developing countries as its main objective; (2) be concessional (compared to market terms) and have a grant element of at least 25 per cent.

110 More up-to-date figures portray an even grimmer picture, stating that only 29 per cent of the foreign aid budget for FY 1994 goes to sustainable development (17 per cent) and humanitarian assistance (12 per cent) purposes (Bread for the World Institute 1995, p. 35).

111 The seven nations are: Libya, Syria (since 1980); Iraq (1980–82, 1990 to date); Cuba (1982 to date); Iran (1984-date); North Korea (1987-date), (Elliott 1992 p. 101). Sudan has been the only addition in the 1990s, listed in 1993, though aid to the Khartoum regime had effectively ended in 1991.

112 Sources included: government agency annual reports and other documentation; European Commission documents; ministers' speeches; newspapers and magazines. Information was also gained through interviews and correspondence with government and Commission officials.

113 Definitions of the different types of aid are as follows:

- *Programme aid* is a grant or loan to the recipient government for unspecified purposes, though commonly used as balance-of-payments support to finance a range of imports. It is generally a lump sum payment to recipient governments, much valued by them, though disbursements are frequently made conditional on the implementation of economic policy reforms.

- *Project aid* comprises of grants and loans to specific development projects. Such aid is most commonly channelled through recipient governments, though it can also be disbursed direct to a recipient country NGO.

- *Technical co-operation* (TC) involves the provision of technical expertise, usually in the form of personnel or training. Personnel generally originate from the donor country and training is commonly in a donor country institution, with obvious benefits for such providers.

114 It is most unlikely that new project aid would be suspended and programme aid maintained, given the direct benefit of the latter to the recipient government. If no restrictive measures regarding programme aid are indicated on Table 7.1, it can be assumed that there is no such provision.

115 For a full version of each country case, see Crawford 1997, Appendix 1.

116 See below for a full discussion of aid to Sri Lanka.

117 See speeches by the then Minister for International Development Cooperation, and later Foreign Minister, Mrs. Lena Hjelm-Wallén, in Swedish Ministry for Foreign Affairs 1990 pp. 373–4 and 1991 p. 359. In addition, the Under-Secretary of State for Development Co-operation in the then Social Democratic government, Mr Mats Karlsson, stated the view that democracy is a long-term process which evolves from within and cannot be commanded from outside (interview, 8 November 1994).

118 The full list of 19 cases characterised by a relatively consistent approach are as follows: Burundi, The Gambia, Liberia, Kenya, Malawi, Niger, Nigeria, Rwanda, Somalia, Sudan, Togo, Zaïre, Burma, China, Cuba, Guatemala, Haiti, Peru. Equatorial Guinea is also included, where the EU is the only significant donor, but with its actions not contradicted by any other.

119 Interviews with officials of the European Commission (December 1994) and SIDA (November 1994).

120 See the work of Hufbauer *et al.* (1985) for an investigation of 103 cases of economic sanctions taken in pursuit of foreign policy goals between 1914 and 1984. They identify three main types of economic sanctions: limiting exports; restricting imports; impeding finance, including aid.

121 Donor objectives can be more specific, for example, particular legal or constitutional changes. The global approach adopted here, however, does not allow for impact evaluation of such specific conditionality, which requires country case-studies. From the experience of SAPs, it could be argued that the greater the specificity of objectives, broken down into particular targets and deadlines, the greater the likelihood of effectiveness, and the decreased scope for 'slippage'. Again country case-studies are necessary to carry out such an evaluation. Nonetheless, one observation of the author is that, in comparison with economic conditionality, donors have made less serious attempts in specifying the precise *political* reforms required of recipient governments.

122 A related methodological point is that evaluations here are inevitably based on limited research into the political developments of each of the 29 country cases, which, in some instances, may be subject to qualification or contestation by individual country specialists.

123 Terminology used by Mosley *et al.* 1991.

124 Identified cases have included those where threats of punitive actions were sufficient to achieve intended objectives, for example, in Lesotho, Sierra Leone. It is recognised that there may be other such cases of donor success that escaped detection, where, for example, the reputation effect of donor responses has led to anticipatory action by aid recipients.

125 Criticisms can be made of the Freedom House survey for the ideological bias inherent in their categorisations. It has been used, however, for two reasons. First, there is little alternative – it is the only annual rating for all countries in the world, and itself does use a number of other qualitative sources. The Charles Humana reports are not updated regularly enough. Second, its twofold categorisation of political rights and civil liberties approximates to the concern here with both democratic development and human rights.

126 This additional categorisation is necessary to correspond with the four-point scale of the aid sanctions contribution (below), and is adapted from Hufbauer *et al.* (1985). The scores given in Table 8.1 are my own assessments based on a number of sources, for example, Amnesty International, Human Rights Watch and US Department of State human rights country reports, as well as the Freedom House ratings themselves.

127 The human rights and democratisation trend is rated 0/1 in an additional three countries, Rwanda, Togo and Zaïre, indicating a possible, but scarcely apparent, positive trend during the period examined. Aid sanctions may also have made some impact in two further cases, both rated 0/1: in Peru, on the return to (amended) constitutional rule after Fujimori's 'self-coup'; in Rwanda, aid conditionality may have restrained the trend to more limited power-sharing.

128 Banda's loss of support from the apartheid regime in South Africa was another key factor.

129 Kenya is one of the most manifest examples of where donor pressures for both economic and political reforms, as well as recipient perceptions of these, became entangled. For detailed analysis of the Kenyan case, see Ngunyi *et al.* 1996.

130 A more critical stance has been taken by the US government in the 1990s, but it must be noted that it did not condition its overall bilateral aid package to Guatemala on improvements in human rights or on the successful negotiation of the peace accord.

131 This figure of 18 includes only the zero rated cases and not the ambiguous ones, Peru and Rwanda, where aid sanctions contribution is rated at 0/1.

132 Full suspension by all donors with a government programme occurs in 8 out of the 29 country cases, with an additional 5 cases where full measures are taken by at least one donor. See Crawford 1997, Appendix 1.

133 Following the Dili massacre in East Timor in November 1991, the Dutch government alone suspended aid to Indonesia. The response of the Indonesian government was to itself discontinue Dutch aid projects and unilaterally disband the Inter- Governmental Group on Indonesia (the Dutch-chaired aid consortium), and invite the World Bank to chair a new group. In 1990 and 1991, the Dutch government had been the second largest provider of net ODA, although overshadowed by Japanese assistance, (OECD 1996, p. 111). For more detail, see Landuyt 1995, De Feyter *et al.* 1995, Nordholt 1995, and M. Robinson 1993a.

134 Zaïre could be regarded as an eighth such case, with suspension of new projects since 1992 amounting now to full suspension. Haiti is the only case of successful full suspension.

135 UK government trade policy towards Burma appeared to soften in 1996, providing some financial assistance to British firms, in divergence from its stated 1993 policy of not encouraging trade (*The Guardian*, 5 March 1996). At EU level, however, diplomatic sanctions were imposed in October 1996 and special trading status withdrawn in December 1996, both on human rights grounds, (*The Guardian*, 29 October 1996 and 19 December 1996).

136 Such broader packages also do not guarantee success, of course, but their likelihood of effectiveness is increased.

137 Observers have used the expression of 'electoral coup d'état' to describe circumstances where incumbent regimes have manipulated an uneven playing field to gain electoral victory, for instance, through their control of state resources and the media and by means of more developed party organisations than newly legalised opponents.

138 There is evidence that in fact French aid to countries involved in genuine transition in 1991 (Benin, Niger, Mali) was decreasing, whilst that directed to authoritarian regimes was growing (Togo, Cameroon, Zaïre). See Martin 1995.

139 See Shiddo (1995) for the Sudanese government's views on EU aid sanctions.

140 Detailed country case-studies may reveal attempts by recipient governments to whip up anti-donor sentiment, and enable more precise comment on the relative success of this strategy.

141 This could be accounted for either by a different British diplomatic style or by the closer ties forged by colonialism and a post-colonial alliance.

142   There are also exceptions where less well co-ordinated measures have had some impact. For example, in Zambia, threats of punitive action by the US and UK were not reciprocated by the EU and Sweden, though not contradicted. The US acted alone in Thailand, although here internal pressure outweighed external influence in determining the outcome.

143   In 1999, Obasanjo became the elected President with the return to democratic rule in Nigeria.

144   This does not include Sweden, which has no programme with the government of Nigeria.

145   The new licences entailed a discreditable circumvention and disregard of the EU guidelines in three ways: first, ignoring 'the presumption of denial'; second, the phony distinction of arms sales to the police not military, for example, CS gas and rubber bullets; third, the dubious nature of so-called 'non-lethal' arms. The British government has not denied granting arms exports licenses, but stated unconvincingly that they have not been for the supply of 'lethal defence equipment to the Nigerian armed forces', while refusing to reveal the details (*The Guardian*, 21 July 1995 and 28 August 1995).

146   Indeed, proven respect for human rights has become a pre-requisite for EU membership. Hence, the failure by the EU to condition financial assistance to human rights indicates the predominance of other foreign policy agendas.

147   Correspondence with European Commission official.

148   No aid restrictions have been taken by any of the four selected donors, and generally not by any other donor. In some cases, though, a donor may not provide bilateral (government to government) assistance in the first place, particularly so with Sweden.

149   All aid statistics in these five country cases are taken from the OECD (1996).

150   See Landuyt 1995 for a detailed case-study of Indonesia with regard to development co-operation, human rights and democracy. A summarised version is also contained in De Feyter *et al.* 1995.

151   Estimates of killings vary from 20 per cent of the population (Instituto del Tercer Mundo 1995, p. 222) to one-third (UK World Development Movement, election materials, 1996).

152   The Clinton administration was initially critical of the Indonesian government's poor record on labour rights, threatening suspension of trade privileges under the General System of Preferences in 1993. However, such links were abandoned eight months later despite no improvement in standards (Landuyt 1995, p. 18). At the Consultative Group meeting in June 1994, the US statement did raise the issues of East Timor and workers' rights, but with no aid conditionality (ibid.). After the Dili massacre of November 1991, military training was suspended for FY 1993 and FY 1994 by Congress on human rights grounds, but the ban lifted for FY (fiscal year) 1995.

153   Aside from human rights considerations, this is quite remarkable given that Indonesia is a lower middle income country and that one of British aid's core objectives is 'poverty reduction'. A level of public concern about the aid programme to Indonesia is reflected in the recent investigation and report by the National Audit Office, submitted to the parliamentary Public Accounts Committee.

154 Sweden does not have a programme to Indonesia except small amounts of technical assistance and aid to NGOs.

155 Indeed, the military coup through which General Suharto seized power in 1965 had the stated intention of 'stemming communism', and undertaken with the covert support of the CIA. The Indonesian Communist Party at that time was the second largest in Asia after the Chinese, but the coup left nearly 700 000 of its members dead and another 200 000 imprisoned. Further, high-level US support was evident again in 1975, with the invasion of East Timor following a visit to Jakarta only hours previously by US President Ford, who clearly signalled his approval (Instituto del Tercer Mundo 1995, p. 298).

156 The Sri Lankan government state that the JVP was responsible for over 6500 killings from late 1987 to March 1990. They themselves were responsible for 'disappearances 'and extrajudicial killings numbering tens of thousands (Amnesty International 1991a, p. 209).

157 Human Rights Watch estimates '40,000 people disappeared between 1983 and 1992 after arrest by government forces or abduction by government-linked death squads' (1992, p. 186).

158 For example, the targeting of relatives of known Islamists, particularly women, and generalised retaliatory actions against citizens in areas where armed groups are active (Human Rights Watch 1994, pp. 256–9; Human Rights Watch 1995, pp. 263–6).

159 Algeria is the second largest beneficiary, however, of government credits for the purchase of US agricultural products, generally amounting to $550m per annum, and subject to the same human rights criteria in the Foreign Assistance Act as development assistance. Yet no human rights conditionality has been imposed (Human Rights Watch 1993, p. 276).

160 Correspondence with Commission official.

161 One could foresee, for example, the introduction of cosmetic changes or flawed democratic procedures as sufficient for the EU to state that there is a 'progressive trend' which they wish to encourage.

162 The cancellation of the elections brought no criticism from either the EU or the Bush administration. The latter explicitly made clear its preference for a military *junta* to a democratic process that resulted in a Islamic-dominated legislature. The EU's silence on human rights abuses is in marked contrast to their critical statements on events in many other countries.

163 Also see Amnesty International 1991b.

164 Outside the time frame of this study, in March 1996, the US government 'decertified' the Colombian government for not co-operating fully in anti-narcotics activities, repeated in March 1997. Decertification carries a full prohibition on all assistance (see case-study of Nigeria, below). Somewhat conversely, a Presidential waiver was granted for aid to counter-narcotics programmes, disbursed principally to the Colombian National Police and military. For FY 1998, the Clinton administration sought $3.9 million assistance to Colombia, made up of $3m anti-narcotics aid and $0.9m military training. Yet, no Colombian military unit is devoted exclusively to counter-narcotics operations. The military's first priority is fighting the guerrillas, with the consequence that the hardware supplied by US counter-narcotics aid is also used in counter-insurgency activities, during which hundreds of extrajudicial killings and 'disappearances' occur each year (Amnesty

International 1997). The US Congress responded to this anomaly with legislation, known as the Leahy Amendment, attaching human rights conditionality to counter-narcotics assistance. This stated that anti-narcotics aid cannot be provided 'to any unit of the security forces... [that] has committed gross violations of human rights'. The rigour with which the Leahy Amendment is implemented remains an open question.

165   The Andean Commission of Jurists – Colombian section (CAJSC) analyses annually those cases where perpetrators are known. For the year until September 1992, it found that 40 per cent were attributable to state agents, 30 per cent to paramilitary groups, 27.5 per cent to guerrillas, and 2.5 per cent to others, including drug traffickers (Human Rights Watch 1992, p. 86). In 1995, proportions assigned were similar: 65 per cent to government security forces and 35 per cent to guerrillas, (Human Rights Watch 1995, p. 79).

166   An exception was 1993 when a large concessionary loan from the US reduced this figure to 26 per cent.

167   Suggestions for improving donor practice, some on similar lines, are also made in Moore and Robinson 1994, pp. 153–8 and De Feyter *et al.* 1995 pp. 75–91.

168   As a corollary, and in order to ensure the integration of economic, social and cultural rights into development co- operation, it is suggested that evaluation criteria for aid include the progressive realisation of this set of 'aspirational' rights (see Tomasevski 1993).

169   See Crawford 1995, pp. 51–4. Of particular relevance are the treaty monitoring bodies of the UN human rights system, particularly the Human Rights Committee, the supervisory body for the ICCPR. The reports of the UN Commission on Human Rights are also of importance, though this body has the reputation of being more politicised.

170   The ACP states argued for such a joint decision-making body to investigate perceived breaches of the human rights and democracy clause during the mid-term review of the fourth Lomé Convention. Joint consultation procedures were established, but, disappointingly, without decision-making powers, which the EU retained. See Crawford 1996, p. 507.

171   Stokke (1995, pp. 56–62) discusses the prospects of an international regime administering political conditionality policies, and while not optimistic of its short-term realisation, similarly believes that it would be best situated within the United Nations. The Development Assistance Committee of the OECD may be the choice of donors to perform such tasks, but a more genuinely international body, combining representatives from both developing and industrialised nations, would enhance Southern input and increase its legitimacy.

172   These included neo-liberal policy institutes, for example, the Free Market Foundation in South Africa, and private sector associations, for instance, the Private Enterprise Foundation in Ghana (Hearn 1999, pp. 22–3). She remarks that, 'It is an interesting observation... that donors have calculated that bringing civil society into the [economic] reform process will not undermine it but strengthen it' (ibid., p. 21).

Bibliography

Ake, C. (1991) 'Rethinking African Democracy', in *Journal of Democracy* vol. 2 no. 1, pp. 32–44.

Allison, G. and Beschel, R. (1992) 'Can the US Promote Democracy?', in *Political Science Quarterly* no. 107, Spring 1992, pp. 81–98.

Amnesty International (1990a) *Amnesty International Report 1989* (Amnesty International, London).

—— (1990b) *Sri Lanka: Extrajudicial Executions, Disappearances and Torture 1987–90*, (Amnesty International, London).

—— (1991a) *Amnesty International Report 1990* (Amnesty International, London).

—— (1991b) *Egypt: Ten Years of Torture* (Amnesty International, London).

—— (1994a) *Human Rights Violations Five Years After Tiananmen* (Amnesty International, London).

—— (1994b) *Colombia: Political Violence – Myth and Reality* (Amnesty International, London).

—— (1997) *Issue Brief: FY98 Foreign Assistance for Colombia* (Amnesty International, New York).

Andersson, C. (1986) 'Breaking Through', in P. Frühling (ed.), *Swedish Development Aid in Perspective: Policies, Problems and Results Since 1952*, pp. 27–44, (Almqvist and Wiksell International, Stockholm).

Andreassen, B.-A. and Swinehart, T. (1992) 'Promoting Human Rights in Poor Countries: the New Political Conditionality of Aid Policies', in B.-A. Andreassen, and T. Swinehart (eds) *Human Rights in Developing Countries Yearbook 1991*, pp. vii–xviii (Scandinavian University Press, Oslo).

Archer, R. (1994) 'Markets and Good Government', in A. Clayton (ed.) *Governance, Democracy and Conditionality: What Role for NGOs?*, pp. 7–34 (Intrac, Oxford).

Baehr, P. *et al.* (eds) (1995) *Human Rights in Developing Countries Yearbook 1994* (Nordic Human Rights Publications, Oslo).

Ball, N. (1992) *Pressing for Peace: Can Aid Induce Reform?* (Overseas Development Council, Washington D.C.).

Bangura, Y. and Gibbon, P. (1992) 'Adjustment, Authoritarianism and Democracy in sub-Saharan Africa', in P. Gibbon, Y. Bangura and A. Ofstad (eds) *Authoritarianism, Democracy and Adjustment: the Politics of Economic Reform in Africa*, pp. 7–38 (Scandinavian Institute of African Studies, Uppsala).

Barry, T. (1992) *Inside Guatemala* (Inter-Hemispheric Education Resource Center, Albuquerque).

Barya, J. J. B. (1993) 'The New Political Conditionalities of Aid: an Independent View from Africa,' in *IDS Bulletin* vol. 24 no. 1, pp. 16–23.

Baylies, C. (1995) 'Political Conditionality and Democratisation' in *Review of African Political Economy* vol. 22 no. 65, pp. 321–37.

Beetham, D. (1993a) 'Liberal Democracy and the Limits of Democratisation', in D. Held *Prospects for Democracy*, pp. 55–73 (Polity Press, Cambridge).

——(1993b) *The Democratic Audit of the United Kingdom: Key Principles and Indices of Democracy* (Charter 88 Trust, London).

——(ed.) (1994) *Defining and Measuring Democracy* (Sage, London).

——(1995a) 'What Future for Economic and Social Rights?' in *Political Studies* vol. 43 (Special Issue), pp. 41–60.

——(1995b) *Human Rights and Democracy: a Multi-faceted Relationship* (Centre for Democratisation Studies, University of Leeds).

Beetham, D. and Boyle, K. (1995) *Introducing Democracy: Eighty Questions and Answers* (Polity Press, Cambridge, in association with UNESCO).

Blackburn, R. and Taylor, J. (eds) (1991) *Human Rights for the 1990s: Legal, Political and Ethical Issues* (Mansell, London and New York).

Bossuyt, J., Laporte, G. and Brigaldino, G. (1993) *European Development Policy After The Treaty of Maastricht* (European Centre for Development Policy Management, Maastricht).

Bratton, M. and van de Walle, N. (1992) 'Toward Governance in Africa: Popular Demands and State Responses', in G. Hydén and M. Bratton (eds) *Governance and Politics in Africa* (Lynne Rienner, Boulder).

Bread for the World Institute (1995) *At the Crossroads: the Future of Foreign Aid* (Bread for the World Institute, Maryland).

British Foreign and Commonwealth Office (FCO) (1978) *The Balance Between Civil and Political Rights and Economic and Social Rights: Origins of the Human Rights Declaration and Covenants and Subsequent Developments*, Foreign Policy Document no. 127, (FCO, London).

——(1991) *Human Rights in Foreign Policy*, Foreign Policy Document no. 215 (FCO, London).

British Foreign and Commonwealth Office including Overseas Development Administration (1992) *Departmental Report 1992* (FCO, London).

——(1993) *Departmental Report 1993* (FCO, London).

——(1994) *Departmental Report 1994* (FCO, London).

British Overseas Development Administration (ODA) (1993) *Taking Account of Good Government*, Technical Note no. 10 (ODA, London).

——(1994) *British Aid Statistics 1989/90–1993/94* (ODA, East Kilbride).

——(1995) *Progress Report on ODA's Policy Objectives (1992/93 to 1993/94)* (ODA, London).

Bromley, S. (1997) 'Middle East Exceptionalism – Myth or Reality?', in D. Potter *et al.* (eds) (1997) *Democratization*, pp. 321–44 (Polity Press, Cambridge, in association with the Open University).

Buijtenhuijs, R. and Rijnierse, E. (1993), *Democratisation in Sub-Saharan Africa (1989–1992): an Overview of the Literature* (African Studies Centre, Leiden).

Burnell, P. (1993) *'Good Government' and Foreign Aid*, PAIS Working Paper no. 115 (Dept. of Politics and International Studies, University of Warwick).

——(1994) 'Good Government and Democratization: a Sideways Look at Aid and Political Conditionality', in *Democratization* vol. 1 no. 3, pp. 485–503.

——(1997) *Foreign Aid in a Changing World* (Open University Press, Buckingham).

Carothers, T. (1991) *In the Name of Democracy: US Policy Toward Latin America in the Reagan Years* (University of California Press, Berkeley).

——(1995) 'Recent US Experience with Democracy Promotion', in *IDS Bulletin* vol. 26 no. 2, pp. 62–9.

—— (1996) *Assessing Democracy Assistance: the Case of Romania* (Carnegie Endowment for International Peace, Washington D.C.).

—— (1997) 'Democracy Assistance: The Question of Strategy', in *Democratization* vol. 4 no. 3, pp. 109–32.

—— (1999) *Aiding Democracy Abroad: the Learning Curve* (Carnegie Endowment for International Peace, Washington D.C.).

Cassen, R. *et al.* (1994) (2nd edn) *Does Aid Work?* (Clarendon Press, London).

Chalker, L. (1991) *Good Government and the Aid Programme*, transcript of speech at the Royal Institute of International Affairs, 25 July 1991 (Overseas Development Administration, London).

—— (1992) *Priorities in Development for the European Community*, transcript of speech to the All Party Parliamentary Group on Overseas Development, 25 November 1992 (Overseas Development Administration, London).

—— (1994) *Good Government: Putting Policy into Practice*, transcript of speech to the Royal Institute of International Affairs, 6 July 1994 (Overseas Development Administration, London).

—— (1995) transcript of speech at House of Lords debate on Nigeria, 7 March 1995.

—— (1996) transcript of speech to the Royal Institute of International Affairs, 14 February 1996, (Overseas Development Administration, London).

Charlick, R. (1992) *The Concept of Governance and its Implications for AID's Development Assistance Program in Africa* (USAID, Washington D.C.).

Cheru, F. (1998) Review of 'A Half Penny on the Federal Dollar: the Future of Development Aid' by M. O'Hanlon and C. Graham, in *European Journal of Development Research* vol. 10, no. 1, pp. 238–9.

Chomsky, N. (1991) 'The Struggle for Democracy in a Changed World', in *Review of African Political Economy* no. 50, pp. 12–20.

Clayton, A. (ed.) (1994), *Governance, Democracy and Conditionality: What Role for NGOs?* (Intrac, Oxford).

Congressional Research Service (February 1995) *Sudan: Civil War, Famine and Islamic Fundamentalism* (The Library of Congress, Washington D.C.).

—— (March 1995) *China–U.S. Relations* (The Library of Congress, Washington D.C.).

—— (March 1995) *El Salvador and U.S. Aid: Congressional Action in 1993 and 1994* (The Library of Congress, Washington D.C.).

Council on Hemispheric Affairs and the Inter-Hemispheric Education Resource Center (1990) *National Endowment for Democracy: a Foreign Policy Gone Awry* (Resource Center, Albuquerque).

Courier, The, no. 128, July–August 1991, edition on 'Human Rights, Democracy and Development' (European Commission, Brussels).

—— no. 139, May–June 1993, 'ACP-EC Joint Assembly in Gaborone', pp. 7–10 (European Commission, Brussels).

—— no. 155, January–February 1996 (European Commission, Brussels).

—— no. 170, July–August 1998 (European Commission, Brussels).

Cox, A. and Koning, A. (1997) 'Understanding European Community Aid: and Policies Management and Distribution' (Overseas Development Institute, London, European Commission, Brussels).

Crawford, G. (1995) *Promoting Democracy, Human Rights and Good Governance Through Development Aid: a Comparative Study of the Policies of Four Northern Donors* (Centre for Democratisation Studies, University of Leeds).

——(1996) 'Whither Lomé? The Mid-Term Review and the Decline of Partnership', in *The Journal of Modern African Studies*, vol. 34, no. 3, pp. 503–18.

——(1997) *Promoting Political Reform Through Aid Sanctions: Instrumental and Normative Issues* (Centre for Democratisation Studies, University of Leeds).

——(1998a) 'Human Rights and Democracy in EU Development Co-operation: Towards Fair and Equal Treatment', in M. R. Lister (ed.) *European Development Policy*, pp. 131–78 (Macmillan Press, London).

——(1998b) *Aid and Political Reform: a Comparative Study of the Development Co-operation Policies of Four Northern Donors* (PhD thesis, University of Leeds).

Cumming, G. (1996) 'British Aid to Africa: a Changing Agenda?', in *Third World Quarterly* vol. 7 no. 3, pp. 487–501.

Dahl, R. (1971) *Polyarchy: Participation and Opposition* (Yale University Press, New Haven).

De Feyter, K. *et al.* (1995) *Development Co-operation: a Tool for the Promotion of Human Rights and Democratization* (Belgian Ministry for Development Co-operation, Brussels).

Diamond, L. (1991) *The Democratic Revolution: Struggles for Freedom and Pluralism in the Developing World* (Freedom House, New York).

——(1992) 'Promoting Democracy', in *Foreign Policy* no. 87, Summer 1992, pp. 25–46.

Dias, C. (1994) 'Governance, Democracy and Conditionality: NGO Positions and Roles', in A. Clayton (ed.) *Governance, Democracy and Conditionality: What Role for NGOs?*, pp. 53–64 (Intrac, Oxford).

Dicklitch, S. (1998) *The Elusive Promise of NGOs in Africa: Lessons from Uganda* (Macmillan Press, Basingstoke)

Donnelly, J. (1993) *International Human Rights* (Westview Press, Boulder, Colorado).

Echenique, J. (1994) 'NGOs and Pro-Democracy Movements in Latin America', in A. Clayton (ed.) *Governance, Democracy and Conditionality: What Role for NGOs?*, pp. 111–12 (Intrac, Oxford).

Edwards, M. (1994) 'International NGOs and Southern Governments in the New World Order', in A. Clayton (ed.) *Governance, Democracy and Conditionality: What Role for NGOs?*, pp. 65–84 (Intrac, Oxford).

Elliott, K. A. (1992) 'Economic Sanctions', in P.J. Schraeder (ed.) (2nd edn) *Intervention into the 1990s: US Foreign Policy in the Third World* (Lynne Rienner, Boulder and London).

Eide, Asbjorn (1994) 'Human Rights and Development – and in Development Co-operation', in *Forum for Development Studies*, nos 1–2, pp. 167–90.

Eidmann, G. (1993) 'Democratisation in Africa and Human Rights Conditionality in Development Aid – Old NGO Tasks Take On a New Guise', in R. Tetzlaff (ed.), *Human Rights and Development: German and International Contents and Documents*, pp. 123–50 (EINE Welt, Bonn).

Euro-Cidse (1993) *News Bulletin*, September 1993, November–December 1993 (Euro-Cidse, Brussels).

——(1994) *News Bulletin*, September 1994 and October–November 1994 (Euro-Cidse, Brussels).

European Commission (1991) Communication to the Council and Parliament on *Human Rights, Democracy and Development*, 25 March 1991 [Doc. no. SEC(91) 61] (European Commission, Brussels).

—— (1992a) *Report on the Implementation of the Resolution of the Council on Human Rights, Democracy and Development adopted on 28 November 1991* [Doc. no. SEC (92) 1915, 21 October 1992] (European Commission, Brussels).

—— (1992b) '*Propositions d'orientations pour l'utilisation des moyens financiers disponibles pour la promotion des droits de l'homme et de la démocratie dans les pays en voie de développement*', 13 March 1992 (European Commission, Brussels).

—— (1993a) Communication from the President and the Commissioner for External Relations to the Commission *Sur la prise en compte des droits de l'homme et des valeurs démocratiques dans les accords entre la Communauté et les pays tiers* [Doc. no. SEC (93) 50/4, 22 January 1993], (European Commission, Brussels).

—— (1993b) *Note de dossier sur l'utilisation de la ligne budgétaire B7–5078*, 15 December 1993, (European Commission, Brussels).

—— (1994a) *Report on the Implementation in 1993 of the Resolution of the Council on Human Rights, Democracy and Development adopted on 28 November 1991* [Document number COM (94) 42, 23 February 1994], (European Commission, Brussels).

—— (1994b) Communication to the Council *Towards a New Asia Strategy* [Document number COM (94) 314, 13 July 1994], (European Commission, Brussels).

—— (1994c) *Memorandum on the Community's Development Aid in 1993* [to the Development Assistance Committee], (European Commission, Brussels).

—— (1995a) Communication *On the Inclusion of Respect for Democratic Principles and Human Rights in Agreements between the Community and Third Countries* [Document number COM (95) 216, 23 May 1995], (European Commission, Brussels).

—— (1995b) Communication to the Council and Parliament on *The European Union and the External Dimension of Human Rights Policy: From Rome to Maastricht and Beyond* [Document number COM (95) 567, 22 November 1995], (European Commission, Brussels).

—— (1995c) *Memorandum on the Community's Development Aid in 1994* [to the Development Assistance Committee], (European Commission, Brussels).

—— (1996) *Report on the Implementation in 1994 of the Resolution of the Council on Human Rights, Democracy and Development adopted on 28 November 1991* (European Commission, Brussels).

—— (1998) Communication to the Council and Parliament on *Democratisation, the Rule of Law, Respect for Human Rights and Good Governance: the Challenges of the Partnership between the European Union and the ACP States*, [Document number COM(98) 146 final, 12 March 1998] (European Commission, Brussels).

European Parliament (1991) *Resolution on Human Rights and Development Policy, adopted 22 November 1991* [Document number PE 155.084], (European Parliament, Luxembourg).

—— (1993) *Suivi des Résolutions D'Initiative Adoptées par le Parlement Européen de Juillet 1989 à Juillet 1993* (Document de Travail).

—— (1995a) *Report on Human Rights in the World in 1993–94 and the Union's Human Rights Policy* (Imbeni Report), [Doc. no. PE 211.973], (European Parliament, Luxembourg).

—— (1995b) *Human Rights Clause in External Agreements*, Summary record of presentations made at the Public Hearing, 20–21 November 1995, (European Parliament, Luxembourg).

—— (1996) *Report on Human Rights Clauses in EU Agreements with Third Countries* (Aelvoet Report), [Committee on Development and Co-operation, February 1996], (European Parliament, Luxembourg).

European Research Office (1994a) *Promotion of Human Rights, Democracy, Good Governance and the Rule of Law* [Lomé IV Mid-Term Review Position Series], (ERO, Brussels).

—— (1994b) *Modification of Instruments* [Lomé IV Mid-Term Review Position Series], (ERO Brussels).

European Union Council of Ministers (Development) (1991) *Resolution of the Council and of the Member States meeting in the Council on Human Rights, Democracy and Development*, 28 November 1991 [Doc. no. 10107/91], (European Commission, Brussels).

European Union Council of Ministers (Development) (1993) *Declaration on Human Rights, Democracy and Development*, 25 May 1993 [Doc. no. 6705/93], (European Commission, Brussels).

European Union Council of Ministers (General Affairs) (1995) 29 May 1995 [Doc. no. 7255/95], (European Commission, Brussels).

Evans, P. (1992) 'The State as Problem and Solution: Predation, Embedded Autonomy and Structural Change', in S. Haggard and R.R. Kaufman (eds) (1992) *The Politics of Economic Adjustment*, pp. 139–81 (Princeton University Press, Princeton).

Financial Times (28 January 1994) 'Sweden stops aid for ANC after 20 years' (*Financial Times*, London).

Forsythe, D.P. (1988) *Human Rights and US Foreign Policy: Congress Reconsidered* (University of Florida Press, Gainesville).

—— (1989) 'US Economic Assistance and Human Rights: Why the Emperor has (almost) no clothes', in D.P. Forsythe (ed.) *Human Rights and Development: International Views*, pp. 171–95, (Macmillan, Basingstoke).

Fowler, A. (1997) *Striking a Balance: a Guide to Enhancing the Effectiveness of Non-Governmental Organisations in International Development* (Earthscan, London).

Fox, L. (1995) *Civil Society: a Conceptual Framework* (USAID, Washington D.C.).

Freedom House (annual survey) *Freedom in the World: Political Rights and Civil Liberties* (Freedom House, New York).

Frühling, P. (ed.) (1988) *Recovery in Africa. a Challenge for Development Co-operation in the 90s*, (Swedish Ministry for Foreign Affairs, Stockholm).

German, T. and Randel, J. (eds) (1995), *The Reality of Aid 1995: an Independent Review of International Aid* (London: Earthscan).

Gibbon, P. (1993) 'The World Bank and the New Politics of Aid', in G. Sorensen *Political Conditionality*, pp. 35–62 (Frank Cass/EADI, London).

Gills, B., Rocamora, J. and Wilson, R. (eds) (1993) *Low Intensity Democracy: Political Power in the New World Order* (Pluto Press, London).

Ginter, K., Denters E. and de Waart, P.J.I.M. (eds) (1995) *Sustainable Development and Good Governance* (Martinus Nijhoff, Dordrecht).

Goodwin-Gill, G.S. (1994) *Free and Fair Elections: International Law and Practice* (Inter-Parliamentary Union, Geneva).

Gordon, D.F. (1997) 'On Promoting Democracy in Africa: the International Dimension', in M. Ottaway (ed.) *Democracy in Africa: the Hard Road Ahead*, pp. 153–65 (Lynne Rienner, Boulder, CO).

Guardian, The (14 December 1994) 'Plan for US aid cut set to spark battle' (*The Guardian*, London).

Haggard, S. and Kaufman, R.R. (eds) (1992) *The Politics of Economic Adjustment* (Princeton University Press, Princeton).

Haggard, S. and Webb, S. (eds) (1994) *Voting for Reform: Democracy, Political Liberalization, and Economic Adjustment* (World Bank, Washington D.C.).

Hansen, G. (1996), *Constituencies for Reform: Strategic Approaches for Donor-Supported Civic Advocacy Programs* (USAID, Washington D.C.).

Häusermann, J. (1994) 'NGOs and International Policy Reform', in A. Clayton (ed.) *Governance, Democracy and Conditionality: What Role for NGOs?*, pp. 95–7 (Intrac, Oxford).

—— (1998), *A Human Rights Approach to Development* (Rights and Humanity, London).

Healey, J. and Robinson, M. (1992) *Democracy, Governance and Economic Policy: Sub-Saharan Africa in Comparative Perspective* (Overseas Development Institute, London).

Hearn, J. (1999) *Foreign Aid, Democratisation and Civil Society in Africa: a Study of South Africa, Ghana and Uganda* IDS Discussion Paper 368 (Institute of Development Studies, Brighton).

Heinz, W.S. (1995) 'Positive Measures in Development Co-operation: United States and Germany', in P. Baehr *et al.* (eds) *Human Rights in Developing Countries Yearbook 1994*, pp. 27–42 (Nordic Human Rights Publications, Oslo).

Heinz, W., Lingnau, H. and Waller P. (1995) *Evaluation of EC Positive Measures in Favour of Human Rights and Democracy* (German Development Institute, Berlin).

Held, D. (1987) *Models of Democracy* (Polity Press, Cambridge).

Hjelm-Wallén, L. (1988) 'Introductory Statement', in P. Frühling (ed.) *Recovery in Africa: a Challenge for Development Co-operation in the 90s*, pp. 11–18 (Swedish Ministry for Foreign Affairs, Stockholm).

Hoffman, J. (1988) *State, Power and Democracy: Contentious Concepts in Practical Political Theory* (Wheatsheaf, Brighton).

House of Lords Select Committee on The European Communities (1993) *EC Development Aid* (HMSO, London).

Hufbauer, G.C., Schott, J.J. and Elliott K.A. (1985) *Economic Sanctions Reconsidered: History and Current Policy* (Institute for International Economics/MIT Press, Washington D.C.).

Human Rights Watch (1990) *Human Rights Watch World Report 1991: Events of 1990* (Human Rights Watch, New York).

—— (1991) *Human Rights Watch World Report 1992: Events of 1991* (Human Rights Watch, New York).

—— (1992) *Human Rights Watch World Report 1993: Events of 1992* (Human Rights Watch, New York).

—— (1993) *Human Rights Watch World Report 1994: Events of 1993* (Human Rights Watch, New York).

—— (1994) *Human Rights Watch World Report 1995: Events of 1994* (Human Rights Watch, New York).

—— (1995) *Human Rights Watch World Report 1996: Events of 1995* (Human Rights Watch, New York).

Huntington, S.P. (1991) *The Third Wave: Democratization in the Late Twentieth Century* (University of Oklahoma Press, Norman).

Hurd, D. (1990) Transcript of speech at the Overseas Development Institute, London, 6 June 1990 (Foreign and Commonwealth Office, London).
——(1993) Transcript of speech to the Nigerian Institute for International Affairs, Abuja, 5 January 1993 (Foreign and Commonwealth Office, London).
Hydén, G. (1988) 'State and Nation under Stress', in P. Frühling (1988) *Recovery in Africa: a Challenge for Development Co-operation in the 90s*, pp. 145–58 (Swedish Ministry for Foreign Affairs, Stockholm).
——(1992), 'Governance and the Study of Politics', in G. Hydén and M. Bratton (eds) *Governance and Politics in Africa* (Lynne Rienner, Boulder).
Hydén, G. and Bratton, M. (eds) (1992), *Governance and Politics in Africa* (Lynne Rienner, Boulder and London).
IDS Bulletin vol. 24 no. 1 (January 1993) *Good Government* (Institute of Development Studies, Brighton).
IDS Bulletin vol. 26 no. 2 (April 1995) *Towards Democratic Governance* (Institute of Development Studies, Brighton).
Instituto del Tercer Mundo (1995) *The World: a Third World Guide 1995/96* (Instituto del Tercer Mundo, Montevideo).
Inter-American Development Bank (1996) *Modernization of the State and Strengthening of Civil Society* (IDB, Washington D.C.).
——(1997) *Frame of Reference for Bank Action in Programs for Modernization of the State and Strengthening of Civil Society* (IDB, Washington D.C.).
Inter-Parliamentary Union (26 March 1994) *Declaration on Criteria for Free and Fair Elections* (IPU, Geneva).
International Institute for Democracy and Electoral Assistance (IDEA) (1998) *Dialogue for Democratic Development: Renewing the ACP-EU Partnership for the 21st Century* (International IDEA, Stockholm).
International Monetary Fund (1997) *Good Governance: the IMF's Role*, (IMF, Washington D.C.).
Kiloh, M. (1997) 'South Africa: Democracy Delayed', in D. Potter *et al.* (eds) *Democratization*, pp. 294–320 (Polity Press, Cambridge, in association with the Open University).
Klinghoffer, A.J. (1998) *The International Dimension of Genocide in Rwanda* (Macmillan, Basingstoke).
Lancaster, C. (1993) 'Governance and Development: the Views from Washington', in *IDS Bulletin* vol. 24 no. 1, pp. 9–15.
Landuyt, K. (1995) *Development Co-operation: a tool for the promotion of human rights and democracy? A case-study on the Republic of Indonesia* (Working Paper, Institute of Development Policy and Management, University of Antwerp).
Leftwich, A. (1994) 'Governance, the State and the Politics of Development' in *Development and Change* vol. 25, pp. 363–86.
Leftwich, A. (1996), 'On the Primacy of Politics in Development' in A. Leftwich (ed.) *Democracy and Development: Theory and Practice*, pp. 3–24 (Polity Press, Cambridge).
Lindgren, L. (1991) *Local Government Goes South: a Study of Swedish Development Assistance in the Field of Public Administration* (Gothenburg University, Gothenburg).
Lipjhart, A. (1984) *Democracies: Patterns of Majoritarian and Consensus Government in Twenty-one Countries* (Yale University Press, New Haven and London).

Lipset S.M. (1959) 'Some Social Requisites of Democracy', in *American Political Science Review* no. 53, pp. 69–105.

Ljunggren, B. (1986) 'Swedish Goals and Priorities', in P. Frühling (ed.) *Swedish Development Aid in Perspective: Policies, Problems and Results Since 1952*, pp. 65–84 (Almqvist and Wiksell International, Stockholm).

Lone, S. (1990) 'Donors Demand Political Reforms', in *Africa Recovery*, July–September 1990, vol. 4 no. 2, pp. 3/28–9.

Lowenthal, A.F. (ed.) (1991) *Exporting Democracy: the US and Latin America* (Harvard University Press, Harvard).

Luckham R. (1995) 'Dilemmas of Military Disengagement and Democratization in Africa' in *IDS Bulletin* vol. 26 no. 2, pp. 49–61.

Mayo, M. and Craig, G. (1995) 'Community Participation and Empowerment: the Human Face of Structural Adjustment or Tools for Democratic Transition?', in G. Craig and M. Mayo (eds) *Community Empowerment: a Reader in Participation and Development*, pp. 1–11 (Zed, London).

Madeley, J., Sullivan, D. and Woodroffe, J. (1994) *Who Runs the World?* (Christian Aid, London).

Martin, G. (1995) 'Continuity and Change in Franco-African Relations', in *Journal of Modern African Studies*, vol. 33 no. 1, pp. 1–20.

McGoldrick, D. (1994) *The Human Rights Committee: Its Role in the Development of the International Covenant on Civil and Political Rights* (Clarendon Press, Oxford).

Moore, M. (1993a) 'Introduction', in *IDS Bulletin*, vol. 24 no. 1, pp. 1–6.

—— (1993b) 'Declining to Learn from the East? The World Bank on 'Governance and Development', in *IDS Bulletin*, vol. 24 no. 1, pp. 39–50.

—— (1995) 'Democracy and Development in Cross-National Perspective: a New Look at the Statistics', in *Democratization* vol. 2 no. 2, pp. 141–58.

Moore, M. and Robinson M. (1994) 'Can Foreign Aid Be Used to Promote Good Government in Developing Countries?', in *Ethics and International Affairs* vol. 8, pp. 141–58.

Morfit, M. (1993) *Usable Knowledge: Theory and Practice in Government Policy to Support Democracy* (Paper for American Political Science Association annual meeting September 1993).

Morphet, S. (1993) 'The Non-Aligned in "the New World Order": the Jakarta Summit, September 1992', in *International Relations* 1993, pp. 358–80.

Mosley, P. (1987) *Overseas Aid: Its Defence and Reform* (Harvester Wheatsheaf, Hemel Hempstead).

Mosley, P., Harrigan, J. and Toye, J. (1991) *Aid and Power: the World Bank and Policy-based Lending*, vol. 1 (Routledge, London).

Muñoz, H. (1993) 'The OAS and Democratic Governance', in *Journal of Democracy* vol. 4 no. 3, pp. 29–38.

Munslow, B. (1993) 'Democratisation in Africa', in *Parliamentary Affairs* vol. 46 no. 4, pp. 478–91.

Museveni, Y.K. (1997), *Sowing the Mustard Seed: the Struggle for Freedom and Democracy in Uganda* (Macmillan, London and Basingstoke).

Murray K. with Barry T. (1995) *Inside El Salvador* (Inter-Hemispheric Education Resource Center, Albuquerque).

Muzaffar, C. (1995) 'EU policy: a perspective from Asia', in European Parliament *Human Rights Clause in External Agreements*, Summary record of presentations made at the Public Hearing, 20–21 November 1995 (European Parliament, Luxembourg).

Napoli, D. (undated) *Eléments d'une Politique Externe de l'Union Européenne en Matière de Droits de l'Homme* (mimeo).

Nelson, J. and Eglinton, S. J. (1992), *Encouraging Democracy: What Role for Conditioned Aid* (Overseas Development Council, Washington D.C.).

—— (1993) *Global Goals, Contentious Means: Issues of Multiple Aid Conditionality* (Overseas Development Council, Washington D.C.).

Ngunyi, M. *et al.* (1996) *Promoting Democracy through Positive Conditionality* (Centre for Democratization Studies, University of Leeds).

Nherere, P. (1995) 'Conditionality, Human Rights and Good Governance: a Dialogue of Unequal Partners', in K. Ginter *et al.* (eds) *Sustainable Development and Good Governance*, pp. 289–307 (Martinus Nijhoff, Dordrecht).

Nordholt, N. G. S. (1995) Aid and Conditionality: the Case of Dutch-Indonesian Relationships', in O. Stokke (ed.) *Aid and Political Conditionality*, pp. 162–200 (Frank Cass/EADI, London).

Nordic Ministers of Development Co-operation (1990) 'Communique' from meeting in Molde, Norway, 10–11 September 1990.

Nugent, N. (1994, 3rd edn), *The Government and Politics of the European Union* (Macmillan, Basingstoke).

Nwokedi, E. (1993) 'Political conditionalities: Vectors or Constraints on Development in sub-Saharan Africa', in R. Tetzlaff (ed.) *Human Rights and Development: German and International Contents and Documents*, pp. 161–86 (EINE Welt, Bonn).

O'Donnell G., Schmitter P. C. and Whitehead L. (eds) (1986) *Transitions from Authoritarian Rule*: Volume 3 *Comparative Perspectives* (Johns Hopkins University Press, Baltimore and London).

Official Journal of the European Communities (various editions) (Official Office for Publications of the European Union, Brussels and Luxembourg).

Oloka-Onyango, J. and Barya J. J. (1997) 'Civil Society and the Political Economy of Foreign Aid in Uganda', in *Democratization* vol. 4 no. 2, pp. 113–38.

Organisation for Economic Co-operation and Development (OECD) (1991) *Development Co-operation: Efforts and Policies of the Members of the Development Assistance Committee* (1991 Report), (OECD, Paris).

—— (1992) *Development Co-operation: Efforts and Policies of the Members of the Development Assistance Committee* (1992 Report) (OECD, Paris).

—— (1994) *Development Co-operation: Efforts and Policies of the Members of the Development Assistance Committee* (1994 Report) (OECD, Paris).

—— (1995) *Draft Orientations for Donors from the Uppsala Workshop on Civil Society and Democracy* [document: DCD/DAC (95)5], (OECD, Paris).

—— (1996) *Geographical Distribution of Financial Flows to Aid Recipients 1990–94* (Development Assistance Committee/OECD, Paris).

—— (1997a) *Evaluation of Programs Promoting Participatory Development and Good Governance* (Synthesis Report, DAC Expert Group on Aid Evaluation), (Development Assistance Committee/OECD, Paris).

—— (1997b) *Final Report of the Ad Hoc Working Group on Participatory Development and Good Governance* (Development Assistance Committee/OECD, Paris).

Ostergaard, C. S. (1993) 'Values for Money? Political Conditionality in Aid – the case of China', in G. Sorensen (ed.) *Political Conditionality*, pp. 112–34 (Frank Cass/EADI, London).

Overseas Development Council (1990) *U.S. Foreign Aid in a Changing World* (ODC, Washington D.C.).

Overseas Development Institute (ODI) Briefing Paper (January 1992) *Aid and Political Reform* (Overseas Development Institute, London).

Oxfam UK and Ireland (1993) *Africa, Make or Break: Action for Recovery* (Oxfam, Oxford).

Pateman, C. (1970) *Participation and Democratic Theory* (Cambridge University Press, Cambridge).

Pearce, J. (1990) *Colombia: Inside the Labyrinth* (Latin America Bureau, London).

Pipkorn, J. (1995) 'Legal Aspects of the Application of the Human Rights Clause', in European Parliament *Human Rights Clause in External Agreements*, Summary record of presentations made at the Public Hearing, 20–21 November 1995 (European Parliament, Luxembourg).

Potter, D. (1997) 'Explaining Democratization', in D. Potter *et al.* (eds) *Democratization*, pp. 1–40, (Polity Press, Cambridge, in association with the Open University).

Ramos, V. (1995) 'Outline of the EU's policy objectives', in European Parliament *Human Rights Clause in External Agreements*, Summary record of presentations made at the Public Hearing, 20–21 November 1995 (European Parliament, Luxembourg).

Randel J. and German T. (eds) (1994) *The Reality of Aid: an Independent Review of International Aid* (ActionAid, London).

Robertson, A. H., revised by Merrills, J. G. (1989) (3rd edn), *Human Rights in the World* (Manchester University Press, Manchester).

Robinson, M. (1993a) 'Will Political Conditionality Work?', in *IDS Bulletin* vol. 24 no. 1, pp. 58–66.

—— (1993b) 'Aid, Democracy and Political Conditionality in sub-Saharan Africa', in G. Sorensen (ed.) *Political Conditionality*, pp. 85–99, (Frank Cass/EADI, London).

—— (1994) 'Governance, Democracy and Conditionality: NGOs and the New Policy Agenda', in A. Clayton (ed.) *Governance, Democracy and Conditionality: What Role for NGOs?*, pp. 35–52 (Intrac, Oxford).

—— (1995a) 'Strengthening Civil Society in Africa: the Role of Foreign Political Aid', in *IDS Bulletin* vol. 26 no. 2, pp. 70–80.

—— (1995b) 'Political Conditionality: Strategic Implications for NGOs', in O. Stokke (ed.) *Aid and Political Conditionality*, pp. 360–76 (Frank Cass/EADI, London).

—— (1996) *Strengthening Civil Society Through Foreign Political Aid* [ESCOR Research Report R6234], (Institute of Development Studies, Sussex).

Robinson, W. I. (1996) *Promoting Polyarchy: Globalization, US Intervention and Hegemony* (Cambridge University Press, Cambridge).

Roniger, L. (1994a) 'Conclusions: the Transformation of Clientelism and Civil Society', in L. Roniger and A. Günes-Ayata (eds) *Democracy, Clientelism and Civil Society*, pp. 207–14 (Lynne Rienner, Boulder and London).

—— (1994b) 'Civil Society, Patronage and Democracy', in *International Journal of Comparative Sociology* vol. 35 no. 3/4, pp. 207–20.

Rueschemeyer, D., Stephens E. H. and Stephens J. D. (1992) *Capitalist Democracy and Development* (Polity Press, Cambridge).

Sandbrook, R. (1990) 'Taming the African Leviathan', in *World Policy Journal* vol. 7, pp. 673–701.
—— (1993) *The Politics of Africa's Economic Recovery* (Cambridge University Press, Cambridge).
Santiso, C. (1999) *Strengthening Democracy and Good Governance in the Americas: the Contribution of the Multilateral Development Banks* (unpublished manuscript).
Schimpp, M. (1992) *A.I.D. and Democratic Development: a Synthesis of Literature and Experience* (USAID, Washington D.C.).
Schmitz, G. J. and Gillies, D. (1992) *The Challenge of Democratic Development: Sustaining Democratisation in Developing Countries* (North-South Institute, Ottawa).
Schrijver, N. (1995) 'The dynamics of sovereignty in a changing world', in K. Ginter *et al.* (eds) *Sustainable Development and Good Governance*, pp. 80–9 (Martinus Nijhoff, Dordrecht).
Sénecal, N. (1993) Keynote statement to the International Conference on Development Co-operation for Human Rights and Democracy, in *Development Co-operation for Human Rights and Democracy*, Report from International Conference, Stockholm 22–24 February 1993 (Ministry for Foreign Affairs, Stockholm).
Shiddo, A. A. (1995) 'Sudan's View of EU Policy', in European Parliament *Human Rights Clause in External Agreements*, Summary record of presentations made at the Public Hearing, 20–21 November 1995 (European Parliament, Luxembourg).
Smith, T. (1994) *America's Mission: the United States and the Worldwide Struggle for Democracy in the Twentieth Century* (Princeton University Press, Princeton N.J.).
Sorensen, G. (1993a) *Democracy and Democratisation* (Westview Press, Boulder).
Sorensen, G. (1993b), 'Introduction' in G. Sorensen (ed.) *Political Conditionality*, pp. 1–5 (Frank Cass/EADI, London).
—— (1993c) 'Democracy, Authoritarianism and State Strength', in G. Sorenson (ed.) *Political Conditionality*, pp. 6–34 (Frank Cass/EADI, London).
—— (1995) 'Conditionality, Democracy and Development', in O. Stokke (ed.) *Aid and Political Conditionality*, pp. 392–409 (Frank Cass/EADI, London).
Stankovitch M. (1996) *The European Union and ASEAN – a Background Paper* (Catholic Institute for International Relations, London).
Stohl, M., Carleton D. and Johnson S. E. (1984) 'Human rights and U.S. Foreign Assistance from Nixon to Carter', in *Journal of Peace Studies* vol. 21, no. 3.
Stokke, O. (1995) 'Aid and Political Conditionality: Core Issues and State of the Art', in O. Stokke (ed.) *Aid and Political Conditionality*, pp. 1–87 (Frank Cass/EADI, London).
Sudworth, E. (1993) *Human Rights, Development and Democracy and the Lomé Convention* (Euro-Cidse, Brussels).
Swedish International Development Authority (SIDA) (1991) *Making Government Work: Guidelines and Framework for SIDA Support to the Development of Public Administration* (SIDA, Stockholm).
—— (1993a) *SIDA's Strategy for its Programmes of Assistance in Support of Democracy and Human Rights* (SIDA, Stockholm).
—— (1993b) *SIDA's Programme for Public Administration and Management* (SIDA, Stockholm).

—— (1993c) *Sweden's Development Assistance in Figures and Graphs, BSD 1991/92* (SIDA, Stockholm).
—— (1994a) *Support for Democracy and Human Rights* (mimeo).
—— (1994b) *Sweden's Development Assistance in Figures and Graphs, BSD 1992/93* (SIDA, Stockholm).
—— (1995) *Sweden's Development Assistance in Figures and Graphs, BSD 1993/94* (SIDA, Stockholm).
—— (1996) *Sweden's Development Assistance in Figures and Graphs, BSD 1994/95* (SIDA, Stockholm).
—— (1997) *Justice and Peace: SIDA's Programme for Peace, Democracy and Human Rights* (SIDA, Stockholm).
Swedish Ministry for Foreign Affairs (1990) *Documents on Swedish Foreign Policy 1989* (Ministry for Foreign Affairs, Stockholm).
—— (1991) *Documents on Swedish Foreign Policy 1990* (Ministry for Foreign Affairs, Stockholm).
—— (1992) *Documents on Swedish Foreign Policy 1991* (Ministry for Foreign Affairs, Stockholm).
—— (1993a) *Sweden's Development Assistance 1992/93* (Ministry for Foreign Affairs, Stockholm).
—— (1993b) *Development Co-operation for Human Rights and Democracy*, Report from International Conference, Stockholm 22–24 February 1993 (Ministry for Foreign Affairs, Stockholm).
—— (1993c) *Current Trends in Swedish Development Policy: Democracy and Human Rights* (Ministry for Foreign Affairs, Stockholm).
Tetzlaff, R. (ed.) (1993) *Human Rights and Development: German and International Contents and Documents* (EINE Welt, Bonn).
Thomas, A. (1992) 'Non-Governmental Organisations and the Limits to Empowerment', in M. Wuyts *et al.* (eds) *Development Policy and Public Action*, pp. 117–46 (Oxford University Press, Oxford).
Tomasevski, K. (1989) *Development Aid and Human Rights* (Pinter, London).
—— (1993) *Development Aid and Human Rights Revisited* (Pinter, London).
—— (1997) *Between Sanctions and Elections: Aid Donors and their Human Rights Performance* (Pinter, London).
Tordoff, W. (1997) (3rd edn) *Government and Politics in Africa* (Macmillan, Basingstoke).
Ul Haq, M. (1993) Keynote statement to the International Conference on Development Co-operation for Human Rights and Democracy, in *Development Co-operation for Human Rights and Democracy*, Report from International Conference, Stockholm 22–24 February 1993 (Ministry for Foreign Affairs, Stockholm).
United Nations, (1993a) *World Conference on Human Rights, Vienna, Austria, June 1993: Information Pack* (UN, New York).
—— (1993b) *Vienna Declaration and Programme of Action, 25 June 1993* (UN, New York).
—— (1996) *The United Nations and Rwanda 1993–96* (Dept. of Public Information, UN, New York).
United Nations Development Programme (UNDP) (1990) *Human Development Report 1990* (UNDP, New York).
—— (1991) *Human Development Report 1991* (UNDP, New York).

—— (1992) *Human Development Report 1992* (UNDP, New York).

—— (1997) *Governance for Sustainable Human Development* (UNDP, New York).

United States Agency for International Development (USAID) (1990) *The Democracy Initiative* (USAID, Washington D.C.).

—— (1991) *Democracy and Governance* (USAID, Washington D.C.).

—— (1993) *Economic Reform in Africa's New Era of Political Liberalization*, Proceedings of a Workshop for SPA Donors, April 14–15 1993, Washington D.C. (USAID, Washington D.C.).

—— (1994) *Strategies for Sustainable Development* (USAID, Washington D.C.).

—— (1994a) *Democracy Sector Review*, September 22 1994 (mimeo).

—— (1994b) 'Section 116(d)(3) Report' [USAID Human Rights Report to Congress 1994], (mimeo).

—— (1994c) *Weighing in on the Scales of Justice: Strategic Approaches for Donor-Supported Rule of Law Programs* (Center for Development Information and Evaluation, USAID, Washington D.C.).

—— (1996) *Constituencies for Reform: Strategic Approaches for Donor-Supported Civic Advocacy Programs* (Center for Development Information and Evaluation, USAID, Washington D.C.).

—— (undated) 'Appendix 1' document on Democracy Project Inventory, obtained March 1995 (mimeo).

United States Department of State (1995a) *Tools for Promoting Democracy: Program Resources in 1995* (US Department of State, Washington D.C.).

—— (1995b) *Country Reports on Human Rights Practices for 1994* (U.S. Department of State, Washington D.C.).

—— (1996) *Country Reports on Human Rights Practices for 1995* (U.S. Department of State, Washington D.C.).

Uvin, P. (1993) 'Do as I say, Not as I do: The Limits of Political Conditionality', in G. Sorensen (ed.) *Political Conditionality*, pp. 63–84 (Frank Cass/EADI, London).

Van Boven, T. (1995) 'The International Legal Context of the EU's Evolving Policy', in European Parliament *Human Rights Clause in External Agreements*, Summary record of presentations made at the Public Hearing, 20–21 November 1995 (European Parliament, Luxembourg).

Van Rooy, A. and Robinson M. (1998) 'Out of the Ivory Tower: Civil Society and the Aid System', in A. Van Rooy (ed.) *Civil Society and the Aid Industry*, pp. 31–70 (Earthscan, London).

Van Tuijl, P. (1994) 'Conditionality for Whom? Indonesia and the Dissolution of the IGGI: the NGO Experience', in A. Clayton (ed.) *Governance, Democracy and Conditionality: What Role for NGOs?*, pp. 85–94 (Intrac, Oxford).

Vincent, R. J. (1986) *Human Rights and International Relations* (Cambridge University Press, Cambridge).

Waller, P. P. (1992) 'After East-West Détene: Towards a Human Rights Orientation in North-South Co-operation?', in *Journal of the Society of International Development*, vol. 24. no. 1, pp. 24–32.

—— (1993) 'Human Rights Orientation in Development Co-operation', in R. Tetzlaff (ed.) *Human Rights and Development: German and International Contents and Documents*, pp. 53–78 (EINE Welt, Bonn).

Weir, S. and Beetham D. (1999) *Political Power and Democratic Control in Britain* (Routledge, London).

White, G. (1994) 'Civil Society, Democratization and Development (I): Clearing the Analytical Ground', in *Democratization* vol. 1 no. 3, pp. 375–90.

Whitehead, L. (1991) 'The Imposition of Democracy', in A. F. Lowenthal (ed.) *Exporting Democracy: the US and Latin America*, pp. 356–82 (Harvard University Press, Harvard, CT).

—— (1986) 'International Aspects of Democratisation', in G. O'Donnell *et al.* (eds) *Transitions from Authoritarian Rule*: Volume 3 *Comparative Perspectives*, pp. 3–46 (Johns Hopkins University Press, Baltimore and London).

Wiseman, J. (1997) 'The Rise and Fall and Rise (and Fall?) of Democracy in sub-Saharan Africa', in D. Potter *et al.* (eds) *Democratization*, pp. 272–93 (Polity Press, Cambridge, in association with the Open University).

World Bank (1988) *Report on Adjustment Lending*, Doc. R88–199 (World Bank, Washington D.C.).

—— (1989) *Sub-Saharan Africa: From Crisis to Sustainable Growth: a Long-Term Perspective Study* (World Bank, Washington D.C.).

—— (1992) *Governance and Development* (World Bank, Washington D.C.).

—— (1994a) *Governance: The World Bank's Experience* (World Bank, Washington D.C.).

—— (1994b) *Adjustment in Africa: Reforms, Results, and the Road Ahead* (World Bank, Washington D.C.).

—— (1996) *World Bank News*, June 27, 1996 (World Bank, Washington D.C.).

—— (1997) *World Development Report 1997 – the State in a Changing World* (World Bank, Washington D.C.).

World Development Movement (1995) *Gunrunners Gold*, (World Development Movement, London).

—— (1997) *Submission to the Committee of Public Accounts on National Audit Office Report on Aid to Indonesia* (World Development Movement, London).

Index

Italics indicate figures or tables. **Bold type** indicates main or substantial references. Under the headings EU, Sweden, UK and USA, (all) after a reference indicates that the particular donor is discussed together with the other three.